"Now, thanks to medicine, a woman may outlive her ovaries by many years. But many women still—symbolically—play the role that nature has written for them. Although not dying in body at the time of ovarian failure, they die in spirit, ambition, self-image, sexuality, vitality, and stamina. We are treading on new ground. Now that a woman can live a third or more of her life in a nonreproductive capacity, the time has come to make those years *better*—more vital, productive, and comfortable."

—Barbara Edelstein, M.D.
from the Introduction

THE WOMAN DOCTOR'S MEDICAL GUIDE FOR WOMEN

"A realistic, unsensationalized explanation of the bodily phenomena that occur when women age, including hormonal changes, estrogen replacement, sexual difficulties, medical problems, stress, depression, and fatigue. Dr. Edelstein provides a sensible, well-balanced diet for weight loss and because she is a strong advocate of good medical care, she often suggests that a physician be consulted; the chapter on finding the right doctor is as helpful and enlightening as the rest of this valuable guide."

—American Library Association *Booklist*

"Practical, informative and candid. . . . Especially helpful in raising a woman's consciousness about her body."

—*Publishers Weekly*

Bantam Books of Related Interest
Ask your bookseller for the books you have missed

ANATOMY OF AN ILLNESS
by Norman Cousins

MY BODY, MY HEALTH:
The Concerned Woman's Book of Gynecology
by Felicia Stewart, M.D., Felicia Guest,
Gary Stewart, M.D., and Robert Hatcher, M.D.

THE PILL BOOK—2nd Edition
by Harold M. Silverman, Pharm.D. and
Gilbert I. Simon, D.Sc.

WOMEN AND THE CRISIS IN SEX HORMONES
by Barbara Seaman and Gideon Seaman, M.D.

WOMAN'S BODY: An Owner's Manual
by the Diagram Group

QUANTITY PURCHASES

Companies, professional groups, churches, clubs and other organizations may qualify for special terms when ordering 24 or more copies of this title. For information, contact the Direct Response Department, Bantam Books, 666 Fifth Avenue, New York, N.Y. 10103. Phone (212) 765-6500.

THE WOMAN DOCTOR'S MEDICAL GUIDE FOR WOMEN

How to Look Better, Feel Great, and Get the Most Out of Life

Barbara Edelstein, M.D.

A PERIGORD PRESS BOOK

BANTAM BOOKS
TORONTO • NEW YORK • LONDON • SYDNEY

This low-priced Bantam Book
has been completely reset in a type face
designed for easy reading, and was printed
from new plates. It contains the complete
text of the original hard-cover edition.
NOT ONE WORD HAS BEEN OMITTED.

THE WOMAN DOCTOR'S MEDICAL GUIDE FOR WOMEN

A Bantam / Perigord Book / published in association with
William Morrow & Co., Inc.

PRINTING HISTORY

Morrow / Perigord edition published September 1982

The medical, health, and dietary procedures contained in this book are based on the research and recommendations of responsible medical sources.

The author and publisher, however, disclaim responsibility for any adverse effects resulting from the use of the procedures contained herein and urge each reader to consult his or her personal physician before implementing any procedures.

Bantam / Perigord edition / September 1983

All rights reserved.
Copyright © 1982 by Barbara Edelstein M.D., P.C.
Cover copyright © 1983 by Bantam Books, Inc.
This book may not be reproduced in whole or in part, by
mimeograph or any other means, without permission.
For information address: Bantam Books, Inc.

ISBN 0-553-23487-0

Published simultaneously in the United States and Canada

Bantam Books are published by Bantam Books, Inc. Its trademark, consisting of the words "Bantam Books" and the portrayal of a rooster, is Registered in U.S. Patent and Trademark Office and in other countries. Marca Registrada. Bantam Books, Inc., 666 Fifth Avenue, New York, New York 10103.

PRINTED IN THE UNITED STATES OF AMERICA

O 0 9 8 7 6 5 4 3 2 1

For David, Jeffrey, Heidi

Acknowledgments

Thanks must go to my editors, Eunice Riedel and Grace Bechtold, for making me rewrite and rewrite; to David Edelstein, for thorough and justifiably impatient editing; to my colleagues who gave of their time to answer urgent questions; to Carol Mull, my nutritionist, for her excellent research; to Dr. Frank Davidoff, Professor of Medicine at the University of Connecticut, and Chief of Medicine at New Britain General Hospital, who graciously agreed to read the manuscript and give me his valuable insights; and to all my patients and friends who shared their time and opinions with me.

Contents

PART II THE MEDICAL PROBLEMS

Introduction

One hundred years ago, nobody would have written a book for the mid-life woman. On the average, women lived only to age forty-five, often dying much earlier in childbirth, and any female over thirty was considered "past her prime." But two things happened in this century: medicine took enormous strides, extending the average female life span to about seventy-five years; and women began to call for and to take a more active, public role in running this country, instead of devoting their lives to raising children and propping up men.

And yet, today, a woman's greatest enemy is not man, but her own childbearing body. Biology, alas, does not provide for her after her ovaries fail (an event we label "menopause"): her bones become brittle; her brain chemistry may change; and she is suddenly vulnerable to a host of swift, debilitating diseases. There is no "natural" model for menopause. In nature, the female animal is pregnant whenever she is capable, and at the end of her reproductive usefulness she is discarded—left to die or be destroyed by the other animals when anemia and infection have weakened her.

Now, thanks to medicine, a woman may outlive her ovaries by many years. But many women still—symbolically—play the role that nature has written for them. Although not dying in body at the time of ovarian failure, they die in spirit, ambition, self-image, sexuality, vitality, and stamina.

We are treading on new ground. Now that a woman can live a third or more of her life in a nonreproductive capacity, the time has come to make those years *better*—more vital, productive, and comfortable.

After all, it's not all downhill. After forty, a woman is far more interesting than she was twenty years earlier, and not just because she's lived longer. Until now, she has been attached to and, to some extent, ruled by her reproductive organs. If she has followed the rules, she has had babies. If she hasn't—from either lack of interest or lack of opportunity—she often worries about what she has missed, and about the consequences of not fulfilling her "natural" function. By age forty this preoccupation has usually passed, and a woman begins untying the psychological strings that have bound her to her uterus. What emerges is a new self: a woman of increased independence and awareness.

It is tragic when a woman comes to *believe* in and, hence, to live the stereotype of the aging, forgotten, asexual female—that infuriating tag our society has pinned on the "menopausal woman." Sometimes male physicians perpetuate it: ads for estrogen in medical journals depict the over-forty woman sitting at home and staring out the window while her mate continues his active, productive business life. Think of how differently we perceive an older man and an older woman: the salt-and-pepper hair and rugged character lines of the male become drab gray and mere wrinkles on the female.

Every day in my medical practice, I see women who are terrified of the limitations and changes brought on by aging when they should be thrilled at the prospect of a new and fuller life. In an era when we can elect a seventy-year-old man to the presidency of the United States, aren't we putting our women out to pasture far too early?

The majority of letters I received in response to my first book, *The Woman Doctor's Diet for Women,* came from women over forty. They were confused and angry about what was happening to their bodies. Their figures were changing, they wrote; they were gaining weight in strange places. They were beset by unfamiliar aches and pains, occasionally incapacitating. Some were having their breasts, uteri, or gallbladders removed and feared the consequences. Some were shaken up by severe hot flashes and didn't know where to turn—to a psychiatrist? To estrogen? To God? Many women were frightened of losing their attractiveness and being rejected by their husbands; and some were going to extraordinary expense and trouble to improve their appearance with hair coloring, antiwrinkle creams, or plastic surgery.

Their needs, in short, were changing—physically, emotionally, sexually, and nutritionally—and they were all having difficulty coping with these changes. They didn't know what to expect, what was real and what was "imagined," what was normal and what was cause for alarm.

This book will help you to understand what's really happening to your body; what changes to expect and how to cope with them; what diseases you have a risk of acquiring and how to cut some of those risks in half. I'll tell you when drugs can help—when they can change your life, in fact—and when they can only make things worse; and when exercise and eating habits can make all the difference in the way you think and feel.

And I'll discuss the psychological traumas that most women undergo as they move into their forties, fifties, and beyond, traumas that can often lead to divorce, depression, or drinking if you're not equipped to deal with them.

I'll also help you to cope with the most serious nutritional problem you face: obesity. I'll give you diets to lose weight, diets to maintain your weight, and diets to keep you healthy, whether you're normal, diabetic, or have heart trouble and whether you've always had a weight problem or have suddenly shot up twenty pounds.

The way to win the aging game is to function well, to love an idea, to glow, and to understand and anticipate the major and minor annoyances that nature has in store for you. A little knowledge can give you the confidence to age more vigorously, more gracefully, and more sensually.

Part I

THE ART OF AGING

Chapter 1

Ages and Stages

A very useful book for new parents once divided a baby's early months, from birth to two years, into distinct stages to help them monitor their infant's development. Although it would be convenient at age forty-three or sixty-one to refer to a similar chart, there is often a huge gap physically between any two forty-three- or sixty-one-year-old women. Each has her own peculiar personality traits, heredity, and state of health, and each of these can influence the way she ages. So it's impossible to break down these years into too many stages; my real reason for dividing them into four—from forty to fifty, fifty to sixty, sixty to seventy, and above seventy—is to give you a broad introduction to some of the symptoms and physiological processes I'll treat in greater depth elsewhere in this book.

Stage One: Ages Forty to Fifty

The forties are a pleasant surprise for many females who look with trepidation on the aging process. Few obvious physical differences exist between a woman in this decade and one in her thirties. Most women feel good—so good, in fact, that they often take up new sports. Freed for the first time from having to care for children, or from the frenetic pace of building a career, they often undertake new and strenuous hobbies and thoroughly enjoy the healthy fatigue they feel after hard play. The nice thing about the forties is that you can still take a fall without necessarily breaking an arm or a leg. A great deal of elasticity remains in bones, joints, and skin (and aging, when you come down to it, is just losing elasticity). Cell structure and metabolism remain intact at this stage, and tissues continue to function efficiently. Biology, however, is relentless, and there are little clues that the organism is slowing down.

A change in visual acuity is often the most irritating development in the first stage, and it is particularly hard on women who have never worn glasses. The realization that something's wrong can come when you are trying to look up a number in the phone book and everything blurs together, or when you suddenly have difficulty threading a needle. When this happens, most women don't rush out immediately to get glasses. They pretend it will go away, sometimes waiting until they have to stand up to read while the paper lies flat on the table. Sometimes they stop reading altogether. It's probably such a shock to people because it's the first physical change that's completely beyond their control. For many women, it is the only reminder of aging in this stage.

Subtle memory lapses sometimes occur at this time. Helen, one of my friends, said to me, "I've never felt better in my life. I run every day, I never eat fat, and my marriage is great. But I'm losing my memory. I sometimes look at friends and can't remember their names, or I go to the store and forget half the things I came in for."

I, too, have experienced that sudden loss of recall, and it can be very troubling. Sequential numbers are often the first to go. I have learned to *write things down*—it really helps. If you're introducing two parties, and you forget the name of one, just seize the name you remember and say, "Myersons, this is the . . ." and usually the other couple will rush to the rescue. This really is the only significant mental change. It's very common and it doesn't go much further.

Skin is just beginning to lose its elasticity at this time, and fine lines often appear around the eyes and mouth. These are not unattractive, however, and often make many blandly pretty faces interesting for the first time. The skin on the inside of the thighs, however, doesn't fare so well. I don't know why that goes so quickly; it's not exposed to the sun, which medical literature assures us is the only thing that ages skin rapidly. Perhaps that small, primitive, undeveloped inner thigh muscle simply shrinks to nothing, leaving the skin without anything to hang onto. Unless you're a fan of bathing suits, this should be of little consequence to you, but many women get all torn up about it.

The forties are the period when lumps may start to appear on the uterus, thyroid, and elsewhere, but only about 60 percent require surgery. Uterine fibroids, as they are called, are usually benign tumors that appear in the muscle layer of the uterus wall. Usually they just sit there, responding to the ebb and flow of estrogen. You can have regular periods with them, get pregnant with them, and most of the time they are harmless. They regress normally in the fifties when there is less estrogen in the body, so there is no reason to have them removed unless you don't want to take a chance on their bleeding or growing rapidly.

Hair begins to grow finer in texture and to turn gray. This happens according to a very rigid genetic clock and has little to do with stress, fatigue, hard work, or environment. Long hair doesn't look great on women at this age; it's too straggly. The one treatment is cosmetic: a good short cut and body wave. Conditioners and bleach promise much but deliver practically nothing. Female balding is rarely as comprehensive as male balding, but the hair can thin significantly over the entire head. Unlike men, women have no "external rim" (that outer circle of think hair that remains even when a man loses everything on top), so there isn't even a site from which to take a hair transplant.

Hair loss, both on the head and, to a lesser extent, in the pubic area, can be very traumatic for some women, especially if they've always had thick, luxuriant locks. A friend of mine almost had a breakdown when her thick hair began to go. She spent thousands of dollars and hours having needles stuck into her head and creams rubbed into her scalp—to no avail.

Although my friendly periodontist denies a trend, all my forty-plus associates seem to be having gum surgery. Maybe they just couldn't afford it before, but I've rarely seen a woman over forty leave a dentist's chair without a requisition for a few thousand dollars' worth of fancy scalings. That gums deteriorate at this age is logical, because the ground substance that is the basis of all connective tissue starts loosening. A collagen that could reinforce sagging gums may be on the horizon. Collagen is a tough, resistant kind of connective tissue. Biogenetic engineering has made it possible actually to synthesize this material so that it can be used to repair living tissue damage, much as cement is used to fill cracks in pavement. It's simple, of course, to avoid the whole mess and expense with vigorous daily flossing and good mouth hygiene. Gums respond well to both, plus occasional deeper scaling (removing the plaque from the teeth and cleaning the gums) by your dentist.

Fat cells constitute the one biologic group of cells—with the exception of cancer cells—that just keep reproducing with age. Most of the time the new fat is stored in totally inappropriate places (cosmetically speaking), and the traditional bulges get bigger. It's also more difficult to lose weight—a subject I treat at great length in the second half of this book.

This is a time when many women, particularly married women, reassess themselves. Single women probably went through this phase years earlier and by this time are quite practiced at shifting gears. That's why they can achieve phenomenal success in this period if they don't worry too much about aging. All women realize that this is the last time they can rely on a reasonably cooperative body and high energy levels, and the luckiest manage to find an outlet.

Married women often say, "I feel better than ever about myself"; "I know who I am"; and "At last I have time to think about *me*." The stirrings of freedom, however, are often accompanied by guilt: "My husband and children need me, but *I* need me, too"; "Should I go back to school and not be around when the kids come home?"; or "I deserve a little fun, but will my family survive without me?" It can sound like the stuff of television drama until it actually happens to you or to someone you know. Your husband and children may be marvelous human beings, but they can feel possessive toward you even as they applaud your new vitality and achievements. Don't retreat from your course or reaffirm your dependence; that's as good as locking yourself indoors and drawing the shades for the rest of your life. This is, perhaps, the last phase in which you *can* cope with every problem that arises.

Whatever you term the end of this stage—ovarian failure, post-reproductive life, the climacteric, or menopause—it usually begins in a burst of physical and emotional energy that constitutes the most dramatic shift since adolescence: overbleeding or underbleeding, severe premenstrual tension, swollen breasts, hot flashes, false pregnancy tests, anxiety, depression, relief, sadness, and joy; lots of forces and counterforces, a biochemical *Ben Hur*. This is a decade in which to live as fully as possible, so that no matter how difficult the next stage is, you'll still recall the myriad sensations of a rich and active life.

Stage Two: Ages Fifty to Sixty

For some women, the honeymoon of the forties ends now. This really is what aging is all about. If you haven't made major changes in your life-style over the previous decade, alternations will be more difficult now. It takes a lot of energy to make changes, and energy is in shorter supply at this age. Biologically, energy systems grow old, too—they don't yield so much, they lose their reserve capacities. The spirit is willing, but we know the way of all flesh. Little things become power struggles with your body.

In the fifties you must integrate your past life with the life to come, making adjustments to maintain biological, social, and psychological equilibrium. Battle fatigue is common. Ways of coping that take a heavy toll in energy must be abandoned. Acceptance and accommodation are the norm: women in stage two would rather switch than fight. "I don't give a damn," many women rationalize. "I finally have my priorities straight. I don't waste time anymore on meaningless contacts."

On one side there may be aged parents and their debilities; on the other, college-age children and their vitality. Death and life—and just when you need to balance yourself in the middle of the seesaw, your energy levels drop.

Reproductive life ends during this stage, with a whimper if you're lucky, with a bang if you're not. Your menopause could be a gentle cessation of menses, with just a few drops of blood and periods that come further and further apart; or it could be marked by fierce and uneven hormonal bursts, causing problems I will discuss at length in the next chapter.

This is the decade when your cast-iron stomach rebels. The foods you used to polish off with alacrity can cause all kinds of digestive disturbances. Some foods spontaneously become irritating to the intestinal tract (onions, for example); some provoke a sudden allergy (citrus juice); others require enzymes, which you lose in the normal process of aging, to digest—lettuce, certain raw fruits, milk and milk products, can all produce sudden abdominal cramps and diarrhea.

Luckily, most of these "functional" bowel problems (there's no actual disease) can be cleared up by changing eating habits and/or foodstuffs. And almost every food you give up to protect your gastrointestinal tract either has a reasonable substitute or may be altered to make it more acceptable to the digestive system. For instance, raw spinach is a good substitute for lettuce if the latter starts irritating your gut. And simply removing the skin from certain raw fruits can make them digestible. Other foods have to be avoided.

You don't need to become a food cripple, though—someone

who surrenders without a fight, proclaiming, "Anything I eat gives me gas, diarrhea, or cramps." It's not that you can't eat *anything*. Usually it's easy to detect the offending food, but the search should be systematic, with certain foods eliminated and then added back to the diet. If you don't *want* to give up the offending food, certain commercial preparations could prove helpful. Mixed digestive enzymes taken after meals can often ease the digestive process. These are available in small amounts from health-food stores, or by prescription from your doctor. (If you can't tolerate milk, yet enjoy it on cereal and need the calcium and nutrients it contains, there are many artificial lactase preparations you can substitute; see the section on lactose intolerance in Chapter 5.) Learn to live with your new digestive tract. Remember, as humans, we have a lot more options in our diets than other mammals. Imagine the problems of a cow that is allergic to grass!

This is the age when intestinal diverticuli appear more frequently. These are "outpouchings" of the intestines, the combined effect of an inherent weakness in the intestinal wall and the loss of elasticity that occurs with aging. These little pouches can fill with undigested food and become infected, causing lower-abdominal pain and fever. After you've treated the infection with antibiotics, a high-fiber, low-fat diet will stimulate the intestine and move food through at a more rapid pace.

All intestinal problems can cause changes in bowel habits. You should report any major ones to your doctor, even if you think you know what's causing them. At the very least, you should take a stool specimen to check for occult blood, which is blood you can't see with the naked eye. This should be done annually after the age of forty. Any doctor will have little packets that you can take home, fill with the sample, and send back. If the test result is negative (no blood found), no further steps are needed—unless the symptoms persist. In that case, a checkup is a good idea.

Many females over fifty think that they have arthritis, but most have no clear-cut disease. They just have more aches and pains—occasionally severe. The complaint is so prevalent that I have devoted a section to it later in this book

(Chapter 8), but I mention it here because it invariably begins during the fifties. Most of the time these pains are not crippling—not that it's much fun to walk around in agony, but at least you can walk. It's a tough problem to cope with, because existing methods of treatment are not very effective. No wonder women buy copper bracelets and snake oil; nothing else does much good. The best that science has to offer is still a tub of hot water and aspirin for pain.

This is the period of greatest change, and along with it comes the realization that you can't go back. You must move forward: with the wind if you can accept it, or against the wind if you're up for a good struggle. But you must move. Biologically, your body is in a degenerative state, but this can be a slow process, and you probably have many years left. Socially and psychologically, you will continue to grow—as long as you let yourself.

Stage Three: Ages Sixty to Seventy

What limits the life span of a cell? The over-sixty woman would probably like to know even more urgently than the rest of us, and the physician often becomes the most important person in her life. But if she has no chronic disease she feels good—often better than her fifty-year-old sister.

By the year 2000, almost half our population will be over sixty, and then, perhaps, the woman at this age will not feel so strongly that "the world belongs to the young." Today, though, in the married female, excitement and the drive for self-realization are often lost, and more and more she sees herself in terms of her family. I interviewed more than thirty women before I found one who didn't define her feelings about herself by invoking the condition of her marriage or what her children were doing. Of course, few of these women had "careers," though many of them had worked. As more career women reach this stage, the over-sixty female population may come to be more vital and engaged as a whole.

Stage three is the age when cancer starts to become more common. All organisms, if they survive long enough to be exposed to enough noxious stimuli, can get it. Whether the insult to the cell is environmental or viral, something makes it change so that it multiplies like mad, with the total approval of the other cells—cells that often won't hesitate to reject a lifesaving transplant if it feels "foreign." It's not fair or logical, but cancer is a mean, relentless customer, and there's not much you can do to stop it. It has been suggested that moderately high does of vitamins A and C afford protection against some tumors. There is no question that sun not only ages skin rapidly but stimulates new growths that could be malignant. Low-fat, high-fiber diets seem to play some role in preventing cancer of the colon.

Regular checkups and immediate investigation of any change, lump, bump, or thickening are essential. Some researchers believe that stress can weaken the body's immune system, which is fairly weak at this stage anyway. So be "mellow." It could actually prolong your life.

Bones get thinner in the sixties, particularly if you are slender and white. If you have not been taking estrogen for this condition, called osteoporosis, it's too late to start now. But doctors may soon have an answer to the problem of how to rebuild bone in fluoride. Calcium, appropriate doses of vitamin D, and as much exercise as you can do will slow the demineralization.

The central nervous system really suffers in the sixties. Tremors and loss of equilibrium are almost untreatable. Hearing and sight become less acute; memory sometimes slips a little; but thinking, reasoning, intuition, and interest are intact in most women. They can even improve. Remember, only 10 percent of elderly people become technically "senile." Many others who often act like it simply withdraw, out of fear, frustration, or depression.

Often, undiagnosed and treatable diseases can affect the nervous system. I knew one elderly female who was unsteady on her feet and had severe tremors. She was found to have a serious potassium deficiency that had been brought about by the use of a diuretic—a pill used to help the kidney excrete water. Another woman, in her early sixties, was extremely confused and forgetful. It turned out that she was having episodes of irregular heartbeats (arrhythmias), which were depriving her brain of oxygen and causing her confusion. Still another, who had been diagnosed as hopelessly senile, was found to be hypothyroid. Thyroid hormone cleared up her "dementia" in two weeks, and she was more lucid than ever.

Although this is the age of coronary heart disease (hardening of the arteries) in women—approximately ten years later than in men—the female heart condition is generally milder and responds very well to drugs (which are excellent for this disease and are getting even better). You can still have sexual intercourse with heart disease, by the way. Intercourse causes the same amount of exertion as climbing two or three flights of stairs. Just don't try it underwater or while you're eating.

Though the stage-three woman may resent her biological "station," she soon realizes that she can do the same things at rest that she always could. Sometimes she can do them better. She knows it takes longer to refuel after expending energy, but she has learned to be patient with her body. Perhaps she has become more philosophical about life and death. Resignation at this age—which implies realism, not "quitting"—is far healthier than denial. The women who withdraw into the family unit are the most vulnerable to being left alone. Companionship and social intercourse are extremely important for all over-sixty women, and the circle of friends shouldn't be limited to other over-sixties. One of the saddest symptoms of our society is the tendency of older people to confine themselves to "old-age communities."

Stage Four: Over Seventy

The average male life span is 68.7 years; the average for the female, 76.4. So it's logical to assume that the majority of persons over seventy are women. Yet very little research has been done on the general well-being (not just physical health) of the seventy-year-old female. What is she really like? What are her needs, her desires, her ambitions, her conflicts, her fears? Doctors have talked *to* them, but not *with* them.

Biologic aging alone, although obviously significant, has given everyone a confused picture of the capabilities, determination, and stamina of the women in this age group.

There is no doubt that cell size is shrinking, that collagen (connective tissue) fibers are becoming less elastic, and that the organism is becoming frailer. What people don't realize is that the physical organism too often hides mental acuity. Many people—including the women themselves—dwell on the negatives, not the positives. They are surprised when a woman in the eighth decade is shrewd, clever, outgoing, and interested in new ideas. In Arthur Kopit's heartbreaking play *Wings,* for example, a woman who has had a stroke can neither talk nor move, but her thoughts are coherent and intelligent. The audience is permitted to share these thoughts with her and is forced to watch how she is infantilized and patronized because she is physically unable to express herself. She can only cry.

On a recent trip, because of a shortage of tables I was seated at breakfast with a retired schoolteacher. When I tried to converse with her, I realized that she had some neurological disease and could barely make herself understood. Poor woman, I thought, how could she come on a trip so debilitated and so alone? I later found out that the "poor woman" could walk faster and farther than people much younger—including me. She could shop longer and bargain better than those who could talk clearly, and she was the only one in her sightseeing group to return to the hotel, not to nap, but to swim. She was a brave woman, and my first evaluation of her was stupid. She had developed her areas of strength, and she understood and lived with her limitations. She took risks—something many older people are afraid to do.

The medical literature on the eighth decade adopts a tone that can best be described as "gingerly," "apologetic." Researchers have been led to believe that older people perform tasks more slowly and not so well, have worse recall and poorer retrieval of stored information, and overall are not as intelligent or competent as younger people.

It would be useless to plead that there is no falling off in speed, energy, or overall competence as people age. But, remember, that's in relation to *themselves,* not to others. A seventy-five-year-old woman may not be as quick to comprehend things as she was at age twenty, but she may be a lot quicker than some twenty-year-olds. To make a blanket assertion that seventy-year-olds as a group are less competent than twenty-year-olds as a group doesn't say very much about individual seventy-year-olds. It's not just inhumane; it's downright misleading.

The quality of life and perception does often decline after seventy, but the reasons are as much cultural and sociological as they are physical. Most women can't see as well as they used to, and a large percentage of them never have their glasses adjusted. Then they don't read as much, and reading is a major source of new ideas. Night vision is a problem, so they don't drive or go out to the theater, movies, or concerts. Thus, another source of learning is eliminated. You think watching movies on television is the same? No way. Most television is brain rot, and even when it isn't, you still miss the public experience of responding to a work of art with other people. Even waiting in line is a learning process, you can talk or listen to people, and the moderate stress you feel is the kind that keeps your pulse rate up and your arteries clear—the kind that keeps you younger. American culture is becoming more and more private, more geared to home entertainment; and the homebody is apt to be more ignorant, self-centered, suspicious of others, and resistant to new ideas and experiences.

Hearing in females starts to go at age thirty-seven, and by the seventies the loss is probably noticeable. If you don't hear so well, you may misinterpret much of what goes on around you; or, even worse, you may confabulate, making up stories about what you think you heard. You also tend to get suspicious or paranoid, because the mind plays funny tricks on you when you can't hear. Ear problems sometimes affect equilibrium as well. And people in their seventies do have balance problems, which is a primary reason that many of them don't like to go out—they're afraid of tripping. Tripping to a seventy-year-old female can be trouble, because her bones can break pretty easily. The more inactive she is, of course, the more easily they break.

It is important in these years to have all the technical help you can get. *Get good glasses*. Don't live with opacities or cataracts. Find somebody who will fight to preserve your sight. Investigate new forms of lens surgery. Get a hearing aid. Most hearing aids, unfortunately, aren't very effective, but they're better than nothing, and it has always surprised me how much women resent having to wear hearing aids when they think nothing of wearing glasses. Hearing is the essence of communication, and you should do *anything* to keep your ability to communicate unimpaired.

One of my happiest professional experiences involved a seventy-year-old woman whose son brought her to me in desperation to lose weight. She was a virtual recluse, never leaving her house, hardly moving. "Mother is like a vegetable," her son told me. "Maybe if she loses weight she will be better." Not only did the "vegetable" end up losing eighty pounds, but we discovered that she couldn't see very well. Her glasses were small, outdated, and uncomfortable. At my insistence, she changed eye doctors and got the correct prescription (although she reminded me how unflattering she thought her newfangled glasses were). Now, two years later, she is a frequent visitor to my office. Yet she drives here alone. She is active, outgoing, and takes care of a demanding eighty-five-year-old aunt, and she loves every minute of her "servitude."

Nutrition also plays an extremely important role in the energy levels and overall functioning of the seventy-plus female. Older people eat too much mush. They ought to consume more fiber for good, sturdy bowels and to eliminate constipation (see the high-fiber diet in Appendix 2); lots more calcium and appropriate doses of vitamin D for bones; and more B_{12} (never underestimate B vitamins, with the exception of niacin, because they make people feel good). They should consume fewer total calories and divide their meals into smaller feedings.

One of the most overlooked problems in older women is their extreme sensitivity to all medications. Adverse reactions to prescribed drugs are called *iatrogenic,* which means "caused by the physician." One aspirin can cause intestinal bleeding, which can lead to anemia, which can cause weakness, fatigue, and confusion. Drugs that lower blood pressure can lower it too much, interfering with the flow of oxygen to the brain and causing a kind of ministroke. Tranquilizers often end up causing stupor. It is tragic that the segment of the population needing the most chemical assistance can tolerate the least.

If you are having unpleasant symptoms and the doctor can find no obvious cause, make sure that you are not overreacting to a drug or having a bad reaction to a mixture of two or more drugs. A woman I knew began to faint repeatedly, and everybody thought she was having a stroke. When they hospitalized her and ran some tests, doctors discovered that she had become very sensitive to a drug she was taking for a severe tremor. Her body had stopped producing platelets (a necessary component in blood clotting, which keeps you from bleeding to death), and her fainting spells were caused by a loss of blood through the intestine.

Exercise is extremely important during the seventies. It keeps your brain well oxygenated and your bones sturdier. It doesn't have to be frenetic exercise—just lifting some small (two-pound) weights to strengthen those fragile muscles; walking outdoors in nice, moderate weather, and indoors (try a shopping mall) when the weather gets bad. (If you don't live near a mall, walk around a big discount store.) And don't forget to stretch, to limber up stiff joints.

When you are seventy, your problem-solving abilities may be slower, you might have to learn new methods of doing old tricks, and your reaction time might not be so fast. But you are still an intelligent and capable human being, and you probably have many productive and fun years ahead of you. Although your health might be fragile, civilization and modern technology can give you back what nature has taken away. Take advantage of both.

My seventy-year-old friend Birdie took a course last year in Greek and Roman mythology at a local community college. (Students over sixty-five could take courses for free.) Birdie was worried because the names of the gods and goddesses confused her. Should I tell her they confounded me, too, when I was twenty?

Chapter 2

The Hormone Upheaval of Mid-life

We have done women a terrible injustice. It's a wonder many of them didn't go crazy. For years we believed that menopausal symptoms were strictly emotional and shrugged them off.

—A male gynecologist at an
endocrinology conference

When I was in medical school, people used to say that busy, well-adjusted, productive women didn't have menopausal symptoms; it was only the psychologically unstable who suffered so much. We were taught to counsel women in all seriousness that if they were psychologically prepared for the end of reproductive life, they'd have no symptoms. What a joke! The reason "stable" women didn't complain so loud or so long as their "unstable" counterparts was that they had a reputation of stability to maintain. They suffered alone and in silence, because if they didn't, they would have been labeled weak and neurotic like the rest.

The majority of women will have severe menopausal symptoms *no matter how well adjusted they are*.

Post-reproductive life syndrome (a term I'll use, whenever possible, to replace menopause) has two phases: acute and chronic. In the acute phase, symptoms can appear ten years before the menses cease and persist until a year or two after the last drop of menstrual blood. A thirty-six-year-old patient of mine once complained to me that her gynecologist had told her she was "too young to have menopausal symptoms." But she did! She was scared to death about what terrible disease was causing her hot flashes, weakness, severe premenstrual tension, and breast tenderness. In this phase, irregular bleeding patterns often develop. Excessive bleeding may be relieved with hormones or a minor surgical procedure known as a D and C (dilation and curettage), in which the uterine wall is scraped. If the bleeding continues unabated, a hysterectomy is sometimes necessary.

To understand the hormonal changes of menopause, it's necessary to know something about the female reproductive system. The reproductive cycle is essentially controlled by the body's production of four hormones, chemical substances with a specific effect on certain target organs. These hormones include estrogen and progesterone, which are manufactured by the ovaries; and FSH (follicle-stimulating hormone) and LH (luteinizing hormone), which are manufactured by the anterior pituitary gland. The last two are called gonadotrophins, which means "gonad nourishers." (Gonads are sex organs.)

Estrogen has many functions in the body, but its most important role is to stimulate the growth of the female reproductive tract, which includes the uterus, breasts, urethra, vagina, and ovaries. It helps to maintain all these reproductive organs, to keep them functioning smoothly. It also affects the heart, the central nervous system, and the skeletal muscles.

The gonadotrophins regulate activity in the ovaries. Inside the ovaries are follicles, which are little cavities that contain eggs. In the first stage of the menstrual cycle, FSH stimulates the ovary to develop a fully mature follicle for ovulation, the process that culminates in the discharge of a mature egg (ovum) into the fallopian tube for fertilization. The growing follicle and the ovary, in turn, produce increasing amounts of estrogen. This estrogen, together with the FSH, then stimulates the second pituitary hormone, LH. At the correct moment, when the egg is mature enough to be discharged from the ovary, there is a surge of FSH and LH. This induces ovulation. The egg, unfertilized but mature, is ready for its journey to the uterus. After ovulation, the empty follicle is luteinized (by LH, of course) and becomes something called a corpus luteum ("yellow body"). The corpus luteum is a short-term gland that secretes large amounts of progesterone and small amounts of estrogen for fourteen days. Progesterone builds up the lining of the uterus (the endometrium) in preparation for the egg. Without fertilization, the corpus luteum degenerates, the estrogen and progesterone levels drop, and the uterine lining sloughs off. That's menstruation. FSH is then activated and the cycle begins anew.

Post-Reproductive Life Syndrome

Stage I: The LH Stage

(Can occur normally anywhere from ages thirty-five to fifty and last up to ten years)

Now, what does all this have to do with menopause? The major physical event in menopause is ovarian failure, which means *no more eggs* are produced. The follicles are used up or dead. Without growing follicles, estrogen levels drop. Remember, the gonadotrophins stimulate the ovaries to produce estrogen; so the sharp decline in estrogen levels causes a frantic rise in gonadotrophins, and it is the burst of LH, and perhaps its activation of other body chemicals trying to activate the dying ovary, that causes the hot flashes and flushes experienced by 80 percent of all women during this period.

This can be an incessant warmth when you've always been rather cold, a hot sensation in the face that makes you think you have a fever, or simply a "happening" with a distinct beginning, climax, and finale. It can make you drip with sweat. The worst thing about the hot flash, however, is that it can partially wake you ten to twelve times a night, disturbing REM sleep—a deep, restful, dream-filled part of sleep. Often you don't remember these moments; the next morning you wake up and wonder why you're so tired, irritable, and depressed, why you can't think straight or cope. This is when many women become hooked on pills or alcohol to alleviate the incredible tension which they've been told is all in their imagination.

There are also psychological symptoms, such as anxiety, depression, and headaches, which are not supposed to be hormonally induced. They are *supposed* to be responses to the children leaving home, signs of aging, and the reality of approaching death. All of these play a part, I'm sure; but I think they're exacerbated by what's happening chemically.

Weight gain is also a problem at this time. The woman who weighed 125 a year earlier can easily weigh 140. Fat distribution is different as well, also the result of hormonal stimulation.

The overweight female, though, has an easier time with the physical symptoms of post-reproductive life syndrome because she has a fair amount of estrogen that's being converted by her fat. Once doctors believed that estrogen no longer circulated when the ovary stopped manufacturing it. Now we know that although much less estrogen is available, there is still some in the bloodstream. It's produced in certain tissues by the conversion of another hormone, androstenedione, which continues to be secreted by both the ovary and the adrenal gland, even after menopause. One of the most important of these estrogen-converting tissue sites is fat. The more fat you have, the more estrogen you seem to manufacture. Thus, the body does make some attempt to compensate for falling estrogen supplies. Well-padded women frequently have pretty, unlined skin (also because it's puffed out). Their mid-life sex problems are less severe because their vaginas are wetter, and they don't experience pain, dryness, and loss of orgasmic response. This is primarily because the female hormone ensures a rich supply of blood to the vagina, which is an important factor in achieving orgasm. That's the good news. The bad news is that the obese post-reproductive female has a four to five times greater risk of having uterine cancer than her thin counterpart—the major drawback of chronic estrogen exposure.

Stage II: The Estrogen-Deficient Stage
(Can start six months to one year after total cessation of menstrual periods and continues on)

Chronic symptoms begin to appear one to two years after cessation of the menses. These symptoms include a loss of elasticity and dryness of the wall of the vagina, stress incontinence (a loss of urine when you cough or laugh), painful uterine spasms, more facial hair, and increasing loss of bone calcium. All of these effects can be traced to a decline in estrogen.

Menopause Is Just a Hormonal Crisis The real crisis in post-reproductive life syndrome, then, is estrogen depletion—but men can make it worse. When a couple has endured for, say, twenty-five years, the male, usually several years older and at the height of his career (if he is successful) or the depth of his depression (if he is not), can withdraw love, support, and attention from his wife—who is otherwise beset with severe physical symptoms (never mind the *normal* anxieties of aging). It's the combination that kills. A loving spouse or lover may not alleviate the physical symptoms, but he (or she, for that matter) can help to cushion the psychological ones. Men directly account for much of the anxiety in this period; studies have shown that there is less anxiety and depression in unmarried females at this age, even though the physical symptoms are the same.

Crisis Intervention I: Estrogen What can relieve these physical symptoms? Estrogen replacement therapy. *Hormone* is a dirty word today to many women who have been brainwashed into giving up the only thing that can help keep them physically younger. Yes, it's artificial. Yes, it's unnatural. Nature, remember, never intended for females to live beyond their reproductive organs. But they do, and now medical science should work to make those years more comfortable. If you are a candidate for estrogen therapy, it can be good for you from head to toe: its benefits include more energy, more elastic skin, no hot flashes, improved sleep, less depression, better concentration, increased memory, and a moister, more responsive vagina (and, hence, no pain during intercourse).

But, most important, estrogen is necessary for your bones, especially if you are a slender, white, inactive female who smokes cigarettes. Estrogen protects the bones from the parathyroid hormone, which is a calcium Robin Hood, robbing from the rich (the bone) and giving to the poor (the bloodstream). Without a lot of estrogen, parathyroid hormone thins the bone matrix and decreases bone strength, leading to a disease called osteoporosis—a decrease in the mineral content (primarily calcium of the bone). This leads to an increased incidence of bone fractures, with their attendant suffering and even death in women over fifty. There are other hormonal and chemical influences active in osteoporosis, but it gets very complicated and nobody is too sure about exactly what goes on.

But what about estrogen and cancer? Scientists think the higher the dose, the greater the risk. In very low doses there seems to be no increase in cases of uterine cancer. Unfortunately, doses that are too low don't protect against osteoporosis. Therefore it is crucial when you are on estrogen replacement therapy, to use the smallest amount that will still do the job. This may vary from woman to woman. There is a small risk that estrogen buildup on the uterine wall will lead to cancer. But look at the statistics: three thousand women die annually of endometrial (uterine) cancer; *fifty thousand* die as a direct result of osteoporotic fractures. The incidence of hip fractures rises dramatically after fifty; pelvic and long-bone fractures and vertebral collapse are also common. And osteoporosis is often not diagnosed until after the fracture has occurred, when estrogen can no longer help. (Some researchers report that fluoride treatments can help rebuild collapsed bone—an exciting treatment, but not yet widespread.) Estrogen therapy can stop the disease from progressing and will often correct the calcium loss, but it will not repair already destroyed bone.

I think that estrogen is so useful to the post-reproductive female that it's almost worth getting your uterus out if you're going to worry about uterine cancer. The new therapy, however, in which estrogen is given for twenty-one days and progesterone for ten, might make this unnecessary. The progesterone, remember, causes you to shed your uterine lining every month, making estrogen buildup almost impossible. Yes, you can continue to have artificial periods. Won't it be fun when you're eighty and having your period the same week as your granddaughter? Recent studies report that the incidence of uterine cancer in women who use the estrogen-progesterone combination is actually *lower* than in women who use nothing. Progesterone may also strengthen bones. Some studies, however, suggest that it increases the risk of heart attack or thrombotic episodes. The risk could be diminished by using progesterone at less regular intervals—every two or three months, for example.

There are, of course, other problems with estrogen therapy. One of them is that it promotes weight gain. But it's easier to gain weight in post-reproductive life anyway, so if you can't win you might as well be comfortable.

Estrogen is usually given in pill form and should be started no later than one to two years after cessation of the menses, or sooner if severe menopausal symptoms occur.

Crisis Intervention II: Alternate Therapy If you can't take estrogen because of vaginal bleeding, previous estrogen dependent tumors, phlebitis, heart disease, strokes, serious liver disease, or, perhaps, a high risk of any of these, or if you just *don't want to,* you can always take progesterone alone. But this is probably less effective and can cause more complications. Although it alleviates hot flashes, it also causes weight gain, fluid retention, depression, and possibly thrombotic complications (blood clots). Other than estrogen and progesterone, little else has been particularly effective in controlling hot flashes. The only other substance that has shown some promise in relieving hot flashes is clonidine, a drug primarily used to lower blood pressure, when given in small doses.

If you can't, or won't, use estrogen, *exercise* can keep your bones in better condition. This, in addition to calcium—at least 1,500 milligrams a day—with Vitamin D to increase its absorption, is an effective regimen. If you can't tolerate milk or milk products, eat plenty of other high-calcium foods such as broccoli, clams, oysters, collards, canned salmon (eat the bones), and spinach. The parathyroid hormone, which robs the bone of calcium, is known as the "thief that steals in the night" because it is more active while you sleep, so it might be a good idea to have those calcium snacks (or pills) at bedtime. If calcium upsets your stomach (and it tends to), consume it during meals.

What about your vagina if you can't take estrogen? Well, as one sex therapist put it, "There's always spit." Male sex therapists say sex, sex, sex will keep it moist, although for some reason the women I talk to don't agree. Vaginal estrogen creams are effective and potentially less risky than other estrogen therapies. However, since estrogen can be absorbed through the vagina into the bloodstream, there is reason to believe the manufacturer's suggested dose is too high. Instead, many doctors prescribe one-fifth to one-tenth of the recommended amount, with excellent results.

Chapter 3

Sex

Libido or sexual appetite is like food appetite: there are wide variations within the norm. There are high-desire and low-desire people; the problem is that in our society everybody's supposed to be high-desire, or at least to conform to the national average of 3.2 orgasms per week. When a low-desire person marries another low-desire person, everyone is happy until they start comparing their experience with the average. When a high-desire marries a high-desire, the rest of us are flooded with tales of what a blast it is every night—until the high-desire people aren't satisfied with one partner.

The female libido seems to conform to the three *R*s: responsiveness, receptivity, and relaxation. That's why sex gets better with age. Some researchers think that a woman can't reach the true height of her sexuality until she has had children, when there is greater capacity for pelvic congestion, which means she has more blood vessels in her genital tract that fill with blood during intercourse and make orgasm more intense.

Orgasm has been the magic word of the last few decades. Must you reach one? How many can you have in a night? Virginia Johnson created quite a ripple when she described the male orgasm as "a rose is a rose is a rose." The male population was highly insulted and claimed that there were levels to their orgasms, too. I don't know about male orgasms because I've never had one, but there are certainly levels to the female variety. There are many different kinds: mellow orgasms, angry orgasms, mini-orgasms, painful orgasms, grateful orgasms, even thank-you orgasms, which are the ones you get after being given a diamond bracelet or a new washing machine.

Is sex better for the older woman, or is it downhill? Because reproduction was once considered the sole reason for sexuality in women, those who passed their childbearing years were automatically considered asexual. If a woman is expected to lose interest sexually, she often does. Her self-esteem may diminish ("I'm old and worthless"), she may be discouraged by physical limitations ("I can't do it hanging from the chandelier anymore"), and she may be embarrassed by changes in her body ("What is my stomach doing around my knees?"). The last is often the final straw.

The older female starts to lose her sexual identity when she assumes the traditional guises of late life. The role most devastating to her femininity is the "grandmother." It is hard for a woman playing grandmother to cross over and become a wife, because grandmothers don't screw—right? They are considered "lovable" in our culture, but they are definitely not sex objects, and often they come to see themselves the way others do. A grandmother *should* be a sex object—at least to a grandfather. One of my father's old medical-school classmates is seventy-four and has recently started a new family. He's got kids aged two and five, so someone must think he's quite manly. Men are able to separate their various roles; father, grandfather, lover, and wage earner can coexist in the same body. But women have trouble with this, maybe because they have traditionally defined themselves in terms of the way *men* see them. In time, perhaps, they, too, will be able to distinguish their various roles.

Physical Changes

The direction sex takes usually has a lot to do with what it was like before menopause. If you were active sexually and orgasmic when you were younger, you are more likely to be when you're older, even though there may be changes in your physical responses. Lubrication of the vagina, the first sign of sexual excitement, may take longer to occur. The labia minora do not become engorged; the Bartholin's glands, responsible for some vaginal lubrication, stop secreting; the vagina expands less; and the vaginal lining (mucosa) is thinner and more sensitive. In other words, the vagina becomes dry, floppy, and fragile. This makes intercourse painful.

But do most women complain? No; their groans of pain are masked—and interpreted—as groans of pleasure.

If the male senses his mate's discomfort, withdrawal, and pain, he can become resentful and even impotent. The wife then worries about her husband's impotence. The husband blames it on his wife's dry vagina. Despite the fact that *she's* the one who's been suffering, it's *his* unhappiness that sends her to a gynecologist for treatment.

You retain your orgasmic potential as you age and are still capable of multiple orgasms. You are an ideal sexual partner if you don't have vaginal problems—and estrogen replacement or vaginal estrogen cream (available by prescription only) often does a beautiful job of clearing them up. But women at this age have difficulty finding available, healthy, and interested partners. Unfortunately, older men are often out chasing younger women.

Some women get irritable durng the post-reproductive years, particularly before the climacteric. They develop changes in perception and sensory awareness, and they may not like to be touched or caressed as before. They convey the message "Don't come into my space." This, indeed, could be a demand for privacy; after years of acquiescing and submitting, the woman wants a little time to herself to reorganize her thoughts about her changing body.

Two areas of your body can become extremely sensitive: the clitoris and the breast. Women who have previously enjoyed clitoral stimulation could find it irritating, painful, and unpleasant. Breast stimulation, which has always been overrated as far as women are concerned, can become annoying. Breast stimulation excites the male, but its effect on the female is unpredictable. There are many females who are never turned on by having their breasts tweaked and nibbled. But, aware of the fragile male ego, women are loath to interrupt their enthusiastic partners for fear of hurting their feelings; and they feel guilty because they have such "insensitive" breasts. A realistic problem is that no woman likes to have flabby, saggy breasts manipulated. It reminds her of what she had before and makes her feel inadequate. The solution lies in honest communication and in finding new ways of making love.

Self-Image Problems

It is difficult for a woman who has had a previously unrewarding sex life to have a good one after menopause. She probably never had much confidence to begin with, and aging can only make things worse. And a woman whose husband has cheated on her will rarely feel kindly toward him in bed. Some people think that an extramarital affair helps sex life at home, but this is often not the case for the older female, whose feelings of rejection and anger can diminish her capacity for sexual stimulation.

Depression can make females less interested in sex. Illness, disappointment, fear of the future, anxiety over aging parents, or aging in general can also suppress libidinous urges. If her partner is active sexually, however, she can fake well—and does, too many times. Unfortunately, women do a lot of faking. They are not permitted the luxury of just not feeling like sex. Too often the partner takes that as an accusation of sexual inadequacy. Many men think they're capable of bringing women to orgasm anytime.

A sixty-two-year-old woman was sent to me by her internist to lose weight. She confided that she had lost her sexual urge and was ashamed to talk about it with her male doctor. She was taking an antihypertensive medication and did not want to discontinue the drug because the doctor was worried about her blood pressure. But *she* was worried about her sex drive. Because she was in a weight-loss program (weight loss often brings down blood pressure), and her blood pressure was stable, I withdrew her medication so that she would feel sexy again. Her internist became extremely irritated and ordered her back on the medication. The patient, meanwhile, was getting very agitated because her husband resented her lack of sexual interest.

I couldn't take her off the blood pressure medication again, so I gave her a small dose of testosterone to see if it would help her feel sexier. It helped, but her internist was livid because I had prescribed a "hormone." He informed me that the loss of her libido was not terribly important, because she was older, and women can always pretend when they have sex.

That statement was made by a man who *dares* to treat women. It would never have been said about a male patient. When a male loses his interest in sex while on medication, there is an enormous scramble to find different drugs to correct the problem. When an older woman loses her libido, the attitude has been "Tough—she doesn't need it anyway. She can fake it."

Psychoanalysts think that women who need to have sex often at this age are looking for reassurance—they want to know they're wanted, that someone will take care of them. It's called "dependency strivings." Supposedly these women are lonely and inhibited—like adolescents—and are grasping at sex to overcome those long-standing feelings of inadequacy in a rather pathetic search for happiness after evaluating their successes and failures to date. With the shrinks, in other words, you can't win. If you're undersexed, they call you neurotic; if you're sexually active, you have "dependency strivings."

More realistically, women experience increased sex drive when they no longer fear pregnancy, when their children are not home interrupting them every minute, when they can have sex in the afternoon, and when financial pressures have eased. One of my patients in her sixties told me that when you wake up in the morning and find out you haven't been struck by lightning, you haven't got a horrible disease, and you're not pregnant, sex is fun! Some women are made to feel so guilty when they get "horny" that they have to consult with their physicians to make sure it's all right.

The afternoon is a very good aphrodisiac for women. Night sex was invented by our puritanical ancestors who thought the whole process should be relegated to the dark. But that just isn't a female time. Your enzyme systems are often depleted, and they need restoration from sleep. For males, an orgasm is very restful; but it isn't for a woman, especially if she has to toddle out of bed in the middle of a cold night to go to the bathroom so that she won't get cystitis. A lot of women at this age would feel much sexier if they had sex before supper and were allowed to go to sleep at bedtime.

Problems with the Mid-Life Male

Many mid-life men I've talked with have had bouts of boredom with sex. If there are no organic (disease) reasons for impotence, this disinterest is the result of having the same mate for twenty to fifty years. It has little to do with the quality of the wife. She may be loving, innovative, attractive, thin, and clean, but it doesn't seem to change the course of male restlessness. As she ages, she may also become less "feminine"—that is, more assertive and independent—which can be frightening to the man who feels less masculine.

Women whose husbands stop making sexual advances or become impotent often feel inadequate and rejected, and many try all the traditional turn-ons: lace underwear with holes in the appropriate places, long stockings with garters, porno movies, lascivious books, and even some aphrodisiacs (although, as of this writing, there are none that do any kind of reasonable job). Relax. Men who live with the same woman for this long generally fantasize about younger women, drool at girlie shows, and sometimes seek prostitutes to prove to themselves that they can still perform. What a pity their masculinity is so dependent on their sexual performance. This is just the time, if you're unlucky, that somebody new comes along who can excite them. Then you've got big problems, which you can ignore or wait out. Some of my friends have lost (temporarily), and they were good-looking, vivacious women. Monogamy laws were made to protect older women and young children, but they haven't been doing a great job.

As if all this weren't trouble enough, the marketplace is filled with pills that lower sex drive for men. The medicines that have the most devastating effect on male sexuality are the antihypertensive drugs, which cause loss of libido, impotence, or inability to achieve orgasm.

What can arouse male interest? Testosterone, touted as the ideal aphrodisiac, will not cure or improve impotence unless the male has an actual hormone deficiency. It can help libido in women, but it has to be given in large amounts—and there are side effects, such as hair growth and lowering of the voice. Alcohol inhibits sexual reflexes in men, causing depressed libido and impotence. Certainly impotence. Even Macbeth's drunken porter reported that alcohol "makes 'em and mars 'em," meaning it makes a man horny but renders his organ a flaccid tool. So a drink before sex is not the answer. Marijuana, however, can enhance sexuality in three ways: it slows down the perceived passage of time; it improves the sense of closeness between partners; and it increases tactile sensitivity. This is subjective, however, and quite variable.

One famous doctor gave me his ginseng formula for libido. I'll pass it on—but it never worked for those I hopefully gave it to: 6 capsules ginseng, 1,200 units vitamin E, 6 milligrams folic acid, and 60 milligrams zinc.

Diabetes is the most important organic cause of male impotence. It causes interruptions of certain neurogenic pathways that affect the filling of the penis with blood. (That's how men have erections.) Although some sexologists claim diabetes interferes with women's sexuality as well, recent studies show it has little effect. Diabetic women, even if they have some of the most severe neuropathies, do not seem to lack sexual interest or the ability to achieve orgasm. Penile erection, the sword of male sexuality, is much more sensitive to external stimuli—psychological, biological, and physical—than the female vagina.

And So To Bed . . .

Generally, mid- and late-life women can have a great sex life *if* (1) they had a good sex life when they were younger; (2) they understand and cater to the fragile male ego; (3) they take estrogen locally or systemically if their vaginas are sore and dry; (4) they have an available, warm, loving sex partner; (5) they feel attractive; and (6) they aren't depressed or chronically worried. Sex at this time of life can be especially sweet, because there is no worry about pregnancy. No matter how good birth-control methods are, many of them aren't foolproof. Also, you should be old enough, free enough, to drop your old hang-ups and try a few different methods. You might be pleasantly surprised. And, remember, there are satisfactory substitutes for men; many older women are looking to other women as a source of caring, love, and even sexual pleasure.

If you had a lousy sex life before forty and you have the same partner, your chances of having a good sex life after forty are bad *unless* you get a lover (younger or older) or change mates. For the woman over forty to get a mate, she must be fairly seductive. Sexuality is extremely attractive at this age and depends upon a vigorous, healthy, warm, interested personality. All the mid- and late-life women I know who have remarried after divorce or the death of their husbands have exhibited these traits. Mothering, masochism, and narcissism don't sell well at this age.

Chapter 4

Fatigue

"I'm tired," my patient said.

Do you know how many women over forty say, "I'm tired"? Do you know what goes through a doctor's head when a woman says that? It goes something like this: "Is she sick? Is she anemic? Is she bored, or frustrated, or depressed? Is she working too hard, or not enough? Are her ovaries drying up? Is she hypoglycemic? Is she hypothyroid? Is she sleeping well? Is her husband treating her okay? Is this the first sign of a major disease? Should I give her a complete physical examination with blood and urine tests, or just try to reassure her that she's fine?"

Fatigue could be caused by any of these things, or none of them.

The most severe fatigue in females is related to viral disease, postviral states, anemia, or hypothyroidism; or in conjunction with changing hormonal states during adolescence, early pregnancy, just after pregnancy, or during post-reproductive life syndrome.

There are four important tests your doctor should administer to determine whether your fatigue is physically related:

1. A *blood test* will show whether you're anemic. It will also reveal leukemia or a viral or bacterial infection.

2. A *serum-potassium test* will reveal a potassium deficiency, a major chemical cause of fatigue.

3. A *monostat* will test for mononucleosis. A popular misconception is that this is a teenage disease. Women over forty contract it all the time, though once you've had it you can't get it again.

4. A *blood-sugar test* will reveal diabetes or hypoglycemia.

There are a couple of interesting theories on short-term, nonspecific fatigue. One is that when muscles and organs are depleted of enzymes (for any reason), they require time to regenerate. Fatigue is their signal to the brain to give them time. Another theory is that fatigue comes and goes according to cyclical biorhythms. Every process in the body is cyclical; fatigue marks the end of one cycle and the beginning of another.

How do you treat fatigue that has no organic basis? Appropriate rest, food, and exercise. This is the important trio for relief of "life-cycle" fatigue. Appropriate food for a female means a 1,500-calorie, low-fat, high-fiber diet—an adequate amount of food to feel comfortable, but *not* a weight-loss diet. Complex carbohydrates (starches), which form a large part of this diet, supply more pep than simple sugars and are also more filling. Call it "energy eating." Vitamins, iron, and a good attitude can also help, but after that you should respect your body and allow it to rest. Sometimes, however, fatigue may be the result of *too much* rest, in which case a brisk walk for at least half an hour a day should make you feel better. Analyze your sleep habits. Remember, the less work you do, the less sleep you actually need.

Fatigue makes women frequent more than one physician's office in search of an instant medical explanation—which is usually not forthcoming. At that point, the earnest doctor will often try to ease the patient's anxiety and to make her feel more comfortable. So a clever fifty-year-old woman can walk away with an armory of pills that would drive a teenage junkie to glassy-eyed ecstasy. I know a lady who collected *fifteen* different kinds of medications, including sleeping pills, tranquilizers, antidepressants, iron, thyroid, a psychic energizer, PABA, calcium tablets, and even an amphetamine. The sad part was that most of them didn't come within striking distance of her problem. She was tired despite adequate sleep and a healthful diet. Her body was cycling down, and she didn't want to admit it. She wanted her former energy levels. After a few years of assurances that she was perfectly healthy, she made peace with her new body and accepted her new capacities. And, mentally, she felt as good as ever.

If fatigue is unrelated to disease, the longer it persists, the more likely it is that the cause is psychological. If you feel wiped out for six months but don't have mono, anemia, or anything else, you may need a change in life-style. It's time to take steps on your own to correct the problem. The answer is not to take pills, which can make you more fatigued (unless there is a more important symptom than fatigue, such as panic or depression). Drinking is definitely not the answer, either. Alcohol is a depressant, and it acts on all your muscles; it certainly won't give you more energy.

Think about your life-style and what needs to be altered. Such changes will be hard, but you're on the defensive now, remember. If you are not working, a job might be the answer. I'm not being glib. It's often a hassle, I know, to look for work. But it's worth the effort. Look for a small job to start with; going from no-time to full-time is often disastrous. If you do have a job, try to do something different with it, or change jobs if you won't lose a lot of benefits. Even if you lose some benefits, it might be better to change if the fatigue is overwhelming. A long vacation if you can arrange and afford it might also do the trick.

Fatigue could also be the tip of the iceberg—the iceberg being a more serious disease. If it is, you'll know it soon enough; the fatigue will not abate, and the progression of the disease will be relentless if left untreated. On the following pages I'll discuss the most common and serious diseases that affect mature women and give you important information that could easily change your life.

Part II

THE MEDICAL PROBLEMS

Chapter 5

The Minor Annoyances

Although mentally or physically uncomfortable, the minor annoyances are usually not life-threatening. Yet women are always rushing to see their physicians at the first sign of trouble. I think you should realize that life is not free from pain, and that the more you know about what happens in your body, the less anxious you'll be. Anxiety can make minor pain even worse. You also won't spend a fortune running around trying to find answers.

Lactose and Assorted Food Intolerance

I once had a run-of-the-mill intestinal virus that took a long time to go away. My symptoms were a pain in my midsection, right above my belly button, and a constant feeling of nausea. Gas bubbled in my upper and lower intestines, and the cramps were unbearable. Even though I was eating the blandest food I could find—custard, pudding, and yogurt—I felt no better. Indeed, I felt worse. Finally, after weeks of suffering and treating myself, I told a gastroenterologist (stomach doctor) about my problem.

The first thing he asked was "What are you eating?"

"Bland milk products," I replied.

"Ha," he said. "You must have developed a lactose intolerance." (Lactose is the type of sugar found in milk.)

I looked at him in disbelief. I, who had been a milk lover for years—not milk alone, but milk in cereal, milk with cookies, and, of course, milk with chocolate cake. But I was in agony and willing to try anything, so I cut out all milk from my diet—and the symptoms went away. All of them. My stomach was as calm as the sea after a storm. "How could milk do this to me?" I asked. "Where did I get this crazy deficiency?"

It's often difficult to give up the idea that milk isn't "the perfect food," as the dairy council would have us believe. True, it contains most of the nutrients required by babies, and many of the vitamins and minerals. Yet *lactase,* the intestinal enzyme necessary for the breakdown of lactose, diminishes with age. Most mature women, particularly those of black or Eastern European extraction, have very little lactase activity, probably enough to handle small quantities of milk products but not enough for any sizable amount.

Normally, lactase breaks down milk sugar so that it can be absorbed. If the milk sugar is not broken down in the small intestines, where this process should occur, it moves, undigested, to the large intestine. There it is attacked by bacteria, split, and fermented, and the result is gas, abdominal distension, pain, spasms, and diarrhea. In fact, for years the milk recommended for ulcers—to "coat the stomach"—was probably causing as many symptoms as it cured.

Lactose, by the way, is present not only in milk but in milk products such as yogurt and soft cheese, in prepared dips, pudding, dried foods, instant potatoes, and instant breakfast drinks.

Occasionally, a viral disease destroys lactase temporarily. This is what happened to me. Some of its activity can be restored, but it rarely returns to previous levels. Now when I exceed a certain quantity of milk, I can feel the distressing side effects.

One problem with a lactase deficiency is that as a female gets older, her calcium requirements jump from 800 to 1,500 milligrams per day because of potential bone deterioration. Milk used to be a quick, painless way to get calcium, but it's not so painless if you have a lactose intolerance. The best solution is to take calcium supplements. If you must drink milk, you can take a commercial lactase that predigests the milk for you.

Symptoms of lactose intolerance are sometimes confused with irritable bowel syndrome (I.B.S.), formerly called spastic colon. I.B.S. symptoms are also abdominal distension, abdominal pain relieved by bowel movement, more frequent loose stools, mucus, or a sense of incomplete evacuation. I.B.S. is probably caused by an interruption of bowel motility as a result of dietary habits, heredity, and stress. It sometimes responds to a low-fat, high-fiber diet, particularly if you eat smaller meals. An antispasmodic medication can also help.

Both lactose intolerance and irritable bowel syndrome are more common in women, especially mid-life women, and both become more common and severe with age.

Constipation

One of my worst medical memories is my two-week stint as an intern on the urology service. The ward was filled with little old men recovering from prostate surgery. (The prostate is a gland that sits at the base of the bladder and secretes the fluid that carries sperm.) As a consequence of surgery, anesthesia, inactivity, and temporary loss of bowel tone, all of these men were constipated. No, they were one step beyond constipated—they had fecal impactions. That means the stools were so hard and dry that they couldn't slide out of the rectum, and, like a string of railroad cars, more stools kept piling up inside until there was a real "fecal jam." The poor old men were in agony; they were still in pain from the surgery, and their constipation made them swollen and distended.

What to do? Enema, you say? Not bloody likely—you couldn't get a nozzle past that dense brown mass. Guess again. Somebody had to go in and remove those feces. By hand. And guess who got the dirty job. So I spent two weeks elbow-deep in shit. Pardon me—no other way to put it. Don't feel sorry for *me,* though; feel sorry for those poor old men whose anuses had to accommodate an arm. Once an impaction was scooped out, we were able to get an enema nozzle into the anus and proceed with the cleaning out. That experience gave me a healthy respect for bowel motility (tone and movement).

It's nice to report that because of the change in American dietary habits, constipation is decreasing. The reason is an increase of dietary fiber, that undigestible residue that adds to the bulk of the stool. It has been observed that in cultures where people eat little refined sugar and large amounts of natural, unprocessed grains and leafy vegetables, few complain of constipation.

I often hear patients say that when their bowels don't move for a few days, they feel logy and toxic, almost as if they were absorbing ill humors from their guts. Doctors used to get a big kick out of that—a typical patient misconception. They're not laughing anymore. It now appears that a regular bowel movement is beneficial to your general state of well-being. Stagnation of fecal material in the bowel can actually cause certain fats to become toxic, which can make the cells of the intestinal lining more prone to change. That's often the first step in the development of intestinal cancer. Anyone over forty with previously regular bowel habits who suddenly develops severe constipation ought to get checked out, pronto. That goes for anyone prone to constipation who suddenly has a particularly painful or persistent bout as well.

What causes a stiff, hard, dry stool? Many things besides diet—not eating breakfast, for one. When you eat breakfast in the morning, the food makes the intestine contract, releasing a hormone called cholecystokinin (which is supposed to decrease appetite, by the way). This is followed by a bowel movement, and the entire process is called the gastro-colic reflex. Women who habitually don't eat breakfast and lunch are disturbing this reflex movement of the intestine.

Women also don't like to sit on strange toilets or to go to the bathroom at inopportune moments, so they will delay passage of feces and destroy their natural bowel rhythms. (This reluctance to go to the bathroom can also lead to cystitis.)

Drugs commonly used by females, such as iron, diuretics, and even some tranquilizers, can promote constipation, by drying out the intestinal tract, slowing it down, or both.

And, speaking of drying out, females tend not to drink enough water, for fear of urinating a lot. Adequate fluid intake does much to promote a good BM, though. Dieting also makes women constipated. This is because starches, which contain nondigestible residues like pectins and cellulose, are cut down in a diet. These residues pass intact through the intestines and give bulk to the stools, which become big and soft and easy to move. Also, you lose body water when you diet. Remember all the urinating you do in the first few days of a diet? This dries out your intestinal tract. Dieters have small, skinny stools and a dry intestinal tract, and that combination breeds constipation.

If you're still having menstruals, you are prone to constipation a few days prior to them. As certain hormone levels drop, you lose body water, making the stool and intestinal tract drier—a good constipation "combo."

Stool softeners and bulk formers are now the accepted method of treating constipation. Regular laxatives have fallen into disrepute because they tend to produce movement by irritation. That interferes with the natural rhythm of a bowel movement, which is important to maintain throughout life.

Most constipation can be corrected by the inclusion of bran and bran products in the diet. This helps intestinal mobility and tone, which is extremely important in mid-life and beyond. There's a natural tendency of the bowel wall to lose its elasticity and to become flaccid, and the stimulatory properties of bran can keep it functioning better. The finely ground bran from a health-food store is often much easier to tolerate because it has more surface for the intestinal bacteria to attack and so causes less gas. Start with two teaspoons and work gradually up to two tablespoons of finely ground bran a day. This seems to ensure good bowel function and probably helps to prevent diverticulitis and irritable bowel syndrome. Also, because it lowers the body's absorption of dietary fat and prevents accumulation of toxic fat, bran might even protect against cancer of the colon.

The only people I know who absolutely refuse to eat bran are the ones who are hooked on harsh laxatives. Often they've been taking them for years, and even if they agree to discontinue the laxative, it takes a while for natural bowel movements to commence. That gap often must be bridged by enemas.

Intestinal Gas

Mark Twain's raunchy little story "1601," or "Conversation As It Was by the Social Fireside in the Time of the Tudors," opens with a prestigious group of nobles and literary types gathered around the royal hearth with the king and queen. In the middle of the conversation, somebody passes gas, an extraordinary amount of gas: "In the heat of ye talk—one did breake wind, yielding an exceeding mightie and distasteful stink." The queen then attempts to discover who in the noble company has passed such a magnificent specimen. Everyone denies making that "thundergust," "hurricane," and so on, until Sir Walter Raleigh admits to the deed. But Raleigh doesn't think his fart was all that big a deal—if anything, it was too small to serve such an august gathering. As if to reinforce this, he proceeds to deliver "himself of such a godless and rock shivering blast that all here fain to stop their ears."

Never has human gas been so eloquently or so graphically depicted. Unfortunately, in real life not everyone can be so jolly about flatulence; it is often embarrassing and even painful. Why do some people have more problems? Natural differences in digestive capacity, diet, and even personality all seem to play a part.

Everyone has some gas in the intestine; some people have an abnormal amount. Intestinal gas has five different components: nitrogen, oxygen, hydrogen, methane, and carbon dioxide. Only oxygen and nitrogen come from the atmosphere, and they are probably swallowed. Air swallowing, called aerophagia, is common in people who breathe primarily through their mouths, sigh a lot, talk or drink a lot while eating, eat rapidly, and chew gum. But I don't think swallowing air is as great a source of gas as some people think, because both nitrogen and oxygen are readily diffusible as they pass through the digestive tract and should not cause much trouble.

The other, more troublesome gases are probably generated by the breakdown of certain foods: beans, the "aromatic" vegetables (cabbage, broccoli, and cauliflower), and carbonated beverages, in particular. All these substances yield gas upon digestion.

But the main source of intestinal gas is any food that goes into the large intestine partially undigested. Digestion should be virtually completed in the small intestine, the previous stop in the system, but three things could prevent this: (1) increased bowel mobility, which causes a certain amount of food to pass through the small intestine too quickly; (2) irritation, which inflames the bowel so that it doesn't absorb food products efficiently; and (3) a deficiency of certain digestive enzymes, which means that certain foods aren't broken down completely. The large intestine is a sort of trash compactor that draws fluid from the waste and shapes it into the stool that is eventually excreted. It contains a normal amount of bacteria (called colonic bacteria), which are not supposed to play a role in digestion; but when all that undigested food is dumped in, the bacteria go to work. And this releases gas, which is a by-product of both the food and the bacteria. People have different amounts and types of bacteria, which account for differences in overall flatulence.

If you are bothered by gas (or your friends and associates are bothered by your gas), examine your food intake first. If you are eating or drinking too many of the previously listed foods, cut down on them. If the gas persists, try some packaged digestive enzymes, such as papase or enterozyme, which can be found in health-food stores. Or try simethicone, an inert substance that absorbs gas and is available at drugstores.

Researchers have recently discovered a new source of intestinal gas by accidentally curing it—*then* they figured out the process involved. The cure is cimetidine, the marvelous ulcer medication that decreases hydrochloric acid formation in the stomach. Now many physicians use it for treating just gas, when there is no ulcer disease.

Cystitis

The first time I had cystitis, I thought I was dying. It was an extremely helpful experience, in retrospect, because I have never missed diagnosing a case of it since. The miserable bladder infection makes instant experts of us all. It was awfully painful at the time, though. I had a sudden and terrific urge to urinate, and when I did I felt as if someone were stabbing me in the vagina with a red-hot pitchfork. Once I was out of the bathroom, there was still no relief. I felt I had to push out another drop, but there was no other drop. The burning and the urgency (the feeling I had to urinate again) persisted. I couldn't sit, I couldn't stand, I couldn't scratch. I had a "textbook case" of cystitis.

Cystitis is *overwhelmingly* a female disease, probably because the urethra—the tube through which urine passes—is very short and sits quite close to the vagina and the rectum. It is easy for germs in the rectum or the vagina to trek up the urethra and into the bladder. Once bacteria enter the bladder, they cause an irritation or inflammation, which makes the bladder go into spasm. Then the bladder doesn't evacuate all its urine. So the bacteria sit there in a pool of warm urine and do what all self-respecting bacteria do—multiply like mad. Before you know it, you have raging cystitis.

There are ways to treat it yourself if the infection is still in its infancy. By drinking copious amounts of water (in excess of eight glasses a day), you can wash some of the bacteria away and prevent them from multiplying. And by drinking cranberry juice (4 ounces twice a day), you can alter the pH balance of your urine to make it more acidic. (Some bacteria tend to multiply faster in an alkaline environment.) If this doesn't work, however, and the infection persists, you'll probably have to take prescription antibiotics such as sulfa or nitrofurantoin. Be prepared to take large doses of sulfa in the beginning and to continue the treatment beyond the point when the symptoms stop. They can vanish within thirty-six hours, but that doesn't mean you've cleared up the infection; it can still be present. If the symptoms recur when you stop the medication, the cystitis hasn't been treated long enough or with the right type of antibiotic. This happens all the time. Some doctors prescribe a bladder anesthetic that colors the urine orange and immediately stops the pain. When the pain stops, women feel that the infection must be under control, so they stop taking the medicine—and, of course, the infection and pain reappear.

Sex is a big factor in causing the perpetuating cystitis. You have probably heard of "honeymoon cystitis." (You might have had it if you were unlucky.) The urethra can get traumatized during intercourse, which makes it easier for bacteria to enter it and invade the bladder. Then you roll over, contented, and fall asleep; and all the while the bacteria are multiplying. The trick is to empty your bladder after intercourse, so there's no urine culture brewing. You may have to drink some water beforehand in order to have some in your bladder afterward. Some women have their doctors prescribe nitrofurantoin to take after intercourse to eliminate the possibility of runaway bacteria, and this seems to work very well.

Lots of other things can trigger cystitis. Here are a few of the most representative:

Sauerkraut. Any food that can irritate the intestinal tract can irritate the lining of the urethra. This is a chemical cystitis instead of a bacterial cystitis, but a chemical irritation makes it easier for bacteria to get a foothold.

Stockings. Nylon is a chemical irritant, and it also cuts off air circulation around the vulva and genitals. A warm, moist place, plus a chemical irritation, creates a good breeding ground for bacteria.

Shellfish. Shellfish can give you an allergic urethritis (inflammation of the urethra), which will act in the same way as a chemical urethritis.

Colored toilet paper. The dye in colored toilet paper can set up a chemical irritation when you wipe yourself. Buy only white toilet paper if you're prone to infections.

Wiping from back to front, incidentally—and I can't imagine why anyone would do that, but women do—contaminates the urethra with feces and fecal bacteria, introducing billions of germs to your bladder.

Dirty underwear. Stained, saturated underwear allows vaginal and rectal secretions to rub against your urethra.

Holding urine. Crossing your legs and holding urine in your bladder allow bacteria to multiply. You should try to urinate at least every three hours.

Ten percent of women over forty experience an episode of cystitis, many for the first time. The best treatment is prevention; but don't worry too much if you detect the symptoms. Present chemical treatment is quite safe and uncomplicated.

Insomnia

Insomnia is the inability to fall or to remain asleep. It affects both sexes, though more frequently women. Of several types, the most common is related to specific stress or to a particular situation. It can develop when you change job shifts or have jet lag. It can arise out of anxiety or depression; in fact, a type of insomnia is one of the most consistent symptoms of depressive illness. Insomnias are also related to such diverse medical conditions as arthritis, toothaches, or malignancy. A very common cause of night pain in women is "carpal-tunnel syndrome," which is a prickling or numbness in the thumb and next two fingers. It is caused by pressure on the median nerve as it runs through the ligaments of the wrist and will frequently wake you up. Insomnia can even be stirred up by something as simple as a bad mattress or a midnight snack containing caffeine (which could include chocolate cake).

Situational insomnia, which accompanies a change in life-style, a vacation, or short-term stress (such as an exam or a wedding), generally corrects itself. Psychological insomnia can be corrected with medication for anxiety or depression—or with therapy, if you have the time and money. Medical insomnia may be treated by treating the underlying disease or pain. For the lumpy mattress, try a waterbed.

Insomnia is not a disease; it is a complaint. Sometimes it's not an especially accurate complaint; one of the most common findings in sleep research is a large discrepancy in the amount of time people think they've slept and the amount they actually have. Many people sleep more than they think they do. Others believe they need their eight hours or they'll be tired—and sometimes they will their own fatigue. Actually, you can get by on less than eight hours. A lot of people need only six.

At the sleep research lab of Montefiore Hospital in New York City, scientists have found a new category of insomnia: "delayed sleep phase." People who have this cannot seem to fall asleep until two, three, or four o'clock in the morning, and often they can't get into bed any earlier. After studying their circadian rhythms (which are biological cycles that recur at about twenty-four-hour intervals), Montefiore directs certain patients to reset their biological clocks ("chronotherapy"). On the first night the insomniacs might go to bed three hours later than usual, at, say, five in the morning. They are allowed to sleep as long as usual, and the next night they go to bed three hours later than the night before (at eight in the morning). They continue to move up by three-hour segments until they are retiring at the proper hour (say, eleven or twelve at night). This chronotherapy seems to work, and it's a much better idea than taking naps in the middle of the day—which many of these people found themselves doing when they had only four hours of sleep the previous night.

If you have insomnia, consider the possible causes. It is best to try to treat yourself before running to the family doctor or to a psychiatrist. Prepare a sleep log for two weeks: record your daily activities, the time you fall asleep, and the time you wake up. Record also what you eat and drink at night, and whether you take any drugs. All drugs can keep you up, but the most frequent offenders are decongestants, nonsteroidal anti-inflammatory drugs, alcohol, and anything containing caffeine. In fact, no caffeine after 4:00 P.M. is a good rule to follow.

When the cause or causes of your insomnia are not forthcoming, you have to treat the complaint itself. Barbiturates, the classic sleeping pills, are *not* the answer. Sleeping pills used to be ''sedative-hypnotic'' drugs; the sedative would calm you, and the hypnotic drug would make you drowsy, promoting a quasi-sleep from which you could be easily awakened. Barbiturates don't work specifically on the central nervous system; they depress other excitable tissues as well (although the brain is perhaps the most sensitive), and they interact rapidly and dangerously with other drugs. Their effect on depressed insomniacs was to deepen the depression, and because patients quickly developed a tolerance to them—meaning they had to take more and more to get the same effect—the record of abuse was appalling. Occasionally they helped to prod patients with suicidal tendencies into actually killing themselves.

Benzodiazepines (Valium, Dalmane, and others) are currently our best sleeping pills. They induce a relatively normal sleep with little or no hangover. Although some fuss has been made over their potential for abuse, they have a relatively high level of safety. They are excellent in short-term situations, but their long-term effectiveness has not been proven.

Allergies

As women get older, they tend to develop more allergies. Allergies may be triggered by an endless variety of substances (dust, molds, food, drugs) and may cause an endless variety of symptoms (rashes, asthma, diarrhea, swelling hives).

Sometimes it takes a combination of things to produce an allergic response. I have a friend who is allergic to the combination of lobster and alcohol—but to neither alone.

Food has long been a culprit in allergies. If you swell up when you eat oranges, or break out in hives when you eat strawberries, or have to be rushed to the emergency room when you eat nuts, you know you are allergic and had better avoid those foods.

Recently, researchers have discovered that food allergies can be the source of some illnesses we previously believed were infectious or psychological; for instance, migraine headaches, which doctors used to think were caused by rigid, perfectionistic personality traits, have a definite relationship to the consumption of chocolate, peanuts, and alcohol.

That stuffy, half-sick, tired feeling that many women experience might be a mold allergy. Recently, some researchers have begun to see a connection between the ingestion of products that contain mold, because of curing processes, fermentation, or aging, and nonspecific but debilitating physical symptoms in women. With this information they have developed a mold-free diet adaptable to either a normal or a weight-loss plan. Here it is:

> *Eat:* all fresh foods, fruits, and vegetables.
>
> *Do not eat:* cheese of any kind; mushrooms; vinegar (use lemon juice in salads); cider, wine, or beer; canned juice, especially tomato; leftover cooked food; smoked meat or fish (ham, corned beef, bacon); sauerkraut; yogurt or sour cream; hamburger, unless freshly ground and cooked immediately; mustard, ketchup; dried fruits; leftover canned tuna (okay only if you've just opened it).

If you haven't been feeling right, give this a try for a few weeks. It can't hurt, and it might change your life.

The intradermal, or intracutaneous, skin test is still the most reliable method of assessing allergy; the results must be interpreted by a competent allergist because they are commonly "overread." In intradermal skin testing, a tiny amount of a specific antigen (allergen)—an extract of pollen or cat hair, for example—is injected under the skin. If you're allergic to it, within fifteen minutes you will have a reaction. The reaction is in the form of a wheal, which is a red bump, and it appears, logically enough, at the site of the injection. (Injections are usually given on the forearm.) The degree of allergy is measured by the size of the wheal. A very slight but definite bump is a "one plus." If the bump exceeds 6 to 10 millimeters, it is a "two plus," and so on. Above 15 millimeters is considered a very strong reaction. These are very small numbers, often imprecisely measured, and it's easy to see how this test could be misread.

How do these skin tests work? The injected substance (antigen) evokes an allergic or antibody response. Scientists are not absolutely clear on why certain people become sensitized to certain antigens. When an antigen meets an antibody—a sort of cellular watchdog—there is a fight. The cells are injured, and a chemical compound called histamine is released. This causes a "congested reaction"—redness, swelling, and so on.

The purpose of allergy testing is to identify the offending substance and either remove it from the person's life—as you would a specific food or a feather pillow—or immunize the person by chemically desensitizing him or her to the allergen. This desensitization process is long and costly, however; and today many allergists don't give as many allergy shots. They find the shots are effective only in certain allergic states—the seasonal allergies, for example, which are triggered by trees, grass, weeds, and pollen. They are not as effective in fighting allergies to dust, molds, and animal dander. Most allergists try antihistamines (to block the histamine release and thus stop cell damage) before they jump into immunotherapy.

Skin tests are not an end in themselves; they must be evaluated along with any symptoms you may have, as well as when and where you have them. Physicians and lay people who are not specifically trained in allergies tend to read almost every test as positive, regardless of symptoms (or lack of them).

There has been a proliferation of so-called allergy testing

at nutritional and holistic centers. A woman goes to the center because she doesn't feel well, and she usually receives a test for hypoglycemia, a hair analysis, and at least one or two allergy tests. She rarely leaves the center without one or more of the following diagnoses:

1. One of twelve types of hypoglycemia
2. Allergy to wheat, potatoes, corn, or other foods
3. Chromium, magnesium, selenium, and manganese deficiency, plus too much cadmium, lead, or mercury

Let's take a look at these diagnoses.

1. There are not twelve types of hypoglycemia; there are two. One is true hypoglycemia, where the fasting blood-sugar level (which means unaffected by food intake) is below 50 milligrams percent. However, in this condition, absolute numbers do not mean anything unless accompanied by physical symptoms. This drop in blood sugar is caused by oversecretion of the beta cells (insulin-producing cells of the pancreas), the result of a tumor or hyperplasia (an increased number of secretory cells). This type is dangerous and needs careful evaluation, diagnosis, and active treatment. The other is *relative* hypoglycemia, where the fasting blood sugar is normal. After a test with a 100-gram sugar load, however, it rises and falls precipitously to hypoglycemic levels. This type is treated by diet. But these centers fabricate weird types of hypoglycemia that they claim can be treated only by eating avocados and pine nuts and having enemas.

2. These centers choose a common food to identify as the patient's allergen—something they're sure she eats regularly. So, if someone comes in feeling lousy, the clinicians will say, for example, that she is allergic to wheat. You can be pretty sure she commonly eats foods with wheat in them, whereas it would be patently meaningless to say she was allergic to, say, papaya. Some people do have bona fide corn or wheat allergies, but these centers simply aren't administering the correct test to ascertain that.

3. Nobody has defined a "deficiency state" in these elements, and for many of them, normal human levels have

never even been established. When you don't know how much people need and you don't know what happens to them when they're deficient, how can you tell someone her cadmium level is too low, and that's what's making her depressed?

So alarming is the incidence of bogus allergy testing that the American Academy of Allergy has finally taken a position on it and has condemned the most common tests. In the "cytotoxity test" the center draws some blood, and adds an allergen to it. If white blood cells are destroyed, you're labeled allergic. Actually, it's very easy to cause white cells to self-destruct by throwing any foreign antibody into the blood, so this test is utterly useless. In the "provocative neutralization test" (subcutaneous), they inject an antigen into your blood in sufficient quantities to provoke symptoms similar to those you've complained about. Then they dilute the antigen and inject more of it into you, on the premise that this will cure the original symptoms. It's irrational, irresponsible, and, of course, ineffective—but it costs.

Speaking of costs, there's a "provocative test" that will run you $150. Three drops of an allergenic extract are placed under your tongue. In ten minutes, "allergy symptoms" appear. What are they? Often they consist of your pulse speeding up. Then a "neutralizing" dose is administered and the "symptoms" are expected to disappear in the same sequence in which they appeared. In the first place, increased pulse rate is not a valid indication of an allergy. Caffeine, for example, which is found in chocolate in addition to coffee and cola, makes everybody's pulse speed up. Second, no known immunological mechanism can account for the "neutralizing" effect. In other words, it's a fraud.

These centers will also give you injections of your own urine on the premise that this will relieve allergy, jaundice, constipation, asthma, and migraines. This is not only ineffective and irrational—it's dangerous.

People are very defensive about the value of these tests and the centers that administer them. One woman told me her nutritional center found she was allergic to corn, potatoes, fried foods, white flour, and sugar. She gave all of them up and felt so much better. She also lost fifteen pounds. When I pointed out that she lost weight because she gave up a lot of high-calorie foods, she refused to be convinced. It was the giving up of foods she was *allergic* to, she insisted, that made her lose the weight.

Chapter 6

The Gallbladder

My nurse, Jackie, had her gallbladder removed a couple of years ago. But she still has gallbladder pain two or three times a week. "It's the stump," she explains, popping an anti-spasmodic pill into her mouth. I had learned about the "post-cholecystectomy syndrome" in medical school. This theorized that the little duct that remains after the gallbladder is removed goes into spasm just like the diseased gallbladder did.

But that was twenty-five years ago. We now know that there's no such thing as "post-cholecystectomy (p.c.t.) syndrome," and that if Jackie has the same pain now that she had before her gallbladder operation, the original pain had nothing to do with her gallbladder. Oops. Those uncomfortable symptoms of bloating, gas, a feeling of fullness, and abdominal spasms might be present along with gallstones, but often they are not relieved by the removal of the gallbladder and may indicate another disease or else an abnormality in stomach motility.

"Fair, fat, and forty" was the way the high-risk person for gallbladder disease used to be described. Now it's "fair, fat, forty, and flatulent." Actually, you don't have to be fair and flatulent. Just being female, fat, and forty seems to favor the formation of those nasty little marbles called gallstones that become firmly wedged in (impacted) and infected. The disease favors women two to one, and one-third of all overweight females can expect to suffer from it. Fifty percent of the people with gallstones never have serious symptoms, though, and if these "silent stones" aren't causing you any trouble, they require little attention. If there is a symptom, it is usually intense pain below the sternum (breastbone), the result of a stone's obstructing one of the bile ducts. The pain, called a "biliary colic," can last up to four hours. It can resemble the pain of a heart attack, extending as far down as the lower right rib and as far up as the shoulder blade. Most of these attacks come after a fatty meal, a long diet, or pregnancy (particularly a mid-life pregnancy).

Repeated attacks of the pain, along with jaundice, vomiting, and fever, would constitute a good reason for surgery. Occasional attacks of pain only, along with the presence of gallstones, do not necessarily mean that the gallbladder should be removed. Medicine is now perfecting a way to dissolve stones. It is a long process (it takes several years), and there is no guarantee that the stones won't re-form. (At this point, researchers think that if you lose weight or go through menopause while the stones are dissolving the first time, they won't be so likely to return.)

I don't love surgery, but I think that after a few attacks of biliary colic—even without the fever and vomiting—I might start looking at my gallbladder as if it were a loaded bomb. Gallstones predispose the gallbladder to infection and its painful consequences. You also run a minor risk (1 percent) of developing gallbladder cancer if you leave the stones in. I suppose your decision about whether to opt for surgery will depend on how you like the odds and how close you live to a hospital in case of emergency.

Chapter 7

Diabetes

The following is a heated conversation between a local internist and me.

Me: You have Abbie on 60 units of insulin and she can't lose weight. She weighs 260 pounds and she needs to lose weight—she can hardly walk!

Internist: She's a diabetic. Diabetics need insulin to regulate their sugar metabolisms.

Me: But it's almost impossible to lose weight on that much insulin. It seems to block the breakdown of fat even if she does require it. I have her on as few calories as I dare with that enormous dose of insulin. If I go any lower, she'll go into insulin shock.

Internist: What do you want me to do?

Me: Hospitalize her, take her off the insulin, put her on a 500-calorie diet, and let her lose some weight. Then send her home on a substantially lower dose.

Internist: Are you nuts? I have to treat her *disease*. She can't follow any diet. It's my responsibility to get her blood sugar down.

Me: But her blood sugar isn't even regulated on all that insulin—

Internist: See you. (Click)

This conversation is a variation of the chicken-or-egg problem: which do you treat first, diabetes or obesity? The answer, as far as I'm concerned, is clear. Of all the diseases associated with aging, none is so directly related to obesity as Type II non-insulin-dependent diabetes mellitus. Perhaps you once had a chubby grandmother or aunt who had "sugar." Diabetes now appears to be not one but a group of disorders that have in common an inappropriately high level of blood sugar. This blood sugar, if left untreated, causes a variety of complications in the blood vessels, especially in the vessels of the eyes and kidneys. Circulation and heart problems, as well as sensory disturbances (prickling, tingling, and numbness) are also common.

In the past ten years, diabetes has been split into two types: insulin-dependent and non-insulin-dependent. Type I insulin-dependent used to be called "juvenile" diabetes, and it generally hits people early in life. The non-insulin-dependent diabetes that arrives in mid-life—and the one I'll discuss in this section—is Type II, which accounts for 80 percent of all diabetes in the United States. It generally hits adults over forty, is genetically transmitted, is more common in females, and is usually associated with obesity. In fact, weight gain is a significant risk factor in the development of the disease.

By reclassifying diabetes we have become increasingly aware of the faulty carbohydrate tolerance that marks all obesity, whether the patient is diabetic or not. Only the diabetic, however, has a chronic metabolic disorder, characterized by increased blood-sugar levels of 140 milligrams percent or above in the fasting state, and 200 milligrams percent or above after eating. In contrast, the overweight *non*diabetic has normal blood-glucose levels. But both have strikingly similar metabolisms.

What happens in the metabolism of a Type II non-insulin-dependent diabetic? It's complicated. The cells become resistant to insulin, a hormone secreted by the pancreas that reduces blood sugar. Perhaps the insulin receptor has trouble fitting around an overstuffed cell, but that's a guess—no one knows for sure. When the cells don't accept the insulin, the body manufactures more and more in an attempt to regulate blood sugar. But the cells become even *more* resistant when they're overwhelmed by insulin, and the blood-sugar levels continue to rise.

The high amount of insulin in the Type II diabetic's blood is the opposite of what we used to believe—that all diabetes was the result of *low* insulin levels. (Insulin-dependent, or Type I, diabetes *is* the result of low insulin levels.) So, fifteen years ago, before diabetes was divided into two types of disease, *everybody* was getting insulin.

Insulin resistance is also the result of lack of physical activity, and the more you weigh the less you usually move. And when you're insulin-resistant, you don't burn carbohydrates, fats, or proteins efficiently, making it even easier to gain and more difficult to lose weight.

Diabetic Symptoms

What symptoms will you have if you're becoming a diabetic? One-third of all women have the classic symptoms: weakness, drinking a large amount of fluid (polydipsia), and urinating a lot (polyuria). Whereas younger, insulin-dependent diabetics lose weight, it is weight gain, not weight loss, that accompanies or precedes mid-life diabetes. Diabetes can also cause repeated infections around the base of the fingernails and boils in the groin or under the arms or breasts. More serious complications are arteriosclerosis (hardening of the arteries), neuropathy (tingling and numbness of the hands and feet), kidney problems, and heart disease. The adult female diabetic is far more likely to die of a heart attack than a nondiabetic female.

Treatment

So the treatment of Type II non-insulin-dependent diabetes can center—not surprisingly—on weight loss and be extremely successful. By reducing total caloric intake, dividing calories among the major food groups, avoiding concentrated sweets to minimize fluctuations in blood-sugar levels, and reducing cholesterol and saturated-fat intake to prevent potential cardiovascular problems, we can lick the problem astonishingly fast. An appropriate distribution of calories is 20 percent protein, 30 percent fat, and 50 percent carbohydrates. Increased physical activity is also extremely important in diabetes because it accelerates weight reduction, lowers blood-sugar levels, and increases the cells' sensitivity to insulin. Notice how interchangeable are the treatments for diabetes and for obesity.

If diet alone doesn't work, try getting an oral hypoglycemic agent from your doctor. These agents, called sulfonylureas, are related to the sulfa drugs. Doctors accidentally discovered sulfa's ability to lower blood sugar while using it to treat typhoid fever. Sulfa stimulates the pancreas to secrete insulin; and, unlike insulin itself, which must be injected, the hypoglycemic agents can be absorbed from the gastrointestinal tract, and so can be taken by mouth. But be forewarned. A lot of doctors don't like them. Diet is a far safer and usually more effective treatment for Type II non-insulin-dependent diabetics. The oral hypoglycemic agents are not innocuous—they can stimulate the heart and cause irregularities.

Recent studies have found a link between diabetes and a certain type of obesity: truncal obesity, where the fat is concentrated above the hips, in the stomach, breasts, arms, back, and bosom. Physicians observed that women with this kind of obesity have a much higher incidence of diabetes than overweight women with a different kind of fat distribution. These women have abnormally large fat cells, as opposed to an abnormally large number of normal fat cells. As I'll discuss in the section on overweight, this is the easiest kind of obesity to treat; it's possible to shrink an overstuffed cell, but not to get rid of a surplus. To my surprise, in surveying my own case load, I've found this to be true especially for women in their fifties. In the sixties, however, this relationship is not as clear-cut, and diabetes seems to be equally linked to all types of obesity.

What about insulin treatment? you may ask. No way, except in an emergency (infections or surgery). It is illogical to give insulin to someone who already has too much of it. Although it will lower blood sugar, it will also promote weight gain, leading to even greater insulin resistance. Then blood-sugar levels will continue to rise, the dosage of insulin will continue to be increased, and. . . . You get the picture. Diet is still the best answer. Obesity and Type II diabetes may even prove to be the same disease.

A new test, called the glycosylated hemoglobin test, is now available; it shows how high the blood sugar has been in the past sixty days. It was originally touted as a great diagnostic tool for detecting the obese female who will go on to become diabetic, but it appears to be valuable only in the known diabetic.

Hypoglycemia (The Other Side of the Coin)

Hypoglycemia—abnormally low blood-sugar levels—is really a symptom and not a disease in itself. It can be severe or mild, depending on the disease that causes it; it may also have no cause, in which case it is called *functional hypoglycemia*. In essence, when the blood sugar dips below 50 milligrams percent (the normal being around 60 to 120 milligrams percent), certain symptoms may occur. These include anxiety, pallor, shakiness, sweating, palpitation, and a subsequent, compensating rise in blood sugar. These symptoms are probably brought on by a release of adrenaline, triggered by the rapid drop in blood sugar—nature's way of quickly meeting emergency demands for blood sugar. Needless to say, this condition is sudden, uncomfortable, and frightening.

In the past few years, however, most low-grade, vague, nonspecific cases of fatigue and depression in females have been diagnosed as hypoglycemia. Therefore, since many women have these symptoms, they fervently believe that they are hypoglycemic. Because of this, I found myself practicing defensive medicine and ordering many glucose-tolerance tests—not to rule out diabetes (which is what I formerly used the test for), but to rule out hypoglycemia. I discovered so few hypoglycemics that I virtually discontinued the search two years ago—until I missed diagnosing two patients who actually had hypoglycemia. Now, when fatigue or depression is a prominent symptom, I once again do a routine glucose-tolerance test.

For three days before the blood is to be drawn for a glucose tolerance test, you should eat 150 grams of carbohydrates a day. Many women starve themselves because they know they are getting a blood-sugar test or they are dieting and resent the instructions to eat all those carbohydrates. Sugar deprivation, however, can give you a false positive on the test. So eat.

When you take a glucose-tolerance test, you are given a fixed amount of sugar water to drink, after which your blood and urine are collected at hourly intervals. Physicians look for the following:

1. How high the sugar level goes, at what hour. This is to evaluate how efficiently the body handles a known sugar load and how long it takes to do it. It also gives some indication of your insulin response to sugar: How high? For how long?

2. Whether you spill sugar into your urine. This gives you the renal threshold, or the level of blood sugar at which your kidneys are unable to reabsorb the sugar load. If you spill sugar into your urine, a doctor can tell approximately how high your blood sugar is without having to draw blood for a chemical analysis.

3. How low the blood-sugar level drops, at what hour.

I have found many times that when the blood sugar drops to its lowest level in a woman—but not to the critical level required for the diagnosis of hypoglycemia—certain symptoms occur. Some women get very anxious, some burst into tears, some feel shaky, and some become confused. These symptoms are not psychological, because the woman has no idea that her blood sugar is at its lowest point. I believe, therefore, that a woman can have a *relative* degree of hypoglycemia—relative to her normal blood-sugar level.

It doesn't matter whether you have relative or absolute hypoglycemia; both seem to affect mood and energy levels in females. It is important when evaluating fatigue, therefore, to check any symptoms against your blood-sugar levels. You might be surprised at the correlation. I was.

The treatment for both absolute and relative hypoglycemia

is a diet high in protein with a moderate amount of complex carbohydrates, divided into frequent small feedings (say, four small meals and two small snacks a day). This can also be a good way to reduce your weight and can easily be worked into a diet program. So, if you're on a hypoglycemic diet, you don't need to gain weight! You don't have to eat saltines between meals; skim milk or tomato juice will do just fine. Remember, *sugar is not the answer for hypoglycemia*. In the short term it will elevate your blood sugar, but afterward that sugar will plunge to new lows.

Chapter 8

Aches and Pains

"Something's happened to me since I hit the big five-oh," Sara said. "I never used to have these aches and pains. One of my shoulders hurts, I have terrible pain in my knee, and right now my fingers are killing me." She pointed to the small bones of her fingers. There was no swelling, redness, or other inflammation.

"I'll check you for arthritis," I told her, thinking how frequently I heard those complaints and grateful that most of the time the test for inflammatory arthritic disease was negative.

"You know," she said, "nobody ever told me how painful it is to grow old. Never mind the fears. Never mind my brain—that's clear. At least I think it is. But there's just so much *pain*."

Sara was one of the lucky ones. Her arthritis tests were negative.

Arthritis is the number-one crippling disease in this country. Although generally not fatal, it can inflict immeasurable suffering. Who suffers the most? Women win again. From rheumatoid arthritis to osteoarthritis to fibrositis, women have it three to one, two to one, and six to one.

There is no cure for arthritis, and few adequate treatments exist. Though medical conferences on the subject have become fairly common, no significant advances have been made in the last several decades. The only progress in the field has been in the area of painkillers. I was very pleased to see a new medical magazine called *Aches and Pains,* and I thought that perhaps it would be the beginning of some original research, but it turned out to be a rehash of stuff we've already heard, along with a sprinkling of orthopedics. Plus it's a vehicle for advertisements of the new nonsteroidal anti-inflammatory drugs (NSAIDs). I suppose we should be grateful to drug companies for trying to alleviate the excruciating symptoms of arthritis, even if it is for a huge profit. At least they're doing something.

Arthritis, or inflammation of the joints, takes several different forms, but basically it consists of inflammation and/or degeneration. Arthritis could be caused by a problem with the immune system. Some antibodies, which normally attack foreign substances in the bloodstream, suddenly turn on the body's own connective tissue. Researchers know where it happens, but not why. Sometimes it is a ferocious attack, as in the more serious collagen diseases (which destroy connective tissue) like rheumatoid arthritis. At other times it is a leisurely whittling away, as in osteoarthritis. Most inflammatory arthritis affects younger people. Rheumatoid arthritis, the most widely known of these, strikes women between the ages of twenty and forty. It is a systemic, often crippling disease whose main symptoms are pain, tenderness, and swelling in the joints of the hands, wrists, knees, and ankles. Symptoms come and go, flaring up for a while and then vanishing, only to reappear in weeks or months. The most common arthritic conditions in the mid-life woman are fibrositic disease and osteoarthritis.

Fibrositis: The "I-Ache-All-Over" Disease

Some women get lots of aches and pains in their joints. Bursitis, an acute inflammation around the joint capsule, and tendinitis, a similar inflammation around the tendon, are often a source of annoyance to more athletic women in their forties and fifties. Annoying, remember—not yet debilitating. At least these inflammations are specific entities, they can be identified and treated. But what if you ache all over and nobody can find a reason? Then you might have fibrositis, or the "I-ache-all-over" disease.

Fibrositis is a women's disease six to one, and a recent report tried to link it to tension and anxiety in driving, competitive, meticulous females. This is the same personality type that supposedly suffers from anorexia nervosa, ulcerative colitis, and Type A coronary risk. That's quite a mixed bag. The report insinuated that fibrositis is a neurotic symptom. What we have here, ladies, is another attempt by the male medical establishment to relate a true pathological process to the female personality. (Other examples are the "menopausal woman" and the "hysteric.") Whenever they can't figure out the etiology of an illness, particularly one that strikes females, they give it a psychological basis.

I am quite interested in fibrositis because I do not believe there is anything imagined about the aches and pains of fibrositic women, any more than I believe there's anything imagined about menstrual cramps. Obviously great differences exist in the way women react to and interpret pain. But something—be it a special endorphin or prostaglandin (endorphins are the body's natural painkillers; prostaglandins are its natural pain producers)—makes some women hurt more than others. It's a physical disease, not a state of mind.

There is also a type of fibrositic disease that occurs in conjunction with other diseases such as osteoarthritis, viral diseases, inflammatory bowel disease, and hypothyroidism. Yes, even lack of thyroid hormone can cause diffuse aches and pains. In the last few weeks I have seen two women whose chief complaint was generalized aching. Both had an underactive thyroid, and neither was obese.

If lab tests don't reveal another disease, if physical signs of redness and swelling aren't present, and if your pain is uncomfortable but not crippling, you probably have fibrositis—but we're not sure *why* you have it.

Fibrositic disease is the wastebasket of rheumatology the way hypoglycemia is the wastebasket of endocrinology—anything that can't be understood is generally dumped there. There is presently a controversy even over the name. The ending, *itis,* in *fibrositis* indicates inflammation, and none has been discovered in the connective tissue of women with this disease. The new suggested name is fibromyalgia, which means pain and tenderness in the fibrous tissues and muscles that surround the joint, but no inflammation.

If you have fibrositis or fibromyalgia, you can have generalized aches and pains, tenderness, stiffness after periods of activity (though prolonged early-morning stiffness is often a different disease), and no joint swelling. You particularly feel it in the knees, lower back, shoulders, and hands. Pain is usually worst in the evening and varies with weather, degree of physical activity, and fatigue. A key feature in diagnosing the disease is the presence of certain specific "trigger areas," where muscles are under the most tension, such as in the lower back, the sides of the neck, below the shoulder blades, and around some of the larger joints.

In women, the cause of some of this pain is probably mechanical. The joints are often not well supported by muscle, especially in the out-of-condition female. In the upper extremities, where the joints are subjected to repeated tension, the ligaments, not the muscles, must often pick up the strain, and this results in a "mini-sprain." Pain follows sprain, and many of the surrounding tissues feel it, too. In the lower extremities, though, the muscles are usually more developed, so low-back and knee fibrositic pain is usually the result of extra stress caused by poor posture or obesity. The female form is somewhat unstable because of the swaying, lateral movements of the hips. The sacroiliac joints in the lower back and hip get the bulk of the strain and need the support of the small, undeveloped back muscles. If you're having support problems in this area, these are the muscles you must work to strengthen. I'm an old disc patient myself, and the neurosurgeon suggested exercises to strengthen my lower-back muscles and prevent a relapse; you'll find these under "Back Problems," below.

What else can help? If poor sleep habits are a problem, a mild sedative can help you rest more comfortably, and this will relieve some of the tension and pain. People tell me that waterbeds are terrific for this, too. In fact, a few recent studies have shown that fibrositic women spend less time in stage four sleep (the deepest stage). So improving your sleep can relieve your fibrositis. Aspirin taken on a continuous basis—two pills four times a day for several weeks—will help the pain; so will the NSAIDs; but both tend to be a little hard on the stomach. The problem with taking too many antacids to combat the stomach problems is that these pills need an acidic environment to dissolve and work, and so neutralizing the acid immediately diminishes the strength of the medication.

One of the best nondrug treatments for fibrositis or fibromyalgia is keeping in shape, building up muscle strength, and increasing flexibility. This can be done with stretching exercises like climbing the walls with your fingers (for your shoulders), turning a nonexistent doorknob (wrist and elbow), or kneading bread (fingers). Or try lifting a loaded purse with your feet while seated (knee), or lying on your side with a two-pound weight attached to your upper ankle and raising your top leg (hip). In degenerative disease of the knee, isometric quadricep exercises—pushing the knee against a fixed object—can help prevent major disability.

Pressing on your trigger points can also give you some relief. You can locate these points yourself: just press gently around the affected area, and you'll find a spot that will initially give you more pain with the same amount of pressure. Applying pressure on this area for two or three minutes, three or four times a day, can often relax the tension and break up the pain cycle.

And don't forget warm water. The best pain reliever of all is a big tub where wet heat gets to every part of your body, and it costs a lot less than that fancy ultrasound machine that some uninterested technician massages you with.

Swimming is the best all-around exercise for arthritis; even if you can't swim, try doing these exercises in shallow water, supporting yourself with one hand.

Back Problems

Every creature that walks upright develops back trouble once in a while. It doesn't matter what kind of condition you're in, and the "trauma" that sets the whole thing off can be minimal—turning one way or another quickly, bending the wrong way, or lifting a heavy object. The problem can be as serious as a disc (the little cartilaginous cushion between the vertebrae) that has slipped out of place, or as harmless and fleeting as a muscle spasm. Both usually respond well to bed rest, heat, and, if you need it, pain medication or muscle relaxants.

To prevent back problems, learn to bend and lift properly. It might look more attractive to bend from the waist down, but it puts a terrific strain on your back if those little muscles aren't well developed. So, bend at the knees. Put most of the pressure on your thighs when you lift something. Turn your whole body, not just the top half.

I find the following exercises extremely helpful in preventing relapses of back pain.

Lying flat on the floor on your back and with your knees bent, do five pelvic arches, hardly lifting your pelvis from the floor. Arch, relax, arch, relax.

Still lying on the floor with your knees bent, lift one leg up straight at a thirty-degree angle. Then do the same exercise with the other leg. Repeat five times. It is important to keep your knees bent because lying flat and leaving them straight puts too much strain on your back muscles.

Don't get off the floor yet. Still lying with your knees bent, raise one knee to your chest and return it to the floor. Repeat, using the opposite knee. Repeat the entire exercise five to ten times. These exercises are good for strengthening normal backs, too.

Osteoarthritis

Osteoarthritis, the other important arthritic disease in women over forty, is also a misnomer. This is not an inflammation of the joint as the name implies, but a degenerative joint disease, which again favors women over men by at least two to one. It occurs when the protective cartilage that cushions the ends of bones wears out, causing the bony surfaces to rub together and become irritated. Bone secretes more bone when it's irritated and gives rise to bone excesses called spurs. Spurs at joint surfaces cause a lot of pain and limit motion. Osteoarthritis tends to be more prevalent in the weight-bearing joints of the knees and hips, where there is more stress. Also, for some unknown reason, it has a predilection for the small bones of the hand. The exception is the last finger joint, which has its own variety of osteo called Heberden's nodes, a normally painless, though unsightly, thickening of the joint. Only women get Heberden's nodes, and it's probably a sex-linked genetic trait.

Osteo responds best to a short-term treatment of aspirin and NSAIDs, although in acute situations where only one joint is affected, an injection of steroids gives adequate temporary relief. But no medication has been shown to alter the course of the underlying disease, only the pain and inflammation.

Often it is difficult to tell where fibrositis or fibromyalgia ends and osteoarthritis begins. I have seen many women diagnosed as osteo when they were still fibro. This is depressing, because when you tell someone she has arthritis, you are telling her she has an irreversible degenerative disease that will require medication for the rest of her life. And women resent having to take pills constantly, despite what the newspapers would have us believe. They will take pills to relieve a particular symptom, but if it doesn't go away, they get scared. They also get scared if a pill that works for a while begins to lose its effectiveness. Will they have to take more and more for relief? Are they doomed to a life of pill-taking? What if the pills make them feel lousy?

Rheumatologists often complain about patients who don't

follow orders, such as the command to take large amounts of potentially dangerous pills. One a rheumatologist gave me a bottle of one hundred NSAIDs and said casually, "Here, take these. They'll make you feel better." The bottle scared the hell out of me. He didn't tell me for how long I would have to take them and how I could expect to feel when I finished. I saw myself hooked for life on that little orange pill, and, naturally, I didn't take any. And I suffered.

All osteo seems to be tied to the end of reproductive life. Remember the Tin Woodsman whose joints needed oiling so that he could move? The appearance of osteoarthritis so soon after primary ovarian failure might make you think that estrogen is the "oil of female joints." It's worth considering, anyway.

There may be another kind of medication on the horizon for the treatment of aches and pains, but it's hard to predict its future. It came to my attention when a friend pulled a back muscle while playing golf. We were on vacation in a southern state where medical care was not easily available. Then we saw a sign on a pharmacy door: *DMSO available here*. We all agreed it was worth a try. We walked into the store and found a whole shelf of unmarked bottles filled with a clear liquid that could have been mistaken for water. My friend picked up the bottle and approached the cash register. "Could you tell me how to use this stuff?" he asked.

"We don't know anything about that," said the pharmacist as he was ringing up the sale.

What is it that's sold in drugstores, advertised in large letters on the front door, yet won't stir a response from the pharmacist? DMSO, of course, the controversial by-product of wood pulp being touted by regular users as the miracle drug of the century. But the Food and Drug Administration (FDA) has virtually ignored it. Dimethyl sulfoxide has been used for everything from neurological disease to brain trauma to protecting previously frozen cells from damage. It has shown varying degrees of success in all these areas. It is also a potent solvent and paint remover.

DMSO has the ability to lessen aches and pains in arthritic and swollen joints and in acute injuries to man and animal.

Rubbed on the skin over the area of pain or swelling, it is rapidly absorbed into the bloodstream and has the ability to draw water from the injured site, relieving the symptoms. Other than a funny taste like garlic in the mouth minutes after its application to the skin, there are apparently no noticeable side effects.

Why the reluctance on the part of the FDA to okay it? Except for approved use in a rare bladder condition called interstitial cystitis, the FDA is worried about reports that DMSO can suppress the immune system, leaving the patient vulnerable to other diseases. The drug seems to have the ability to interfere with misguided antibodies that probably cause certain auto-immune diseases, in which the system manufactures antibodies that actually attack the person's own muscle joints, connective tissues, and organs. Osteo and fibromyalgia might have an auto-immune component, which is why DMSO could be effective. But if it also interferes with the *good, protective* antibodies, which are the body's weapons in fighting disease, DMSO could spell serious trouble. So the FDA is moving very, very slowly, and the drug remains unmarked on the shelf.

My friend's rib pain? Gone in thirty minutes.

Chapter 9

The Pump (Better Known as the Heart)

We constantly hear of young men dying of heart attacks, but rarely of women. Isn't this your disease as well? Have you "lucked out," finally? You probably have. Men are four times more likely to have a fatal heart attack than women, and one-fourth of the time it's the first clinical sign of the disease that kills them.

The reason is your estrogen, which has something to do with a protein in your bloodstream called HDL. To understand the importance of HDL, you should know something about cholesterol.

Cholesterol is a form of fat that doesn't just float around by itself in your blood. Something has to carry it, and what carries it determines whether it will go to a cell and be stored or to the liver and be excreted. Your cells need a certain amount of cholesterol; it forms part of their membranes (walls). You also need cholesterol in order to manufacture some of the sex hormones. But too much of it can form thick, fatty deposits on these blood-vessel walls, creating resistance to blood flow and forcing the heart to work much harder.

HDL (short for high-density lipoprotein) is one of the cholesterol carriers. It has been called a "cholesterol scavenger" because it removes cholesterol from the cells and takes it to the liver for excretion. Researchers have associated high levels of HDL in the blood with a low risk of heart disease, and low levels with a high risk. They've also discovered that you have high levels of HDL if you have estrogen, good heredity, are thin, and exercise regularly—factors traditionally linked to a lower risk of heart disease!

The highest risk factors are those associated with LDL (*low*-density lipoprotein), which carries cholesterol *to* the cells. High levels of LDL and low levels of HDL suggest that more cholesterol is being deposited in the cells than is being carried off, which means an accumulation of fat on the membranes. This greatly enhances a woman's chances of having a heart attack or any other atherosclerotic type of heart disease. The following are the most important risk factors.

Heredity Bad genes are one of the most serious sources of heart disease, but there's obviously nothing you can do about them. The first postmortem examination I watched in medical school was of a young physician whose father and older brother had been struck down by heart attacks at very early ages. He vowed never to be in poor physical condition, exercised moderately, and gave up smoking. I saw him for the last time on the autopsy table after he had died of a heart attack at age forty-two, having outlived his father and brother by four or five years, but still unable to retard the progress of the disease. That was before the days of cardiac medicine, though, and we might have kept him alive a lot longer today. But it would still have been a battle.

If there is a history of heart disease in your family, remember that it affects the males more than the females, so your chances aren't *that* bad. But they are *terrible* if you have any of the other risk factors described in this section. You should be extremely careful about your diet and physical condition, and for God's sake, don't smoke.

Cigarettes Smoking damages your blood vessels, and fat accumulates on damaged vessels more easily. Smoking also increases carboxyhemoglobin (where carbon monoxide replaces oxygen) and encourages the release of catecholamines (which are natural body chemicals that make the heart beat faster), both of which put extra stress on the heart by depriving it of oxygen and increasing demands on outflow. If you smoke one pack of cigarettes a day, you have a three times greater risk of a heart attack than a nonsmoking woman. If you smoke two packs a day, you have five times the risk. Give it up. Please. (I did.) Any way you can.

An excellent incentive is to look at a picture of your youngest child and wonder if you'll ever see him or her married, or if you'll ever know your grandchildren. Or picture your husband with another woman—wearing *your* clothes. Or check out the cancer ward of a local hospital. Pick your own scare and march yourself to a clinic or organization (if you'd like supervision and the chance to commiserate) or to a hypnotist, or go cold turkey in your own house. Get rid of the car, get rid of the cigarettes, and wait it out. Stick raw vegetables in your mouth if you have oral cravings. If it's a choice between eating and smoking, eat—you can lose the weight when you've kicked the habit.

Giving up smoking will also make aerobic exercise easier, so you're *twice* as well off.

Diabetes If you are a Type II non-insulin-dependent diabetic (this is usually an adult onset, obese diabetic), or if you have an impaired glucose-tolerance test (which means you're a potential diabetic), getting your disease under control is crucial. Your chances of having coronary heart disease are *twenty times* greater than your nondiabetic counterpart, which makes diabetes a far greater risk factor in women than smoking. Luckily, this type of diabetes is almost always associated with obesity, and weight loss can almost completely control the disease (as well as contributing to overall fitness).

Obesity Obesity is not in itself a risk factor in heart disease, although extreme obesity can put a lot of strain on the heart. A healthy heart, however, can compensate for significant amounts of excess weight *up to a certain age* without apparent sign of breakdown. The big problem with obesity is that it's a major risk factor for other diseases that are risk factors for heart disease. Almost all adult female diabetics are obese, and many obese women have high triglyceride and cholesterol levels along with low HDL levels. And obese women tend not to exercise as much as they should. Obesity, then, could encompass *many* risk factors.

Hypertension High blood pressure can exist alone or be accompanied by obesity. It is measured in pressure units. The top number means the amount of work the heart has to do to pump blood through the arteries. The bottom number denotes the backflow or elasticity of the arteries. The upper limits of normal for the systolic pressure (top number) for women over forty is considered 140 to 150. The top limit for normal diastolic pressure (bottom number) is 90 to 94. Mild hypertension (a diastolic pressure of 90 to 95) is probably not an important risk factor in coronary heart disease and is usually reversible by consuming less salt and/or losing weight. A more sophisticated treatment is the use of a thiazide-type diuretic. (A diuretic is a drug that removes water from the body by blocking sodium uptake in the kidneys.) The thiazide diuretic enhances excretion of sodium and chloride—and thus water—and lowers blood pressure. Why it lowers blood pressure isn't clear, but it obviously has something to do with sodium levels in the body.

Some researchers criticize studies linking hypertension to obesity, claiming that fat people take appetite suppressants that increase their blood pressure. This is absurd, because most hypertensive obese patients would never be prescribed any kind of appetite suppressant. In my practice I have seen little or no hypertension that could be traced to these drugs.

High-fat and high-cholesterol diet Constant fighting goes on within the ranks of experts about whether dietary cholesterol should be restricted, whether it has anything to do with HDL or LDL levels, and whether eating eggs has any effect on anything. Now, with the advent of new chemical tests that distinguish between high- and low-density lipoproteins, it should be easier to figure out why some people with high cholesterol levels never have heart disease, while others with normal levels do. It will probably prove to be a matter of good and bad cholesterol, but nobody is certain yet which is which. Some reearchers think that if you cut out too much cholesterol from your diet (your cells need it, remember), your cells will go into overtime manufacturing it, and your overall level will rise alarmingly. A low-fat diet can lower your cholesterol levels a modest, but effective, 10 to 15 percent and should help you lose weight. But nobody knows if this is *the* answer.

Recent studies indicate that high-fiber diets do an even more efficient job of lowering cholesterol levels than do low-fat diets. Fiber is the undigested residue that reaches the terminal ileum, the last-digesting part of the small intestine. Along the way, fiber actually *absorbs* fat (it has been studied as a possible weight-loss tool, in fact), blocks the absorption of glucose, and increases fecal transit time (the amount of time it takes the feces to pass through the colon). There are three basic groups of fiber: vegetable, bran, and chemically purified. All help lower blood fats, but chemically purified fiber, such as cellulose, pectin, and guar gum, are the most effective. Cellulose, however, has been shown in rats to damage some of the cells that line the intestine, and these cells do not return to normal. Guar gum, which as of this writing is the safest and most efficient fiber to lower cholesterol, isn't available yet in this country. In England it has been baked into a crisp bread, and the results have been dramatic. Meanwhile, you can get pectin in any grocery store (it's used for making jellies) and from apples, or cellulose, which is used as a bulking agent in some over-the-counter diet aids. Bran, though it's great for bowels, is the weakest of the hypocholesterolemic fibers. And, as far as diet goes, new findings suggest that garlic lowers cholesterol, so in the future, garlicky breath could be a sign of cardiovascular fitness.

Your meals should be low in fat, low in salt (if you have high blood pressure), and high in fiber. This will give you the best dietary protection, such as it is, against heart disease. This is considered a "prudent" diet and is the basis of the American Heart Association plan.

Lack of exercise People who exercise regularly have been found to have higher levels of HDL than their sedentary counterparts. Although it has never been proved that exercise prolongs the life of those with heart disease, it has unquestionably improved the *quality* of life. Heart patients who exercise take less medication and feel more confident in their abilities.

Exercise should be started when you're as young as possible, *before* you develop heart disease; then it is prophylactic (preventive). Exercise for at least twenty minutes, three times a week. It is almost unrealistic to talk about jogging to a woman over forty if she hasn't jogged before. Brisk walking is an entirely acceptable aerobic exercise when carried out for longer periods of time (at least one hour). Aerobic dancing can be fun, but it doesn't put the same kind of demand on your heart and body as extended periods of walking or jogging.

Cardiac Symptoms

How can you tell if you're having a problem with your heart before it's too late? The first symptom is usually a peculiar kind of chest pain. Not a sharp, jabbing pain, or a pain that goes through to your back and hovers between your shoulder blades. It is a squeezing, aching, deep pain that can extend up into your neck and jaw, into your arms, down to your fingers, most commonly on the left but occasionally on the right, and sometimes accompanied by sweating. It is often mistaken for indigestion, particularly because it often follows a heavy meal. You can also feel chest pain in periods of stress or in very cold air. On all three occasions, there is an acute, extra strain on the heart. However, 20 percent of people who get angina—the technical name for heart pain—are resting. Resting angina can be the result of blood-vessel spasm and not coronary blockage. Most angina, though, comes from partial blocking of the vital coronary arteries by atherosclerotic plaques—fatty deposits that restrict blood flow to and from the heart.

Cardiac pain is caused by an imbalance; the heart is working desperately to consume more oxygen than it's being supplied with. In the normal heart, obviously, the amount of oxygen supplied is roughly equal to the amount needed and consumed; this is true both at rest and during periods of activity. If you're lucky, your first cardiac chest pain will be angina. If you're unlucky, and your heart is deprived of sufficient oxygen for long enough, your first sign of cardiovascular disease will be a heart attack, which means that parts of the heart muscle are damaged or destroyed.

When Your Heart Skips a Beat

Palpitations, or skipped beats, which plague many females, are only annoying variations of normal heart rhythm caused by stress, caffeine, exercise, or mitral-valve prolapse. They are frightening, but usually not significant.

Mitral-valve prolapse (MVP) is a relatively new diagnosis. Many clinicians, myself included, have often wondered why many females have such irritable hearts—hearts that speed up or palpitate out of proportion to the amount of stimulation. It also seems to take these hearts much longer to return to their resting rate. Physicians, of course, have traditionally felt that this was a product of either female neuroticism or poor conditioning. Restless hearts are frequently accompanied by a faint sound heard with the heartbeat, called a murmur. In the absence of any electrocardiographic changes, these murmurs have been called functional, or without clinical importance. In the past five years, through a new radiologic device called ultrasound, it has become possible to identify heart valves.

On the mitral valve (the valve shaped like a bishop's mitre that separates the two chambers of the left side of the heart) of some of these irritable hearts, radiologists have noticed an extra projection that doesn't belong there. This interferes with the blood flow through the heart and disturbs the perfectly timed valve closing. They have named this condition "mitral-valve prolapse."

Mitral-valve prolapse is now the most common valve disease in adults, and twice as many females have it as men. It means that the leaflets of the mitral valve on the heart don't close as tightly as they should ("floppy valves," they're sometimes called), and this gives rise to a heart murmur. It is not clear what causes MVP. It might be related to an inherited loss of collagen (connective tissue) supporting the structure of the valve, allowing it to stretch and become floppy. Often called an unimportant condition, it can nonetheless cause several distressing symptoms, among them chest pain, shortness of breath, fatigue, dizziness, fainting, palpitating, paroxysmal rapid heartbeats (tachycardia), and an unstable pulse rate during exercise. Because many women have many of these symptoms on occasion, it's nice to know if MVP is the cause.

If you have a mitral-valve prolapse, there are a couple of precautions you should take.

1. If you have any kind of dental surgery, make sure you take antibiotics before and after. Surgery in the mouth releases a large amount of bacteria into the bloodstream, and the bacteria collect like bees on any kind of protuberance—particularly the leaflet of a heart valve. There they vegetate and can cause a serious infection. Antibiotics will kill the bacteria immediately, however, so don't let this stand between you and needed surgery.

2. The only other kinds of surgery that release anywhere near the amount of bacteria into the bloodstream as dental are vaginal, and gynecologists routinely prescribe antibiotics for these patients or for any surgery below the waist.

3. Diuretic therapy—for high blood pressure or to eliminate water retention—tends to deplete body potassium, and this can make your heart rather irritable if you have MVP. So

diuretics, although not absolutely forbidden, should be approached with extreme caution.

Otherwise, MVP is an unobtrusive disease.

Diagnosis and Treatment

After you've had heart pain and survived, you should have a coronary workup. (Or, better yet, if you're over thirty-five, have a routine workup *before* the fact.) This consists of an electrocardiogram (EKG) and perhaps a stress test if your doctor thinks it is indicated. Stress tests, though, are rather inaccurate in some women. Many times no disease is found, so females with chest pain are often diagnosed as having "Syndrome X," a wastebasket diagnosis for pain that resembles angina when no obstruction in the coronary artery has been found. Syndrome X is also known as "small-vessel disease."

Cardiology has become an extremely sophisticated and technical science. There is now, along with the stress test and EKG, a new tool called ultrasound, in which sound waves are able to delineate the size of the heart, the thickness of the heart walls, and the size of the chambers individually, plus hundreds of other measurements that heretofore could be obtained only by cardiac catheterization—which means sticking a tube through an artery directly into the heart.

Treatment for uncomplicated angina is nitroglycerin, which dilates certain small vessels in the heart, allowing a better distribution of the available blood supply; propranolol or beta blockers, which decrease oxygen consumption by the heart (I'll discuss these in Chapter 13); and a new type of drug that has been used with great success in Japan for several years called calcium channel blockers. Muscles (of which the heart is one) need calcium ions to contract (the only function of a muscle). Channel blockers change the flow of calcium into and out of the heart muscle, decreasing heart irritability and allowing arteries to dilate, thus improving the blood flow to the heart. They represent one of the most exciting finds in cardiac medicine yet. Currently they are used to treat angina, heart attacks, and even some very difficult arrhythmias (irregular heartbeats that are otherwise impossible to control).

And if all this doesn't work, there is always bypass surgery, although its use in females is rare—about one to eight, females to males, one of my cardiologist friends estimates. He points out that females tend not to have such severe heart disease, at least prior to their seventies or eighties. At that age, their chances of surviving such a major operation are not good, and most surgeons choose not to operate. He also says that most cardiovascular surgeons would rather operate on males because women have much smaller blood vessels, the operation is more difficult, and the success rate isn't so high.

Coronary heart disease is the number-one killer of men, and in no other branch of medicine—outside the infectious diseases—have there been so many exciting advances. Coincidence? I don't think so.

Chapter 10

The Breast

Benign Breast Disease

If your breasts have a lot of little bumps and lumps that interfere with your attempts to examine them, you probably have fibrocystic disease, the most common disease of the female breast. About 5 percent of all mature women contract it, and it's particularly prevalent between the ages of thirty and fifty, when the ovaries are most active and estrogen levels are high. It can make self-examination quite confusing because your breasts have a "shotty" feel, making it difficult to palpate a true mass. What you're feeling are lots of cysts.

Fibrocystic Disease of the Breast

A cyst is any closed sac with a tough lining that contains liquid or semisolid material. A tumor, in contrast, is usually solid. Cysts have smooth, even borders and are not attached to any underlying structures.

How are cysts formed? The normal breast is filled with

ducts that lead to the nipple. Surrounding each duct are small lobules where milk is produced. Lobules are subjected to monthly hormonal stimulation as the reproductive system readies itself for fertilization of the egg. This stimulation produces a change in the lobules of certain women. The result is often a cyst.

Cysts dot the terminal ducts of the breast tissue like buds on a tree branch, and if you are a "cyst former" you usually have them in both breasts. It's common to have many cysts of all different sizes. A cyst can alter in size rapidly, and it's usually smallest immediately after menstruation; it fills up premenstrually, when estrogen levels are highest.

Fibrocystic disease is uncomfortable, but not serious. Achy breasts and premenstrual swelling are generally the extent of the symptoms. It's only a problem because a lumpy, fibrocystic breast is sometimes difficult to distinguish from a cancerous one. And this means a lot of trouble, expense, and anxiety; mammography, aspiration (removing fluid from a cyst), and, ultimately, excision are sometimes the only surefire means of establishing nonmalignancy. Some researchers believe th[illegible] is a slight relationship between fibrocystic disease and cancer, the theory being that women with many cysts are hypersensitive to hormonal stimulation—and hormones play a prominent role in breast cancer.

Fibrocystic Disease and Caffeine

I have a friend whose breasts are so cut up from biopsies that they look like a road map. She had a lot of cysts, you see, and her ultraconservative, ultra-knife-happy surgeon would cut chunk after chunk out of her. She used to cringe every time a new lump appeared. But in 1978 a report came out that established a causal relationship between drinking coffee and the progression of fibrocystic disease. When the subjects gave up tea and coffee (both of which contain caffeine, from the chemical family methyl xanthine), the majority of their cysts either regressed or disappeared entirely. The report was criticized, of course—mostly for not taking into account the chronic and unpredictable nature of fibrocystic disease, and for not detailing what was going on hormonally in the patients' lives. However, my friend stopped drinking coffee and tea, and she even gave up chocolate (which also contains methyl xanthine). She has developed few new cysts in the last four years, and none have required surgery.

If your breasts feel large, painful, or cystic, especially before menstrual periods, it might be a good idea to try giving up coffee and tea, or to switch to decaffeinated coffee and herbal tea. Remember to check medications you are taking. Cold medicines and some aspirin products, among many others, often contain caffeine, as do many carbonated drinks, including colas. If giving it up doesn't work, you'll have lost nothing but your caffeine addiction. If it does work, your post-reproductive life will be much more comfortable.

Noncystic Breast Enlargement

Many women in their middle to late forties suddenly find their breasts getting bigger, and this enlargement is generally unrelated to weight gain. They get upset when their blouses pop open and wonder what the hell is going on. The reason for this enlargement is an imbalance in the estrogen-progesterone ratio—the same thing that causes breast changes at puberty. At puberty, hormonal surges kicked the ovaries to life; in mid-life, when the ovaries begin to die, hormonal surges try to kick them *back* to life. For the breasts the bottom line is the same—they are the recipients of newly mobilized fat. This is a temporary situation, and there's really nothing you can do about it—except buy a few new blouses. Once your ovaries stop functioning, you can often reduce your breast size by losing weight.

Breast Cancer

In the United States, the average woman was a 7 percent chance of developing breast cancer and a 3 percent chance of dying from it. No wonder it's the subject of so much literature and emotional debate.

Breast cancer might be two separate diseases. Recent studies suggest that the pre-menopausal type differs from the post-menopausal. The first might be related to an abnormality of ovarian estrogens, and the cause is probably genetic. Susceptibility to this disease is easiest to modify early in life, either by early pregnancy, which could possibly normalize the estrogen, or by castration (removal of the ovaries).

Grace was a young, pre-menopausal female with terrible breast-cancer heredity. Her mother and all her sisters had had it before menopause. She had extensive fibrocystic disease, which made it difficult to feel small masses and which distorted the mammography picture. A specialist advised her to have both breasts removed as a precaution. The suggestion horrified her because she was unmarried, childless, and extremely athletic. But after much agonizing, she opted to have it done. When doctors examined the excised breast tissue under a microscope, they found more than a hundred examples of premalignant cells, any one of which could have spelled her death sentence in a few years.

Grace's case is extreme. Most women are never faced with this kind of decision. But if you are, *act quickly,* because pre-menopausal breast cancer can be a rapidly growing malignancy.

The post-menopausal type of breast cancer seems to be related to the nutritional habits of more developed countries. This means there is a far greater incidence of it in, say, the United States and Switzerland than in India or China. It's not genetic; a study has shown that Chinese women who settled in San Francisco now have an incidence of breast cancer comparable to that of American women.

The initiation, or birth, of a malignant cell in the breast may be the result of radiation, a chemical consumed or otherwise absorbed, or perhaps a virus. But malignant mammary cells need a favorable hormonal environment in which to grow and reproduce. So, once initiated, the cell can sit around waiting for hormonal stimulation. In China and India, where bodies tend to be smaller and leaner, breast cancer can be stunted around menopause when the ovaries stop functioning. In this country, however, where bodies are taller and fatter, hormone conditions that can stimulate the growth of a tumor exist even after menopause. This is because fat converts another hormone, androstenedione (manufactured by the ovaries and the adrenal glands), into estrogen. So fatter women have more hormonal stimulation. A good way for the post-reproductive female to reduce her risk of breast cancer is to lose weight.

What else increases your risk of getting breast cancer? Since heredity is a major factor, if you have a family history of the disease, you should monitor your breasts carefully. In pre-menopausal breast cancer, early pregnancy and/or surgical castration (removing the ovaries) are said to modify the risk.

You run a higher risk of breast cancer if you've had a lot of circulating estrogen for a longer-than-normal time—menstrual periods before age twelve and/or beyond age fifty. Also, excessive or prolonged exposure to radiation is always a significant risk. High-fat diets and larger body size—which means increased body fat (although not necessarily obesity)—are also considered moderate risk factors. The use of estrogen supplements does not seem to have a clear-cut relationship to post-menopausal breast cancer.

Having a lot of children, breast size, and breast-augmentation and reduction procedures do not seem to increase your risk of acquiring the disease. They've all been mentioned in the past, but the latest studies have tended to discount them. Breast feeding appears to decrease the risk of breast cancer.

Breast Self-Examination

Ninety percent of palpable breast tumors are detected by self-examination, one of the most important tools in preventive medicine. One of my professors used to say that a woman should know her breasts like the backs of her hands—every lump, bump, and thickening. For some women this is easy: those with small, compact breasts are often able to notice subtle changes. Others, with larger, lumpier breasts, find the procedure distasteful. (Although the porno movies would have men believe that all women love massaging their breasts, this isn't always the case.)

Here are some rules for a proper self-examination:

1. Examine your breasts in front of a mirror. This allows you to observe changes such as dimpling, swelling, asymmetry, skin redness, or peeling of the nipple.

2. Compress your nipple to detect discharge.

3. Palpate (feel by pressing down firmly) your breasts twice, once while standing upright, once while lying down.

4. Examine your breasts *after* your period and not right before. Cysts fill up premenstrually.

You can do the upright palpation most effectively in the shower, when your skin is soapy and your hand will slide easily over the breast and armpit. Place the hand flat against the breast (use the right hand for the left breast and the left hand for the right) and move it in a circular motion from the periphery to the nipple. Complete the palpation by gently squeezing the nipple and feeling for a lump or nodule or discharge of fluid. When you palpate a breast lump, you should be interested in its size, shape, consistency, mobility, and whether it is different from the same area on the opposite breast.

Mammography

Elsie's big breasts dropped over the examining table. "When was your last breast exam?" I asked.

"Too long ago," she said.

My work was cut out for me. I told her to put the heels of her hands together, and I looked for asymmetry and puckering. I saw nothing but mounds of round flesh. She clasped her hands in back of her head, throwing out her bust. No masses were outlined. How could there be? Too much fat hid everything. I began to palpate for masses, my hands going deep into her gelatinous mammaries. I felt lots of shotty little cysts, like bits of buckshot.

"You have a lot of little cysts in your breasts," I told her.

"I know," she said. "They hurt, too."

"Any history of breast cancer in your family?"

"Yes. My mother."

"Ever had a mammography?"

"Too dangerous!" she announced.

Too dangerous! About as dangerous as an airplane ride, and much safer than not bothering about regular checkups—which is suicidal if there's a family history of the disease. Elsie had heard that too much radiation can cause cancer. But at her age (fifty) and weight, and with her family history, would it surprise you to know that she already had it?

Elsie agreed reluctantly to a mammography, and, indeed, a suspicious lesion was found. It was very small, so small that when the surgeon removed it he had to employ special fine markers to make sure he took out the right section. The mass was malignant, but the lymph nodes were negative, which meant the cancer hadn't begun to spread. Elsie had more than a 90 percent chance of survival.

Once a lump is palpable, it has already been growing for a while, which is why routine mammographies are so important. They can detect a lump usually long before you can. It's a low-radiation X-ray, capable of showing early changes in breast architecture and 90 percent of the time distinguishing a benign tumor from a malignant one. It's such a sensitive tool that it can detect cancer too small to be seen by surgeons in tissues actually removed during a biopsy. However, a substantial number of lumps have been found by examination when mammography has been negative. Obviously neither mode of screening for breast cancer is as good as the two together. It can catch the cancer while it's still minimal, before it has invaded surrounding tissue (metastasized), and women undergoing mastectomy for minimal breast cancer (like Elsie) have an excellent chance of being completely cured.

Ten percent of the time the mammography cannot distinguish between a benign and a malignant lesion, and at this stage a surgeon is normally consulted to try to aspirate the lump. Aspirating means taking fluid out, and if this decompresses the lump or if the aspirated fluid contains no malignant cells, nothing further is required except follow-up examinations every three to six months. If the lump is solid or yields very little fluid, or if the fluid contains malignant cells, the entire mass will have to be removed (called a biopsy) and examined under a microscope.

The newest recommendation of the National Institutes of Health is that all women over fifty should have annual mammograms, and that all women over thirty-five should have at least one. It should probably be performed more often on women who are at higher risk—if they have a family history of it, for example, or if they've never been pregnant. Remember, you should have *both* a physical exam and a mammography regularly, not just one or the other.

Treatment

Once malignancy has been established, you'll have to face the controversy about the best surgical procedure to remove it. The original operation was the disfiguring Halsted procedure, or radical mastectomy. This was conceived in 1894 and is virtually unchanged today. It evolved from the idea that breast cancer proceeds in an orderly, stepwise fashion from the original tumor to the lymph nodes to distant sites. Therefore, everything within range of the tumor was systematically removed—breasts, lymph nodes, chest muscles, the works.

The most common method of treatment today is the *modified* radical mastectomy, which is similar to the original except the chest muscles aren't removed. Recently there has been a movement toward preserving the breasts; surgeons remove the lump (a procedure called, appropriately enough, a lumpectomy) and the auxiliary nodes but leave the connective tissue. Then they radiate the breast to try to kill remaining cancer cells (if any) and to give better cosmetic, functional, and psychological results than one would have with surgery. This radiation is called adjuvant therapy, which means preventive treatment when there is no evidence of spread. Chemotherapy (the use of one or several chemicals) and hormone therapy are beginning to show promise as adjuvants with surgery.

Spurred by the idea that surgeons seek to "defeminize" their patients without consent, a very vocal group of lumpectomy enthusiasts has emerged. You're most likely to benefit from this limited surgical removal with radiation therapy if you're a young woman with minimal breast cancer anxious for the best cosmetic results. In some cases, however, a lump with clear margins removed may constitute as great a deformity as losing the entire breast.

It's a shame that so little surgical progress has been made in this disease since 1894, especially since the organ, while useless except for nursing, has such important sexual overtones in our society. To be fair, surgeons have worked very hard to cure and control the disease itself, and the partial mastectomy has been possible only in the past twenty years with the sophistication of radiotherapy. This is a local treatment, like surgery—although doctors can safely radiate a larger area than surgeons can remove—and it preserves the function of the tissues being treated. It's impossible, however, for doctors to measure the amount of tumor foci that might remain after radiation; and it's possible that normal cells may be altered by the radiation and, hence, become cancerous themselves.

One exciting development for women who have had major breast surgery and, two years later, no recurrence of the cancer, is breast augmentation. This sophisticated technique of reconstruction has become so refined that it's no longer a cosmetic tragedy to have a breast removed. And breasts, alas, are cosmetically very important to a lot of women (not to mention men).

Personally, I have trouble relating to the intense feelings most women have about their breasts. Part of their worry, I'm sure, is how their husbands will feel: "Will I be as sexually attractive? Will he be repelled?" It's too bad females have to be slaves to the masculine ego in matters vital to health. I certainly wouldn't want to have my breasts amputated, but I've never attached much importance to them—cosmetic or otherwise. Although the loss of one breast might be a shock to the other breast, those appendages of fat and connective tissues are not the seat of your femininity. If you have breast cancer, there are more important things to worry about than the loss of a breast. It won't affect your sexuality in the least, and if your husband is unhappy, that's *his* problem. Don't let it bother *you;* recent studies suggest that a positive, optimistic attitude plays a role in preventing further outbreaks of cancer.

Chapter 11

The Problematic Pelvis

Vaginal Diseases

The vagina is the tunnel that connects the external sexual equipment to the doorway of the uterus, the cervix. Richly supplied with blood vessels and lubricating glands, it is dark, moist, and warm—thus making it the ideal spot to grow bacteria and yeast or to harbor flagellates (little parasites). Normal vaginal bacteria are actually useful; like the armed forces, they protect the vagina against infection and invasion. Sometimes, however, the precise bacterial balance is thrown off by drugs (antibiotics), natural trauma (intercourse), systemic infection (colds, flu), or metabolic diseases (diabetes). Even the flow of menstrual blood can change the biochemistry of the normal vagina from acid to alkaline, favoring certain kinds of infection. Then you've got problems.

A good, healthy vagina can keep female sexuality at its peak. But with different life-styles and more sexual freedom for women, vaginal infections—both venereal and non-venereal—are becoming much more common.

A popular, grisly movie made in the past few years depicts a beautiful and bored middle-aged housewife who picks up a mysterious stranger in an art museum. After a sexual romp in his apartment, she discovers quite by accident a notice in his desk from the Department of Health. The guy has had sex with a V.D. carrier, it says, and he is urged to come in for treatment.

This may seem ludicrous to many contentedly married women, but it's no joke. Venereal disease is on the rise in the mature female and must be considered if either you or your partner sleeps around. The new sexual permissiveness and an abundance of single mid-life women make sexual intercourse an important part of social intercourse. It's a healthy situation; women are discovering new dimensions in sexuality. They're also discovering new dimensions in vaginal agony.

Most people think of V.D. as syphilis and gonorrhea, which are the diseases that do the most extensive damage. Many other sexually transmitted diseases are less well known but still very common, and a few of them have only recently been classified as venereal.

Except for the chancre sore in syphilis—a painless ulcerated lesion with raised edges that appears on the genitals or in the mouth—symptoms of sexual disease can be very nonspecific. The most common are a pronounced vaginal discharge, pain, and itching. Normal, uninfected females have a vaginal discharge, too, which changes in consistency from thin and white to thick and mucous as ovulation passes. The amount of the normal discharge is quite small.

The abnormal discharge of *gonorrhea*, the most commonly reported V.D., is heavy and resembles semen. That's how it got its name: *gonorrhea* is Greek for "flow of seed." The risk of infection for a female from an infected male is a whopping 85 percent. Symptoms, though, are mild—the said discharge and minor discomfort. Many women don't even seek treatment, and there's the rub. The disease can linger or recede, but a few months later it will pop up as a severe pelvic inflammation. Early treatment is not that much of a hassle; with penicillin or tetracycline it usually clears up satisfactorily.

A *genital herpes* virus infection produces extreme pain and disability but does not have the serious consequences of gonorrhea. Researchers think there may be a link between genital herpes and cervical cancer, however. One type of herpes causes cold sores in the mouth, the other in the genitals. The latter look like the former—little blisters that break and form crusts—but they feel much worse. In the genitals they get wet with acid urine and are constantly rubbed and irritated by the legs. Instead of the seven-to-ten-day cleanup of the oral (mouth) variety, genital herpes can take up to three weeks to clear. There is no specific, consistently effective medication, but fortunately most cases respond to good hygiene and a local anesthetic.

The most interesting thing about the herpes virus is that after you are sexually infected you can be reinfected later without further contact. The virus can lie around and then reproduce itself. The first infection, though, is by far the most painful.

Trichomonas vaginalis is an infection born of a flagellate, which is a little parasite. It is usually transmitted sexually and never seems to afflict adult virgins. Itching of the vulva and vagina is the most persistent symptom, and it can be severe enough to wake you up. Trichomonas often begins just after menstruation, when the vagina is less acidic than usual. You'll notice the discharge: green, frothy, and foul-smelling. The treatment, with an antiflagellate, is very efficient.

Hemophilius vaginalis vaginitis is one of the most common and contagious venereal diseases. It begins with a discharge unrelated to the menstrual cycle—thin and white, with a strong, disagreeable, fishy odor. It does not cause as much irritation as some of the other venereal diseases, but it often inflames the urethra (the tube through which your urine passes), causing burning when you urinate. Although the source of this illness is bacteria, it does not clear up with traditional antibiotic therapy. Treatment is identical to that for trichomonas.

Some vaginal diseases accompanied by a discharge are not transmitted by sexual contact:

Monilia vaginitis (candidiasis). The mold *Candida albicans* may be found in the vaginas of 25 to 30 percent of all healthy women, but not all of them have a monilia infection. You may get monilia symptoms if you're being treated for another infection with antibiotics, which kill vaginal bacteria. Not all vaginal bacteria are bad; they keep the normal vaginal mold in check and vice versa. When all the bacteria are killed, the mold grows freely and creates a new infection. Usually the vulvar area is red and swollen, and the discharge resembles cottage cheese. Diabetics are most prone to monilia because their sugar levels change the pH balance of the vagina. Treatment is with a specific antifungal agent to kill the mold, but the infection, unfortunately, tends to be chronic.

Senile vaginitis (an old and atrocious name) is a nonspecific vaginitis caused by lack of estrogen. Symptoms are a yellowish discharge and burning. Treatment is with estrogen cream or pills.

The Cervix

The cervix is the gateway to the uterus. It looks like a funny knob with a hole in the middle, and it stares in the face of anyone who happens to peek into your vagina. Its only function is as a passageway from the uterus at birth, and it expands astoundingly to allow the baby to travel through it. For an otherwise insignificant little stump it gets into a lot of trouble.

Part of the problem is that the cervix has two different kinds of cells, one on the face of it and one in the cervical canal. The junction of the two is about as placid as your average Middle Eastern border. This is because each type of cell responds differently to changes in hormonal stimulation and vaginal acidity. The area of overlap is confused and volatile, and that kind of chaos makes it vulnerable to infection and neoplasia (a new growth, which could be a cyst or a tumor).

Cervical infections can cause bleeding during or after intercourse and an abnormally large amount of discharge. Your gynecologist can determine the specific type of infection with a culture or cervical secretion smear, but even with a specific vaginal cream these things are messy and tend to hang on for a while. Often they go away and come back. In that case, surgery is the only solution.

Cervical surgery is minor, and it usually works. There are three possible procedures, and each has its adherents. The oldest is cauterization, in which infected tissue is burned off with the surgical equivalent of a hot poker. The second is cryosurgery, which consists of freezing part of the cervix to about minus forty degrees Centigrade, whereupon the infected tissue sloughs off. The newest procedure is laser surgery, in which the infected cells are vaporized. Laser surgery requires expensive equipment, which most hospitals don't have; cryosurgery, although very effective, is considered by many doctors to be too drastic, and occasionally it can lead to complications. Most gynecological surgeons have stuck with cauterization.

Cervical Cancer

Cervical cancer is the easiest internal cancer to detect, and if you get to it early, before the cancer has had a chance to invade surrounding tissues, it's easy to cure as well. The cervix is readily accessible with a speculum, an instrument inserted into the vagina, and this makes Pap smears very simple. In a Pap smear, cells are scraped from the tissue, stained, and examined under a microscope. Ninety percent of the time a Pap smear can reveal a malignancy, even in its earliest stages. If surgeons get to it early enough, they don't even have to remove the uterus, so a younger woman may continue to have children. This year the American Cancer Society has recommended that Pap smears need only be done every three years, after two consecutive negative exams taken one year apart. This infuriated gynecologists who are worried that patients won't come in for their yearly pelvic exam which might be crucial in discovering another disease. So the American Cancer Society does recommend a yearly pelvic exam for women over forty.

The Ovaries and Ovarian Cancer

The ovaries are solid, oval-shaped organs that are responsible for producing eggs and secreting female hormones (primarily estrogen and progesterone). In post-reproductive life they obviously become much less important, although they are never totally inactive. They still secrete the male hormone, androstenedione, which is converted into estrogen in the peripheral tissue. But if you have them removed, it's no big loss; the adrenal gland can take up the hormone slack.

Current surgical thinking holds that after age forty-five the ovaries should go as a means of preventing cancer, ovarian cancer being the fifth leading cause of death in women. The disease is silent and deadly and impossible to predict. It has few, if any, early symptoms. Most of the time it is discovered only because the tumor has become so large that it affects other structures in the pelvis through pressure or blockage, or, more ominously, it has metastasized (spread) to distant organs.

Not all ovarian tumors are malignant, but *all* should be carefully monitored and, if necessary, surgically investigated. Regular pelvic exams will (most of the time) ensure early discovery.

The Uterus

The uterus is the baby carriage of the pelvis. It has a specific, generally short-term use and comes in handy only during a relatively small segment of a woman's life. Yet it is the organ that gives the most trouble to the post-reproductive female. It is a small, muscular, pear-shaped structure that in its good days had the miraculous ability to stretch to many times its normal size and encompass a fetus, and the unique ability to shed its lining (called the endometrium) at monthly intervals. It doesn't seem to manufacture any hormones itself except perhaps the prostaglandins, but it's the target organ for the ovarian hormones and the gonadotrophins (see Chapter 2). It would be nice if it would just quietly shrivel up and die when it is no longer needed, but female organs are rarely very accommodating, and some of the most annoying and costly female illnesses arise during the uterus's slow demise.

Uterine disease is usually manifested in two ways: by tumor formation or by bleeding.

The Bumpy, Lumpy Uterus

Most tumors of the uterus are benign. These are called fibroid tumors and are quite common in women over forty. They form in the muscle wall of the uterus, sometimes jutting into the uterine cavity (the lumen), where they can disrupt the lining and cause bleeding. A majority of fibroid tumors, however, simply grow outward and cause no symptoms. Your gynecologist can feel them at your yearly pelvic exam. Removing them or not is your choice. You can have either a hysterectomy (removal of the uterus with or without the ovaries) or a hysterotomy (scooping out only the tumor, the technique to use if you still want children). Or you can just sit on them.

I am presently sitting on a fibroid tumor the size of a grapefruit, and my gynecologist is eyeing me expectantly. It doesn't hurt or bleed or block any vital organ, though it does make my bladder a little more irritable. The risk I am taking is that the tumor will block my kidneys, or will grow more rapidly or become malignant—which is about as likely as gallstones leading to gallbladder cancer (not too likely). Why am I so stubborn? Well, fibroid tumors are common in women and usually get smaller after age fifty, when the amount of estrogen in the body diminishes. It's not that I'm afraid of surgery. Hysterectomy is the most common major operation in women, and today's gynecological surgeons are decent technicians. But I hate general anesthesia and the six-week post-op convalescence when you can't exercise or drive and *can* eat. If they could get me back to work in two weeks, I'd be strongly tempted to undergo the knife. (See "Hysterectomy," page 103.)

The Bleeding Uterus

The most common cause of uterine bleeding is the monthly menstrual cycle. This occurs at regular intervals when the uterus sheds its lining, the endometrium. The quantity of blood lost varies from individual to individual. Some women are known as heavy bleeders; others have only a scanty flow. However, excess bleeding at any time, bleeding or spotting between periods for more than one cycle, or any bleeding after menopause can be a sign of disease.

The most common source of excessive bleeding in the over-forty female is a benign condition called DUB (dysfunctional uterine bleeding), caused by a hormonal imbalance. There is an excessive buildup of the endometrial lining, which alters the regularity and amount of blood flow. Usually it's a good idea to have a D and C (dilation and curettage or more informally, dusting and cleaning), a minor surgical procedure in which the cervix is dilated and the wall of the uterus is scraped. This procedure is useful in making a diagnosis—the removed tissue can be examined under a microscope to determine if it is malignant—and as therapy, because it removes the excess tissue from the wall of the uterus, leaving a normal base.

Incidentally, a D and C can be done in a doctor's office, but don't believe that "it won't hurt a bit." Even with the best local anesthesia, you'll have cramps afterward. Occasionally, a "chemical" D and C is done instead of a surgical one; high doses of progesterone are injected or administered by pill for seven to ten days and then abruptly stopped. This induces the uterus to slough off its lining. But progesterone in large doses is a hateful drug. It causes bloating, depression, headaches, nausea, and weight gain.

Excessive bleeding from DUB lasts from ten to twenty-one days and can cause spotting, oozing, clotting, and hemorrhaging. You get sick of stained underwear and relentless changing of tampons. If you've had several trials of hormonal therapy and several D and C's and still the problem persists, you might get fed up with the whole messy business and opt for hysterectomy. The problem would pass eventually, but who knows how long that would take? If it's making you tired, cranky, and chapped, there's nothing wrong with having the damned thing removed.

Hysterectomy

This raises an important issue: Is there any medical reason to have your uterus removed for benign tumors or repeated bleeding, even if there's no malignancy? I have a friend who says yes. He is a very competent obstetrician-gynecologist who likes to brag that the reason the incidence of uterine cancer is so low in our part of the state is that he takes out a uterus at the first sign of trouble. "After all," he says, "who needs a uterus after you're through having children? If you don't need it for babies, why hang onto it? I'm not going to sit around while somebody bleeds to anemia from DUB, or watch atypical, often premalignant cells appear. If you don't need it, why keep it?"

That's what they used to say about tonsils. If they're infected and they don't give you immunity to anything, let's take them out. Never mind that it's a miserable, painful, bloody operation. Well, tonsils finally won the battle to stay in place, except in the most extreme circumstances; but the uterus has not.

As you can probably tell, I haven't resolved in my own mind the idea of using a hysterectomy to prevent cancer. The uterus, after all, is the very seat of the female mind, right? At least everyone thought so in Freud's day. The concept of the "hysterical woman" came directly from the belief that the uterus loosened from its attachments and bumped around the pelvis, hitting everything in sight, causing aches, pains, and numerous other female complaints. This is preposterous, of course, yet many women are superstitious about their uteri. And who knows whether it secretes some hormone we haven't yet discovered? My feeling is that a healthy uterus should not be removed; yet if it's gone bad, if it's bleeding or causing other problems, there's no point trying to save it.

The uterus is still removed for complaints as minor as bloating, premenstrual tension, and menstrual irregularities. Before hospitals had surgical review committees, many a totally normal uterus hit the formalin jar. Today, gynecologists must justify its removal.

The Saggy Uterus

There are anatomical reasons for a hysterectomy. Your uterus may drop. Yes, the uterus does loosen up as the Victorians once thought, but it doesn't bounce around the pelvis. Instead, it drops straight through the vagina, and often out, and pulls the neck of the bladder with it, making it difficult to hold urine when you cough, sneeze, or are in the middle of that perfect golf swing. You get up every two hours during the night to go to the toilet, your husband bumps it when you have intercourse, and one day you look down and think you have a penis. Your pelvic ligaments have stretched and no amount of skim milk will make them elastic again. That seems like a good time for a hysterectomy.

Uterine Cancer

If there's a malignancy, obviously, there's no question: the uterus goes. Any post-menopausal bleeding can be a sign of endometrial cancer. (Although there are very rare cancers elsewhere in the uterus, 99 percent of them occur in the lining, the endometrium.) In post-reproductive life, the ovaries stop working—you stop ovulating—and if you have a lot of circulating estrogen there is a buildup of cells (a hyperplasia) in the endometrium. The estrogen can alter them, leaving you with a malignancy. Obesity and diabetes, both associated with relatively high levels of estrogen in post-reproductive life, seem to predispose you to this cancer. The trick is to identify the hyperplasia with a D and C *before* the cells become malignant and invade surrounding tissue. If the hyperplastic cells are normal, high doses of progesterone will cause you to shed the endometrium, and this should take care of the problem. If the cells, however, are "atypical," there's a chance the hyperplasia will lead to cancer, and in most cases a hysterectomy is warranted.

Removing the Uterus: Techniques

If you elect to have a hysterectomy (meaning there's no emergency), you should know that there are two procedures: one performed through the abdomen and one through the vagina.

An abdominal hysterectomy is performed through a nice, neat incision above the pubic hairline that exposes all the pelvic organs—the uterus, tubes, and ovaries. (If your gynecologist is less considerate, though, he can make a long, disfiguring incision that leaves a whopping scar. I used to look at such patients and wonder if the surgeon was trying to remove the tonsils, too). It's very straightforward surgery, but real surgery all the same.

In the vaginal approach, the uterus is pulled down into the vagina, almost the way a sleeve is inverted in a coat, and removed, without an abdominal incision. The contents of the pelvis remain undisturbed. The vaginal approach has a lower risk of complications (such as fever and infection) than an abdominal hysterectomy, and convalescence is shorter by approximately two weeks.

Why aren't all hysterectomies vaginal? Not all conditions lend themselves to it. Extremely large benign tumors of the uterus, pelvic adhesions, ovarian tumors, and most malignancies should be removed via the abdomen. Also, there are many older surgeons (and younger ones, too) who haven't been trained in this method—which is relatively new—and are insecure about using it. So consider your options and choose the procedure most beneficial to *you*, even if it means changing surgeons.

Is There Sex after Hysterectomy?

Damn right, and damn good, too! Just not right away. Males worry about impotence after reproductive-tract surgery, but don't worry—it won't happen to you. Just be sure to wait at least six weeks so that the incision has healed. You might have to wait a little longer for sex after a vaginal hysterectomy because most of the suturing is done in the vaginal wall, but eventually it will heal. Many times your surgeon will tighten up your vagina during a hysterectomy, and that could make sex better than ever. Remember, even if your vagina is a little short, it has a marvelous ability to stretch, and your discomfort should be only temporary.

Libido in the female has absolutely nothing to do with the uterus and cervix. If anything, the cervix can make intercourse painful—it's no fun having your cervix jogged when you're making love. And your uterus is nothing but a big, unresponsive blob. There are those who argue that it can increase orgasmic response by increasing pelvic congestion (see Chapter 3, "Sex"), but the vaginal wall, which is richly supplied with blood, can do all the congesting you need for good orgasm.

I once met a young woman who had had not only a total hysterectomy, but also extensive bowel surgery for cancer of the colon. There was *nothing* left in her pelvis except her vagina. She complained to her doctor that she no longer enjoyed sex, that it was painful and she could no longer have orgasms. All the sex therapists rubbed their hands with glee and began to blame surgery for a loss in pelvic congestion (that's their pet theory, and they champion it). But her gynecologist found that she had a severe monilial infection (see "Vaginal Diseases," above) from the chemotherapy she received for her cancer, and her vagina was swollen and sore. Once he treated the monilial infection, she was able to resume a very satisfying sex life, with no difference in her orgasmic capacity whatsoever.

Every so often somebody suggests that estrogen plays a role in sex drive, but in fact it's not a sexual hormone. When estrogen and progesterone levels drop at ovulation, women are supposed to get sexier—one of nature's little tricks to ensure survival of the species. Post-menopausally (or post-hysterectomy), the ovaries (if they are still in) secrete more androgen (a male hormone) than estrogen, and this, ironically, could *enhance* sexual desire.

Are There Paps and Pelvics after Hysterectomy?

How often should you get a Pap smear and/or a pelvic exam after a hysterectomy? If your ovaries have been taken out with your uterus, there is no need to have a yearly pelvic and Pap smear unless you have other problems. A Pap smear is done to rule out or diagnose cervical and/or vaginal malignancy. Without the cervix, it is necessary to have a Pap smear only every three years, since vaginal cancer is quite rare. If your ovaries are intact, a yearly pelvic is necessary to make sure they are not enlarged.

The Tools of the Trade

The tools of gynecology have become a lot more sophisticated in the past few years, and you'll be hearing more about them soon (if you haven't already). Most women know about the laparoscope, which is an optical instrument with which the abdominal cavity can be viewed through just a small incision in the belly button. The information gained from a laparoscopy used to be accessible only through a major surgical procedure. Certain operations can also be executed through a laparoscope, such as a belly-button operation for sterilization.

A hysteroscope is another optical instrument that allows the physician to look through the vagina and cervix and into the uterus without making a single cut. This is particularly useful in cases of excessive bleeding when no cause is forthcoming. The hysteroscope often reveals a tumor on the inside wall of the uterus that could not be felt by palpation.

Finally, as I mentioned earlier, laser surgery has come to gynecology. Surgeons can funnel electrons into a kind of laser knife that cuts with much less bleeding and scarring, speedily disposing of cysts, abscesses, polyps, and lesions of the cervix.

Chapter 12

Depression

Esther looked like hell. "How are you today?" I asked cheerfully, knowing she'd start to cry if I was anything less than ebullient. I overestimated her. The lightest touch was too much. Tears welled up in her eyes and spilled down her cheeks. "Terrible," she said. "Terrible. Just terrible."

Esther was depressed. No need to have her fill out a questionnaire. No need to ask the usual depression questions ("Appetite poor?" "Sleep disturbed?" "Wake up too early in the morning?"). No need to rate her suicide potential. (Depressed older females are not high suicide risks.)

"What's the trouble?" I asked.

"I can't cope anymore," she said. "Everything is too much for me."

I checked her chart again. She had been stable in the past and had not suffered a recent loss or crisis. Her marriage seemed fine. Her kids were doing what they were supposed to do. Why was she so depressed? I thought about another woman I had seen the previous week, Jenny. She had also sat in front of my desk, crying. Unlike Esther, Jenny had been psychoanalyzed for ten years, and she knew *why* she was depressed. It was her mother.

"My mother has ruined my life," she sobbed. "She has me trapped. I hate her. I hate her!" She pounded on the desk.

"Where is your mother?"

"She's dead—dead for ten years!"

Both of these patients were female and menopausal. Both had moods that were out of proportion to any immediate problems in their environment. Both were responding to some internal . . . "emptiness." We call that emptiness depression.

Depression can manifest itself in many ways. It can be *retarded,* which means the patient experiences withdrawal, fatigue, tears, and difficulty thinking and talking (getting the words out). *Agitated* depression means pacing back and forth, hand-wringing, relentless crying, and feeling unworthy. Depression can have no obvious cause, a cause that is out of proportion to the degree of depression, or a very good cause. It is not, however, to be mistaken for grief. The length of time it persists, its severity, and to what extent it interferes with a person's ability to function determine whether she can treat it herself or should be treated with drugs and/or therapy. Of course, there are different degrees of coping. Some women dissolve under relatively little stress; others manage to live with it; and a few actually seem to enjoy it, because at least it's *some* kind of feeling.

Thirty percent of the population will have at least one episode of true depression in their lifetime, and 77 percent of those will be female. In fact, women have higher rates of depression than men, no matter where they live—country or city, United States or abroad—or how old they are. And the incidence of depression increases with age.

Why? Psychoanalytic theories make sex role the culprit. Women are supposed to think to themselves that "the female role is lousy." Then they're supposed to get really angry because they'll never achieve their goals in life. Then they think—and this is mostly unconscious, you understand—*"I'm a lady,* and ladies can't express anger, so I'll just have to *repress* it." And anger repressed becomes depression.

There's more. Women are dependent on others for self-esteem, say the analysts. It's their nature. When nobody's there to build them up after they've lost a lover, a spouse, or a job, they become depressed. In other words, they no longer have an identity.

Finally, the analysts believe that loss of power also makes women feel helpless, and this leads to depression. They are helpless because they have no power to manipulate life, to change the environment, or to produce predictable results from their actions.

Now there's some truth in all of that, particularly in mild depression. Depressive episodes, it is true, are less frequent in single women and in women who are happy with their careers. A repressive home life or a specific crisis endured alone can cause a kind of "situational" depression. But there has to be more to it than that.

True depression, as I see it, is a prolonged response to physical, social, and biological stress, resulting in the inability to function. Physical stress means disease, social stress means environment, and biological stress means hormones. The hormone theory is particularly important in females because severe depression tends to occur in association with events in the reproductive cycle: the menstrual cycle, the use of contraceptive drugs, the period after a pregnancy, and menopause. All these times are marked by estrogen-progesterone imbalances.

Females even tend to have distinct patterns in the way they express their depression. They eat more instead of losing their appetite (which is the classic symptom); they sleep more instead of hardly at all; they're hostile instead of repressed (which is the psychological model); and, though they tend to shun crowds, they seek support from close friends (unlike their male counterparts).

Depression is not always pure, either. It is often accompanied by anxiety, and sometimes it is difficult to decide which is the predominant symptom. I have a friend who takes an anti-anxiety drug that is making her more depressed. The doctor is treating the wrong disease. Certain classes of anti-anxiety drugs are notorious for making depression worse—as does alcohol.

People use the word *depression* all the time to denote "the blues." But true, clinical depression is quite different and far more serious. What are the symptoms? The depressed person is unhappy, discouraged, pessimistic, wiped out, bored, guilty, disgusted, clumsy, tearful, suicidal, irritable, disinterested, indecisive, unmotivated, sleepless, sexless, helpless, and hopeless. All of the above. *But,* it's a matter of degree. Everyone experiences some of these symptoms sometime. Normal mood swings are *not* clinical depression. Perhaps by putting the word *extreme* or *chronic* in front of those depressive symptoms, we might come out with a better understanding of the real thing.

You can be depressed without having the disease. I used to get depressed on Sundays. This is quite common when you're away from the extended family—and Sunday is a "family" day. I used to crawl under the covers and refuse to talk to anyone. By Monday I was fine. If my behavior had persisted for several weeks, though, if I had refused or been unable to get out of bed, and if I had persistently refused to do anything or to talk to anybody, I would have had a full-blown depression. Everybody gets a touch of "the blues," but if you can reverse it in a few hours or crack a fleeting smile, you don't have the disease.

Mild depression can be alleviated by doing something for yourself. You have some control over it. At the risk of sounding like an advice columnist here are a few suggestions:

Your psyche. Assert yourself with your husband, your mother, or your children. You might have been put on earth to reproduce, but by this time you have either fulfilled that biological function or you haven't—so stop the overkill. Learn to enjoy yourself. Movies are good, libraries are national, and adult education is accessible in many communities. Say what you feel, and don't let anyone tell you you're too fat, too thin, too quiet, too noisy, too vain, or too caring.

Your appearance. Look the way you want to look. Reassess your appearance. A physical change can always make you feel better; highlight a nice feature you've forgotten about. For some women, changing the way they look can make them feel more confident and energetic and can give them that extra push they need to make a new start. I see so many women with big behinds and beautiful ankles who wear pants. So camouflage your behind if it bothers you, and show your ankles. Or whatever—as long as it's appropriate to what you want to accomplish.

Your time. Too many women stagnate at home. They stop learning and growing. One of the healthiest things a mature woman can do is to go to work (if she's not already working). I've talked to hundreds of women who started new occupations at this time, and most have been delighted with the choice. The job does not have to be glamorous. Many women work part-time in health-care facilities, like convalescent homes, where they get a great deal of satisfaction helping someone outside their families.

I think the mid-life woman should work for money if at all possible. There's nothing like earning some cash to boost your self-esteem. To think that someone would pay you for doing something! Being paid gives you the feeling you're appreciated, and that you belong. Volunteers often mill around, with no specific job assignments, which can be frustrating.

When you plan to go back to work, try to choose an area that really interests you, and don't be afraid to be the lowest on the totem pole if you have no skills. Remember, it will be a learning experience, and you will be amazed at how fast you can pick things up. I know a woman who answered an ad to do some minor bookkeeping, and the company she worked for expanded. She is now an executive. Another I know started demonstrating microwave ovens and developed an expertise in the area when the field was new. She is now in great demand.

Some mid-life women don't want to be tied down to a job; they'd rather be available to travel with their husbands, or to cook for droves of relatives during a summer down at the beach. If that kind of life really excites you, there's no need to get a job. Volunteer work is fine, too; try a political campaign, an activist group, or a local symphony or repertory theater. Find a cause that really stirs you.

Many realistic causes of depression will not go away, no matter what you do. Both financial problems and chronic illness have a way of pulling you down with them. But if you succumb to them, you'll only make things worse and become just another casualty of the situation.

Of course, these are only little self-help hints, not heavy stuff at all. And very often what appears to be a mild depression does not respond to this Band-Aid treatment.

Depression without apparent cause is probably related to a genetic defect and is triggered by a malfunction in brain chemistry—and in females, by changing levels of estrogen, progesterone, or other hormones. Mid-life females are among the most depressed segments of society, in part because they are losing their lubricating estrogen. The wheels aren't clicking so smoothly, the brain isn't thinking so clearly, and women don't have their previous resiliency at a time in life when it's necessary to cope more and better. Most important, they have not yet learned to cope with that loss of resiliency itself—they haven't found a new design for living.

One of my patients recently said, "I can't tell you how I feel, so I wrote it in a letter." Her letter was a model of depressive thinking, a kind of free-verse rumination on the nothingness of it all:

Sick for 3 weeks.
Left me feeling
disoriented.
not wanting to get out
to the job
or to sing
Want to give them both up
especially job
afraid I'll be sorry if I give up
Am I going mental?
I know I need help—like I said,
what is it?
Is my mind going?

She was in her post-reproductive phase and was acutely depressed, and her periods had dribbled off to one every four months or so. It sounded like estrogen replacement was the answer. I gave her a tiny dose and sent her home. Two days later she called me back, ecstatic. Her mood had improved startlingly. She was enjoying her work as a salesclerk and was singing as a soloist with the church choir. Now she's only worried about her slightly cystic breasts and the effect the estrogen might have on them. But she has regular breast examinations and is functioning beautifully.

Estrogen deficiency isn't the only hormonal cause of depression. Take the case of Elaine, a normally cheerful, forty-three-year-old woman. She managed to give up smoking, but a strange thing happened to her personality—she became irritable, angry, tearful. "I feel like I've been run over by a truck," she said.

Why was Elaine depressed? Was she upset because she'd lost her nicotine pacifier, or because she thought she would gain weight. Not so easy. She had given up smoking before and had never felt like this.

I studied Elaine carefully and found one difference between this and her previous attempts to quit smoking. She was now at the age when she felt warm all the time, a symptom that is often a forerunner of the hot flash. She was obviously in a state of hormone flux. Because she was still having regular periods, estrogen didn't seem to be the answer. Thyroid hormone, however, diminishes with age and also, if you have been a heavy smoker, when you stop smoking. So I gave her a small dose of thyroid, and it worked. The heaviness lifted.

Let's look at the variety of options in the treatment of severe depression, to see where medicine has come from and where it's going.

The Old Treatment

I have a vivid screen memory—that's a strong memory you have of a specific event during a period in your life about which you don't remember much else. It's about electroshock therapy. My dad was a psychiatrist in the state hospital system (called "snake pits" in popular magazines), and I would occasionally be allowed, as a "state hospital brat," to make rounds with Daddy. Certain days were designated for shock treatment, and I remember the frightened, bewildered patients being led into the treatment room and placed on a flat table with a sheet over it. They were pale, with institutional haircuts and clothing that looked like gunny sacks. Four or five attendants would hold them down. A gray, grainy paste was applied to the sides of their foreheads, electrodes were attached to each temple, and a bolt of electricity coursed through their brains. I saw their convulsions, watched them bite off their tongue depressors (used to protect the insides of their mouths), writhe, then go limp, to wake up dazed and shaken, be handed a glass of orange juice, and be led away. I don't know what I was really thinking as I watched, stolid and wide-eyed, but it gave me nightmares.

I guess when there's nothing to do, something is better than nothing. I can remember my dad's frustration and despair when his only tools for curing psychotic patients were phenobarbital, chloral hydrate, and formaldehyde, while the state hospital was filled with thousands of untreatable and untreated people. Electroshock at least promised a way to get through that maze of abnormal thinking—as if the electrical current would create a vacuum, like a bolt of lightning, and normal thoughts would spill in like thunder.

Shock (as it was affectionately called) persisted for a long time for the treatment of severe depression, even after phenothiazines were discovered. Believe it or not, it had a remarkable success rate for such a barbaric method. But I can't help thinking about how many brain cells were destroyed in those days. But what did it matter? The victims were mostly post-menopausal women anyway. And it was important that they return to their homes to keep house and cook the meals—and you don't need many brain cells for that, right?

Electroshock is still used in certain types of depression and psychotic diseases that will not yield to chemistry.

Current Therapy

Drugs

Biochemistry has come to the rescue of the severely depressed patient. Now there are drugs that can change the levels of brain chemicals. These drugs are called, logically enough, antidepressants. The most common antidepressants are the tricyclics, the MAO inhibitors, and lithium.

The tricyclics (named for their three-ringed chemical configuration) are currently the most popular drugs for treating severe depression. They are quite specific for this illness—normal people who take them become anxious. Unfortunately, these are not innocuous drugs, and they have some disturbing effects on the cardiovascular system, producing a rapid pulse rate and irregular heartbeats. One side effect is weight gain. They also tend to quash your sexual feelings (which is not important, I'm told, in females) and to exaggerate the effects of alcohol and other sedatives. So they can be deadly if mixed.

The MAO (monoamine oxidase) inhibitors are another class of antidepressants that are very effective in treating depression. They are troublesome pills, however, because they clash with many other drugs and foods that contain tyramines (cheese, avocados, wine, or anything cured or aged) and caffeine. Fatalities have been reported when these combinations have inadvertently taken place. How do the MAO inhibitors work? They inhibit monoamine oxidase, which is a chemical in women's brains that increases with age and is an important factor in depression. But MAO inhibitors must be used with extreme care.

Lithium is a salt that is useful in treating a major psychotic depressive illness which is bipolar (meaning it has both a manic and a depressive side). It is not used to treat neurotic depression, the kind I'm primarily discussing in this section.

On a milder note, tryptophan, the essential amino acid used to control binge eating, might prove to be even more valuable as a nontoxic, safe way to deal with mild depression. It is now used in England for this purpose, but is not officially recognized as an antidepressant in the United States (see Chapter 19).

Psychotherapy

Why such radical treatments? you ask. What about psychiatry? Well, I heard one psychiatrist say that talking to a depressed person is only a little better than doing nothing, and my own experience in the field bears this out. You can talk and talk, but however promising an occasional session may be, in the long run it will usually be to no avail. In most cases, delving into the past (the long-term—and I mean *long*—approach used in psychotherapy) just doesn't seem to be the most efficient way of treating the *present* problem. However, the new cognitive therapies, advanced by Aaron Beck and David Burns, might prove to be more successful, in association, perhaps, with a little chemical push.

Cognitive therapy is a therapy in which the patient takes an active part in looking at his or her own distorted thought patterns and in analyzing the distortions. Unlike psychotherapy, it is *brief, present-oriented,* and *practical.* You write down irrational thought processes as they come to you. This allows you to analyze your faulty thinking patterns. It's much easier to see how silly they are when they're "exposed" on paper. For example, one of my depressed patients said, "I don't deserve to eat." (I wish a few more of my heavy patients would say that.) With a little probing, it emerged that she felt she should be punished because she didn't like housework. So I had her follow that line of reasoning to its logical conclusion: anyone who doesn't like housework doesn't deserve to eat; therefore, three million American women don't deserve to eat. But 2,999,999 do eat—only my patient felt she should be punished. The depressed person has an incredible percentage of thought patterns that resemble this one, and having her record and answer to them has proved to be as useful a tool in treating this illness as saying, over the course of a year, "Let's talk about the root of those feelings. . . ."

Exercise

Exercise is now being touted as a possible treatment for depression. Breakdown products of muscle and fat can cause changes in brain chemistry. This would be a much more successful treatment for men, who are physically suited for strenuous aerobic exercise like jogging because of more efficient muscular construction. In jogging, the mid-life woman tends to run the risk of prolapsing her uterus, or putting undue strain on her mechanically imperfect knees, and any lesser exercise wouldn't change the metabolism enough to diminish the symptoms. Brisk walking can be pleasant and distracting, but it is difficult to entice a depressed person to do it.

Chapter 13

A Chemical Carousel: Pills and Alcohol

In the natural history of any drug, there is always a "medication overkill." When it's first introduced, there is intense excitement about its potential. The initial results look miraculous, and every doctor wants to prescribe it. Then, several years later, long-term problems begin to appear, including drug reliance, abuse, and permanent and transient physical side effects. Then the scare begins. Instead of pausing to reevaluate the strengths of the medication, physicians refuse to prescribe it. The press condemns it. The fair-haired child becomes the black sheep, if you'll pardon the mix of metaphors.

This is particularly true when the drug is used to treat "subjective" states such as appetite, insomnia, anxiety, fatigue, or depression. Most of these states, interestingly enough, are suffered by women; and, therefore, most of the drug overkills and sudden withdrawals have been associated with women. In the past twenty years I have watched the evolution of thyroid pills, sleeping pills, diet pills, tranquilizers, antidepressants, and estrogen. All have the same pattern of introduction, abuse, panic, and underuse.

Women are big drug consumers. This is not to imply that they consume too many or take them unnecessarily. Sometimes they do, but more often they take them to be more comfortable and to function better when the alternative is pain and incapacitation.

Let's go over some of the most popular drugs and the reasons women trust them.

Calming Down: Tranquilizers and Anti-Anxiety Drugs

The drug that has received the most criticism in the past few years is the little pill named diazepam, more commonly known as Valium. It is just one of a whole group of minor tranquilizers. Valium is at its best in treating female anxiety disorders, the essential feature of which is a persistent irrational fear of a specific object, activity, or situation and a compelling desire to avoid it. The individual recognizes the fear as excessive or unreasonable in proportion to the actual danger, but that doesn't matter. People can't often talk themselves out of a phobia.

Doris, forty-eight years old, was married to an affluent man, had three children, and seemed to function well. She was gregarious and well liked, and her family was supportive and loving. But Doris suffered severe anxiety attacks. She thought she was going to drop dead, and she didn't want to drop dead where there was no help. Her internist assured her that she was in perfect health, but she didn't believe him. She had been through analysis and her psychiatrist had told her that her symptoms were rage reactions against her mother which she was turning on herself. She listened and understood, but she didn't get any better.

Doris functioned very well when her husband or her friends were with her, or even alone in her large condominium complex. But when she was away from familiar surroundings and alone, she panicked. She started going to a phobia clinic at a neighboring hospital and was placed on a tranquilizer—diazepam. The clinic made her travel increasing distances alone, where at her given destination she would find a social worker or a friend waiting. This was to reassure her that she would have help if she needed it. They gradually increased the distances involved until one day she drove twenty miles alone. All went well. They they took away the diazepam and asked her to repeat the test. What happened? I wish I could say she was forever free of her anxiety, but without her tranquilizer she couldn't drive a mile by herself.

If you were her doctor, what would you do? Worry that she might become addicted? Send her for a thousand more hours of psychoanalysis? Or be happy that, despite an unreasonable but intense fear, she could function successfully in all aspects of her life? Doris didn't want to take the drug. But she needed it, and until she could solve the problem through other means, it helped her to live a normal life.

Diazepam is useful in treating anxiety with mild agitation—but *not* depression. It comes from a class of drugs that was synthesized as early as 1930. Its taming effect on animals led to its use in humans. It is also quite effective as a muscle relaxant. Researchers report that this group of drugs has a remarkable margin of safety, and that before any withdrawal symptoms occur, the drug has to be given in enormous doses for long periods of time and then abruptly withdrawn.

In spite of this, the minor tranquilizers have been targeted by the "moral majority" of the medical population as bad, overprescribed, and addictive, and the trend has been from overkill to abstinence. Who suffers the most at *both* ends of the spectrum? Women, of course, because they are the principal users.

Many of the problems connected to these tranquilizers arise because the drug is misunderstood and carelessly prescribed. It has little or no effect on psychotic states, and increasing the dose to make it effective only causes mental confusion. The drug can also exacerbate depression in already depressed people, increasing their hostility and irritability. And in people who dislike drugs because they feel "out of control" while under the influence, the drug can create more problems than it eliminates.

But for women who must combat many forms of stress in a time of great physiological change, these drugs have often made the difference between successfully functioning and barely functioning at all—or turning to alcohol. Women faced with marriage disruption, job pressures, problems with teen-age and adult children, or the task of caring for aging and dying parents often feel a constant sense of impending doom. Frequently they wake up in the middle of the night with their hearts pounding rapidly, afraid, but with no specific fear. (This is called "free-floating anxiety.") The last thing a woman like this wants to do is to take a pill. She wants to be strong. It's possible to be strong most of the time, but not all of the time; and in a crisis, it's okay to accept some help. When the crisis, or multiple crises, is over, most women happily relinquish their medications. That 1 percent who might be called abusers does not justify denying such high-comfort, low-danger medication to the majority.

Simple anxiety attacks without cause can progress to panic attacks and then to phobias—and then to avoidance of places or situations that give rise to these panic attacks. Avoidance often leads to depression and isolation, symptoms that have always been traced to psychological origins. But many physicians now firmly believe that anxiety, panic, and phobia are biologically induced and must he biologically treated. New research suggests that a lack of certain peptide chains—compounds that yield two or more amino acids and form the basis for proteins—in the brain may cause it to overrespond to fear. Eventually, this fear response can even be triggered *without direct provocation*. Because certain individuals, particularly females and homosexual males, have low panic thresholds, there is a good chance that these reactions are linked to sex hormones.

A new drug, alprazolam, holds promise for the treatment of panic attacks. No longer will it take years of analysis to deal with the panic while the victim withdraws from society. Don't get me wrong—I have nothing against analysis. It's fun and a nice luxury, but the last well-documented success in curing symptoms was probably Freud's "Dora." The true value of analysis—if you can afford the time and money—is in learning to recognize the defense mechanisms you use every day and the role they play in your behavior. Once you understand them, you can try to change them by adopting more mature mechanisms if the ones you use are interfering with successful adaption.

There is now something different to treat anxiety which has nothing to do with its psychological component. It is known as a "beta blocker," and it causes a dramatic change in the cardiovascular response to fear.

It might be useful here to discuss the whole concept behind the "blocking drugs." Our bodies function as a series of chemical actions and reactions. These are initiated by hormones or enzymes that are constantly being released. Lately, medical thinking has been not to stop the initiation of a biochemical process, which is often impossible, but to block one of the receptors that will carry the process to its logical conclusion—very much as in football when somebody tackles the receiver instead of the passer. The new group of "blocking drugs" does just that. Unable to stop panic or oversecretion of certain hormones, they block the hormones' main receptors on the nerve endings or cell walls. (These are often designated as either alpha or beta receptors, depending on their chemical configuration.) The problem with blocking agents is that most are not specific. For example, if you take a pill to block the receptor that causes your heart to beat faster, it may also block the receptors in your skeletal muscles, so it could be harder to lift your legs and arms.

Propranolol is an adrenergic, beta-receptor-blocking drug that is commonly used to treat high blood pressure, rapid or irregular heartbeat—caused by physical as well as psychological factors—and angina or coronary insufficiency. It blocks the stimulating effect (sympathetic or adrenergic) of the central nervous system on certain target organs, such as the heart or blood vessels. It could prove to be the ideal pill for stage fright (because it doesn't make you drowsy, like diazepam), fear of flying, and agoraphobia (fear of crowds) because the heart won't respond to the fear reflex. How can you be scared when the physical scare response is gone? Your heart's not pounding, your palms aren't clammy, your mouth doesn't taste like ashes, and you're not hyperventilating (breathing too rapidly).

This mode of treatment makes the psychiatrists unhappy because they'd rather do a long and costly analysis to discover *why* you're anxious, a question that's often left unanswered or, if answered, is difficult to verify. ("When I was three months of age, my father dropped me on my head; that's why I keep expecting to fall on my face." Or "I'm afraid of flying because that plane looks like a giant penis and reminds me of the time my uncle took down his pants in front of me.") The shrinks argue that you can't control anxiety by controlling heartbeat.

Propranolol has a few disturbing side effects. One of them is weight gain caused by increased fluid retention, and there is a possibility that it blocks the breakdown of fat. Therefore, if the anxiety-provoking situation is short-term or related to a specific event—such as having to give a speech before fifty people—propranolol would not cause any problems. If the situation is chronic, beta blockers might be a better choice, only for anxious *thin* people; and diazepam, which doesn't seem to have any effect on weight, might be better for anxious *heavy* people.

The other disquieting fact about propranolol is that it blocks receptor sites that you don't want blocked. One of these is the skeletal muscle. You can feel wiped out, especially in warm weather, and your legs don't want to move. It also causes spasms of bronchi in the lungs, so asthmatics can't use it. But even nonasthmatics sometimes feel a heaviness in their chests after taking it.

One of my patients who used a beta blocker for blood pressure told me she thought the drug was "unnatural." Last winter she skidded on an icy road and her car hit an embankment. "It was weird," she said. "Here I was in this terrifying situation, and my heart was beating slowly and regularly. I thought, 'This is madness, not being scared out of my wits.' And then I had another thought. If I hadn't been on propranolol, I would probably have died of a heart attack."

Drying Out: Diuretics

Another group of drugs that is high on the list for abuse potential is diuretics. This is interesting because they do not primarily treat mood or pain. They merely increase the rate of urine formation and remove excess fluid. But, as we shall see, excess fluid and mood are often related.

Edema (swelling) or fluid retention is caused by two mechanisms: the circulation signaling the kidneys to retain salt; or renal edema, when a disease of the kidneys prevents them from excreting salt. The use of diuretics to treat these symptoms is therefore logical and necessary.

But what about the more casual use of diuretics to relieve the mysterious "I feel bloated" syndrome so common in women of all ages? And what causes this syndrome, anyway? The mechanics of this kind of fluid retention are unclear. The most likely explanation is that when certain hormones make the capillaries flimsier, the fluid part of the blood (plasma) leaks out and collects in the tissues. Leaky capillaries cause some discomfort, but usually less than many women would have you believe.

Often women simply use diuretics for cosmetic purposes, to make themselves look less puffy. They have learned how to pry them out of their doctors, becoming very persuasive when describing the agony of tight rings, tight shoes, bloatedness, sore breasts, and depression. Physicians shouldn't be manipulated into dispensing diuretics so freely. Often I see patients with prescriptions that may be refilled indefinitely, sometimes for years. When I ask them how often they use a diuretic, they reply, "When I need it." When I ask them when they need it, they say, "When I'm bloated." When I ask when they're bloated, they tend to get angry. Diuretics are now routinely prescribed in general medicine for "bloating," premenstrual tension, swelling in the legs, and high blood pressure.

Women who have been taking diuretics for a long time resent giving them up, and I have had many struggles when I've tried to discontinue diuretic therapy. This is one pill that females enjoy taking; it's nice not to worry about feeling and looking bloated. But where weight loss is concerned, women often have unreasonable expectations. A diuretic won't help you lose weight if you're not following a diet. Diuretics can even be destructive to a diet, because many women will rely on them to lose a few pounds, and won't bother changing their eating habits. A diuretic won't counteract *all* the fluid retention that you get before your period or from taking estrogen. A diuretic will not make you urinate a great deal every day; it will only make you eliminate accessible extra water. There will be a certain amount of rebound water pickup after you stop taking diuretics. The stronger the diuretic, the stronger and more severe the rebound. Diuretics should not be discontinued quickly. Women should be weaned off them slowly so that they don't get the rebound.

Hazards? Allergic reactions are common. Diuretics can deplete body potassium, sodium, and, occasionally, magnesium, causing weakness, light-headedness, and muscle cramps. *Existing* kidney problems may be aggravated, in rare cases producing kidney stones, and sometimes diuretics aggravate latent diabetes as well. But unless there is an underlying metabolic problem, kidneys are normally not affected.

Two stories illustrate the unpredictable benefits and hazards of diuretic therapy. Beverly, aged forty and weighing 160 pounds, wanted to lose weight. Her physician gave her a 1,200-calorie diet, an appetite suppressant, and a diuretic. Her physical examination suggested she was normal. She had always been chubby, but her weight had increased rapidly during her last pregnancy (at age thirty-seven).

She stayed on the prescribed diet and lost twenty pounds; however, she began to notice large blisters on her legs. She also had severe stomachaches after taking the diuretic. When she mentioned both symptoms to her doctor, he told her they had nothing to do with the drugs and that she probably wasn't eating right. He said the blisters were probably burns from her smoking. It didn't sound too logical, but Beverly was a heavy smoker and occasionally would drop ashes on her clothes, so she accepted his explanation. But the blisters became worse and did not seem related to her smoking.

When she complained to her doctor again, he told her she was making a mountain out of a molehill. In desperation she went to a dermatologist, who biopsied her blisters and told her she had a skin disease caused by a drug allergy. Diuretics, he said, could be the cause. So she stopped using them and the blisters cleared up. Her family physician, however, still refused to admit that the diuretics had played any part in the skin eruptions. The skin disease in question, he said, often comes and goes for no apparent reason.

Diane had just passed her forty-second birthday, and her periods were still regular. However, she began to notice that before her periods she was getting more irritable and swollen. She couldn't fit into her shoes or wear her rings. She would cry after the mildest disagreement. Her husband and teenage children agreed that she was becoming impossible to live with.

She heard that these symptoms could be relieved by a diuretic and finally went to her gynecologist to request one. The gynecologist glanced at her chart and pointed out that she'd never had premenstrual tension before, and that there was no reason to believe she had it now. He said flatly that he didn't believe in diuretics and refused to prescribe any. Her mood continued to be erratic for two weeks before her period, finally compelling her to seek psychiatric help. One year later she was still in therapy, but with no improvement. Her marriage was on the rocks. She went again to her gynecologist and begged for relief. He repeated his disapproval of diuretics, but suggested a hysterectomy, since she was no longer of child-bearing age. In desperation she went to an internist. He prescribed a diuretic, and the results were astounding. On a later visit she brought her husband along. "You gave me back my wife," he told the internist.

Beverly and Diane represent two sides of the coin. Beverly was a relatively healthy, uncomplicated dieter who didn't need a diuretic on a regular basis. Her diet progressed well with just an anorectic, or appetite-suppressant, drug. Her physician's refusal to change the drug was an outrage: if a patient has an allergic reaction while on a medication, it's logical to assume the pill's the source until proved otherwise. And, frequently, diuretics evoke allergic rashes.

Diane, on the other hand, really needed a diuretic, and that's *all* she needed. Because of uneven hormone bursts around the beginning of her post-reproductive life, she was retaining more fluid than ever before. The problem was simply remedied with a diuretic a week before her period. Female fluid retention is intimately tied up with the estrogen-progesterone balance and is more severe beginning two weeks before the period. Although some physicians believe in decreasing salt intake, this is ineffective if the symptoms are too severe. Vitamin B_6, about 200 milligrams daily the week before the period, often works, but no one is sure why.

What about diuretics in dieting? They are beneficial, but not *necessary*. Women can diet without them, but the diet will often be longer and more frustrating.

Diuretics should be used cautiously, but responsible use of them in dieting can mean the difference between success and failure. I make this statement carefully because I do believe there is a very real connection between fat loss and fluid retention in the female. The more waterlogged a woman gets, the less fat she seems able to burn. During periods of great water retention, her whole fat-burning system slows down and may virtually stop.

A diuretic can be helpful in a weight-loss program:

1. In women who use birth-control pills or hormones. Dieting while on the pill can often be a seesaw affair, even if the diet stays the same. Diuretics counteract some of the fluid-retaining properties of the pill.

2. After a "big" weekend. Many people eat or drink more than usual on weekends. This can cause the scale to jump five pounds, even though the total calories consumed don't justify that kind of gain. It is obviously related to fluid retention. The judicious use of a diuretic can separate the fat from the fluid. This does not, however, constitute a blanket approval of taking a diuretic every time you overeat.

3. The week before a period. This can be a lost week in a diet, as your weight creeps up relentlessly. At this time a diuretic is not only psychologically but also physically useful.

It is easiest now to gain back weight you have already lost. In a waterlogged state, the thirsty, newly depleted fat cells can fill very quickly.

4. When a chronic dieter begins yet another diet. Often it seems as if her fat cells have become more resistant than ever to breaking down. New research shows that fat-burning enzymes in the body act more effectively when a dieter is in a dry, or dehydrated, state.

5. In the hypertensive overweight. About 50 percent of overweight patients have hypertension, or high blood pressure, which subsides when they lose twenty to thirty pounds. Diuretics can be useful in keeping their blood pressure down to normal levels until they lose the necessary weight. Hypertensives seem to be inherent fluid retainers.

My thinking about diuretics has changed since I started my weight-control practice. In the beginning I was much more heavy-handed with them, enjoying, with my patients, their dry, low weights when they came into the office. I'd never hear cries of "But it's before my period," or "I'm retaining fluid," or "I'm all swollen" when a diuretic was given on a regular basis. However, I began to find out that they made women feel wiped out, particularly during the summer. I began cutting back in the winter, too. Now, even if a patient is taking birth-control pills, I prescribe diuretics only two or three days before a period, and then only one or two pills.

Speeding Up: Thyroid

Females tend to take a lot of thyroid pills. But hypothyroidism, or having too little thyroid, is not a common disease. That statement appears to be a contradiction, but it is true.

The thyroid gland sits at the base of the neck and secretes two forms of thyroid hormone, called T3 and T4. Although T3 appears to be the most active in metabolism, endocrinologists (gland doctors) generally prescribe both T3 and T4 when treating a true thyroid deficiency.

Sometimes the thyroid gland does not put out enough hormone because it's been infected or damaged, so thyroid replacement is straightforward and logical. More often, thyroid is used to shrink an enlarged thyroid gland (called a goiter), an enlarged section of the gland (a "hot spot"), or a growth on the gland (an adenoma). Enlargements occur when low thyroid levels in the blood cause the pituitary gland to pressure the thyroid gland for more. When the thyroid gland can't manufacture any more, it swells. Thyroid pills will satisfy the pituitary, which will ease up on the thyroid gland and allow it to shrink. And everybody's happy.

Most women on thyroid, however, do not have true hypothyroidism (underactive thyroid), goiters, or adenomas. The story of most thyroid therapy involves a woman walking into a doctor's office with one or more of the following complaints: fatigue, sensitivity to cold, puffiness around the face and in the hands and ankles, dry skin, brittle and thinning hair, easy weight gain, and difficulty thinking. All of these *can* be the symptoms of hypothyroidism—as well as of dozens of other diseases, as well as of normal aging. The physical exam and blood analyses are usually normal, except for the thyroid test which is "low-normal." Low-normal is currently medicine's biggest dump bin. Obviously there must be both a low and a high side to the "normal" spectrum. But the patient's symptoms persist, the physician is harried . . . so he gives her thyroid medication, and she usually feels better, or one of the symptoms relents. Is low-normal a legitimate diagnosis, or is the drug a placebo?

This thyroid medication is usually continued for *years*, or until some well-meaning, new, enthusiastic internist tries to discontinue it. Then the woman becomes outraged and panic-stricken. "But I've been on thyroid for years," she pleads.

"Well, let's just discontinue it for three weeks, and then you can take a blood test," the doctor says.

"I can't! I'll die if I go off it for three weeks. I'll fall asleep in the middle of the afternoon! I'll be too exhausted to play tennis!"

And so the battle of the wills rages, and if the patient wins, she will go on taking thyroid ad infinitum—even along with her cardiac medication, if it comes to that. If the enthusiastic young doctor wins, she will be taken off thyroid because her blood thyroid test is normal. And she will revert to her former fatigue.

The use of thyroid to treat a symptom and not a true deficiency is perfectly justified, I think, if the patient feels better with it. As women age, their basal metabolism rate falls, even if it's not reflected in the blood levels. As long as thyroid is not causing a fast pulse, palpitations, nervousness, or anxiety (and it often does), I think it's worth a try in chronic fatigue with no obvious organic or disease origins.

However, T3 does have its drawbacks in treating the mid-life woman whose cardiovascular system might not always be stable. Even in small doses, it is capable of causing palpitations (skipped heartbeats) and a rapid pulse rate. Generally, there are no side effects around the 5-microgram level. In the older patient, however, it is very difficult to increase the dose of T3 significantly. A female in her forties can tolerate about 50 micrograms, when there is no heart disease or hypertension. When she is in her fifties, a woman can tolerate up to 25 micrograms, and a woman in her sixties cannot go much higher than 10 micrograms. I have used it at these lower levels with excellent results.

In small doses, T3 can have a remarkable effect on mature females. Many of them claim they aren't so sleepy all the time and that they think much more clearly. One woman said her life was totally changed by the use of T3. She said she had been forgetting names and numbers and was afraid she was losing her mind. After taking the medication, things seemed so much clearer. She was also able to lose weight more easily. There have been some misdiagnosed cases of depression where the symptoms were actually caused by thyroid deficiency. Six percent of geriatric patients admitted to nursing homes for senile dementia have been found to be hypothyroid, or have *under*active thyroid function, and remarkable recoveries have been made merely by correcting this deficiency.

Finally, we come to the use of thyroid in the dieting female. And what a controversy that touches off! If thyroid tests are normal, yet the patient has some or all of the symptoms of hypothyroidism, plus difficulty losing weight, do we or don't we treat? The purists say *never*. The patients say *please*.

My obese patients seem to feel that thyroid is a very important factor in the breakdown of fat. They also realize that they don't break down fat very efficiently, so they assume they must have a thyroid deficiency or an underactive thyroid. Actually, most of them have absolutely normal thyroid function—at least according to conventional tests—and the few hypothyroids that I do see are usually only slightly overweight.

But T3 can be effective in weight control despite this, even in the person with normal thyroid function. I have many documented cases of patients on low-calorie diets (600 calories a day) who lost weight very slowly (a quarter- or a half-pound a week) until I gave them small amounts of T3. Then they began to lose weight normally (two pounds a week). Some physicians argue that increased weight loss with thyroid is from increased loss of water and body protein. But maybe the original thyroid tests are misleading. Maybe we aren't measuring the right *type* of thyroid.

During a thyroid conference in Boston, several physicians told me that the present blood tests of T3 and T4 did not always give a true thyroid picture and that a test of thyroid-stimulating hormone (TSH) should be administered. Since then, I have done a TSH on many of my slow-losing patients and have frequently found it elevated (meaning hypothyroidism).

I use thyroid to treat overweight patients *only* when combined with diet, in cases of (1) true thyroid deficiency; (2) resistant obesity, which I define as women whose calorie counts have gone below 600 and who are *still* losing only one-quarter to one-half pound per week; (3) recent surgery (women lose weight very slowly for up to a year after a major operation); and (4) women who are in the process of giving up cigarettes. (Nicotine raises the metabolic rate and is an appetite suppressant, so when you stop smoking, you eat more and burn less.)

I prescribe very small doses of T3—5 to 25 micrograms—for weight loss. I have found these tiny amounts to be very helpful. This is especially true when a patient stops losing weight on the same diet that once produced weight loss. We now know that the T3 levels decrease in the dieter to protect body fat, and by bolstering these levels, we can stimulate more rapid weight loss.

I have watched the thyroid picture in diet evolve from the old basal metabolism test, which resulted in almost *everybody's* being put on replacement thyroid, to thyroid blood tests, which rule out the use of thyroid for almost everybody. I fail to find thyroid as dangerous a drug as many would have us believe. Of the hundreds of women who've come into my office already on thyroid, I have yet to see a serious complication when the drug has been used in proper doses under the care of a responsible physician.

Easing Pain: The Old Antispasmodics and the New Treatment of Ulcers

The antispasmodics used to be the major drugs for treating gastrointestinal disturbances, such as stomachaches, ulcers, and diarrhea. They are derived from belladonna, one of the "nightshade plants" that got its name ("beautiful lady" in Italian) from women who took it to dilate their pupils and give them a pale, wan look. They inhibit the parasympathetic nervous system, which controls movement in the gut. But they're not very selective, affecting areas other than the intestinal tract. So you can't treat a stomachache without annoying side effects, such as dryness of the mouth, visual disorientation, increased sensitivity to light, and difficulty urinating.

The antispasmodics have been discredited lately. Detractors say they're effective only if you drool too much. But I have found them useful in treating abdominal pain that is the result of viruses, food allergies, or fat intolerance, which are the most common causes of the old-fashioned stomachache. They are mildly effective in treating diarrhea, but they don't do much for irritable bowel syndrome or biliary colic, and their use in treating ulcers is now being questioned. Tincture of belladonna, the original and oldest antispasmodic, is still the most effective, though the least used.

The degree of relief from antispasmodics is worth the side effects, though these are many and unpleasant. Some drug companies add phenobarbital, which increases sleepiness even further and can be more unpleasant than the side effects of the original drug.

But there is good news for those poor souls with ulcer disease—and there are many—who are now being treated by diet, antispasmodics, and antacids, and who are suffering all the side effects of their medication. A better and more specific method of treating gastrointestinal diseases has been discovered. It is a histamine-receptor-blocking agent called cimetidine, and it has revolutionized ulcer treatment. Cimetidine reduces the secretion of gastric acid and inhibits gastric movement.

Ulcer disease is an erosion of the mucous membrane (lining) of the stomach or intestine that penetrates the muscle, exposing sensitive areas to acid pepsin secretion, which causes pain, heartburn, bloating, acid belching, nausea, and even vomiting. The pain may be described as a steady, deep ache, confined to the midsection. Before cimetidine, the best treatment for ulcers was antacids, and they do provide some relief if taken frequently and in large enough doses. However, the dose has to be a minimum of two tablespoons to neutralize the acid already secreted, one and three hours after meals and at bedtime. So we are talking about seven doses of unpalatable, chalky, diarrhea- or constipation-producing antacids a day. The liquid antacids, by the way, are far more potent than the pills; to get relief with chewable pills, you have to take thirty or forty tablets a day.

Cimetidine can be used in conjunction with antacids, but this is not usually necessary. It can do plenty alone. What's more, monotonous, fattening, bland diets are unnecessary. You can eat almost anything you want. The only thing to avoid in ulcer disease is aspirin and alcohol, which are extremely corrosive to the healing intestinal tract.

Losing Weight: Diet Pills

Diet pills have lost their former popularity in the past few years because of bad press, misuse, and abuse.

Is a diet pill ever absolutely necessary? The obvious answer is no. If they did what they were supposed to do—stop hunger completely—the answer would be an unqualified yes. But in their present form, they only help. The primary effect of diet pills is to reduce appetite. As one of my patients put it, "That's the pill that keeps me from being 'crazy hungry.'" It is not, as some people seem to think, to raise metabolism or to help burn fat. According to the *Physician's Desk Reference*, diet pills can cause the following side effects: "overstimulation, nervousness, restlessness, insomnia, agitation, flushing, tremors, sweating, elevated blood pressure, mouth dryness, nausea, diarrhea, constipation, stomach pain, urinary frequency, dysuria, changes in libido."

I hear these complaints all the time from mid-life women, on or off diet pills! So the pill will probably exaggerate one of these symptoms if you already have it. Remember, though, that a lot of women don't have *any* side effects. The *PDR* warning only says it's *possible* to have them, not inevitable.

Diet pills used to be amphetamines, which are serious uppers and were abused all the time both by physicians and by patients. But in the past ten years they have been replaced with much milder stimulants. Unfortunately, the stigma of misuse still falls on *all* appetite suppressants, as well as the moral judgment of "You should be strong enough to do it on your own." This makes an impartial evaluation of these drugs quite difficult.

I resent physicians who say all you have to do to lose weight is shut your mouth. I invite any male who ever says that to me to join me for three or four weeks on the kind of skimpy eating required of an overweight female to lose weight. Not many will take up the challenge. The first one I proposed it to said, "What? And give up my peanuts at hockey games? Never!" He obviously didn't understand that the restrictive diet a mid- and late-life woman often has to maintain to lose weight represents a dietary and social hardship.

A second problem with diet pills is that they can "collide" with other medications. The mature female is often taking other medications—low back, high shoulder, middle elbow, thyroid, estrogen, progesterone, allergy pills, diuretics, or pain pills. Not all those drugs will collide, but because diet pills, even mild ones, are basically uppers, when combined with other uppers they may stimulate you more than you want. In some people they can be depressing when combined with estrogen. One doctor I know gave a diet pill (an upper) to a patient who was already—unknown to him—taking a muscle relaxant (a downer). The patient actually hallucinated. Luckily, she was a stable individual—an important criterion in evaluating candidates for potentially mood-altering drugs. When the pill's effects wore off in several hours, she was fine. The doctor was very happy she didn't live next door to a lawyer, though.

Diet pills are useful for a group of patients who, either because of high temptation, high stress, low caloric requirements, or high expectations of themselves, can't seem to start a diet without some help. And then they are only good to control real physical hunger. Their side effects are generally not dangerous, only annoying, and can be alleviated immediately by changing the pill, altering the dose, or altering the hour you take the medication. For instance, one woman complained that the pill made her feel nauseated after she took it. In doing a food history, we found that she was eating no breakfast, no lunch, and taking the pill at 10:30 A.M. on an empty stomach. When we required her to eat before taking the medication, the nausea went away. Another patient complained that she couldn't sleep. She was taking her pill at 10:00 A.M. We changed the time to 9:00 A.M., and she had no more problems. Just one hour made the difference.

Diet pills, in the context of a good, total weight-loss program, under careful medical supervision, do have a place in dieting, for certain preselected people who are generally in good health and free from abuse potential. That's a very, very qualified statement—and well it should be. But in my fifteen years of diet practice, I have rarely seen any flagrant diet-pill abuse, except in people who could be spotted as abusers by a nearsighted idiot—for instance, the five-foot-seven, 125-pound male who came into my office with shaking and nicotine-stained fingers and said he needed to lose his "middle" or the man who called from the Bronx (I practice in Hartford) to find out if I had "those black pills," because his own doctor had stopped giving them. Abuse exists, but rarely when a doctor is conscious and conscientious. True overweights like food—they don't like drugs.

Nonprescription Diet Pills

These are usually very small doses of the antihistamine decongestant phenylpropanolamine. They have been declared safe by the FDA and are useful in curbing appetite. They are sometimes combined with caffeine, to give you pep, and a local anesthetic, to dull the taste buds on your tongue.

Some drug companies are selling them to doctors who do their own drug dispensing (a practice far too common among diet doctors). If you buy these pills from your drugstore, they come with a specific diet.

Dangers? Side effects? There have been several fatalities reported when these pills were used in combination with antidepressants, but the antidepressant alone could have caused the problem. I don't particularly like phenylpropanolamine combined with another stimulant, caffeine, because this introduces still another stress factor to a system that is not in equilibrium. We should remember, however, that phenylpropanolamine is merely a decongestant. Nobody got uptight about it when it was used only to unclog noses, but label it a diet pill and the furor is incredible.

To conclude, phenylpropanolamine is a weakly effective anorectic agent that will help some people in the course of a weight-reduction program. In any case it's such a mild substance, it's probably only slightly better than a placebo. The real danger of the over-the-counter diet pill is its unsupervised use by people who might have other health problems. For instance, the older, overweight dieter should not be losing weight without medical clearance, much less taking a pill that has side effects such as speeding up the pulse or raising the blood pressure. Dieting itself causes metabolic changes in the body, and to add the stress of a stimulant to those changes, with no medical monitoring, could cause difficulties.

Alcoholism

Some studies show that there is one female alcoholic for every male one. That's a little hard to comprehend, especially because many times alcoholism is defined only by the problems it creates. Women tend to create fewer problems when they drink; jailed alcoholics are men, twelve to one.

The female drinker is a quiet drinker, and that's why you don't hear too much about her. If she doesn't hold a formal job, she can stay in the house and imbibe all day. Female alcoholics who abuse their children tend to be quite young, and so are their children. Most of the time the mid-life woman abuses only herself. She does abuse her family in a passive sense, however, in that she often neglects their physical and emotional needs. The older children of alcoholic parents learn early to be supportive, protective, and self-reliant.

Alcohol is a drug, a depressant of the central nervous system that is primarily detoxified in the liver. It produces either euphoria or a dulling of external, physical, or psychic pain. Excessive and prolonged consumption can cause problems in the gastrointestinal tract, including the liver, pancreas, and esophagus. Female drinkers tend to have medical problems with less alcohol consumption than males. In other words, they get sicker quicker.

Women drink when they'd rather be somewhere else. Alcohol is supposed to free them from immediate responsibilities and unpleasant thoughts. You are considered an alcoholic when your "social or occupational functioning" is impaired; when you are unable to control the amount you drink and the frequency with which you drink it; when you develop a tolerance, which means it takes more booze to give you the same high; and when you have both mental and physical withdrawal symptoms, including weakness, tremors, seizures, nightmares, confusion, and insomnia. Some women—myself included—have a natural alcohol suppressant in their bodies. Even small amounts give me a feeling of paralysis in my legs and chest, which is unpleasant and frightening. Perhaps this is a modification of the "Chinese syndrome"—a problem that the Chinese have in detoxifying acetaldehyde, which is alcohol in an intermediate, toxic stage of breakdown in the body.

If the disease is manifest before age forty, there could be a genetic tendency—and some ethnic groups really are predisposed to alcoholism. Most female alcoholics, however, tend to become so in mid-life, usually in response to a loss. The loss may be abstract, such as youth or sexuality; surgical, such as a breast or a uterus; or actual, such as death, divorce, or separation. The loss is accompanied by depression, which is probably accompanied by a decrease in estrogen. The progression of alcoholism is rapid in females because there is a tendency to "telescope," or to progress quickly from moderate to heavy drinking. The consequences, physical and mental, can be rapid also.

If a woman resorts to drinking as a solution to her problems, she is likely to be left with more of them. Her health will be rapidly impaired, and she is much less likely to get support from her spouse or friends. Society has learned to tolerate, or at least accommodate, the alcoholic male, but alcoholism is considered "unattractive" in women, and the alcoholic female is more frequently an outcast. No man wants a drunk wife who can't clean, can't take care of the kids, and is no good in bed—even if an unbelievable number of women, in their supreme masochism, will put up with slobbering, extravagant, abusive, drunk husbands and even go to classes to learn how to tolerate their harassment.

Even doctors don't want to recognize alcoholic women. I am guilty of that neglect myself. I once had a lovely sixty-year-old patient whose liver-function studies were abnormal on her blood tests. Immediately I sent her for every exotic test I could think of. In hepatitis, for example, there is an inflammation of the liver, and I thought she must have had a rare case with no external symptoms. When the tests came back negative, I sent her for a liver ultrasound, a test in which sound waves can determine if an organ has a tumor or a cyst in it. That was negative, too.

I was about to send her for a supersensitive, superexpensive CAT scan—the ultimate tool in diagnostic radiology—when her daughter came into the office and casually inquired, "Did Mom tell you she has a drinking problem?" Boy, was my face red. Here I was, looking for some exotic viral disease of the liver or, even worse, a tumor, and what I had was an obvious alcoholic cirrhosis. Extensive alcohol use can cause damage to liver cells, obstructing the bile ducts and making the liver work inefficiently. This makes blood tests abnormal. "Who would have thought such a nice quiet lady . . . ?" I found myself saying. But I was naive. Now, if anyone complains of weakness, insomnia, depression, agitation, disorientation . . . or *anything,* really, I always ask for a history of their alcohol consumption.

Once drinking has become a problem, the best thing to do is to get professional help; often formal dry-out programs are very effective. There are several options: private therapy, clinics, self-help groups, and detoxifying centers. But the alcoholic woman is often too confused even to seek help, and the decision is frequently made by a friend, relative, or spouse. And usually, the choice has more to do with available finances than with the suitability of the program. The self-help groups are cheap and best for long-term counseling and encouragement. In a crisis, and for short-term treatment, many alcoholics find themselves in detoxifying centers, which most health insurance will now cover. Most alcohol detoxifying centers base their programs on a combination of psychiatric counseling and physical and chemical treatment. One chemical treatment, disulfiram, creates an artificial Chinese syndrome, stopping the breakdown of alcohol in the body and allowing it to remain at an intermediate level. This produces toxic effects and severe vomiting. Alcoholics have been known to die while ingesting large amounts of booze after taking disulfiram. It certainly makes drinking unpleasant.

The use of an alpha-adrenergic-blocking agent, a drug that interferes with sympathetic nervous system activity—the excitable part of the nervous system, where impulses from the brain are acted on—has been considered as a means of stopping addictive behavior. A few detoxifying centers have used the combination of phentermine (an appetite suppressant) and an alpha blocker, clonidine hydrochloride. Why an appetite suppressant and a pill to lower blood pressure would be effective together is something of a mystery. But it has proved helpful, much the way methadone is helpful in overcoming heroin addiction, even though you might end up addicted to methadone. Clonidine satisfies the nerve endings (receptors) that drugs affect. It fools them. The alcoholic is still dependent on *something*, but not a dangerous drug; and it's far easier to be weaned off clonidine than alcohol. A few physicians I know have successfully used this combination to help patients stop smoking.

Part III

THE PSYCHOBIOLOGICAL PROBLEMS

Chapter 14

Stress

Every so often we read in the newspaper of a family that has suffered repeated hardships: the father dies in an accident, the mother discovers she has a malignancy, and one of the children commits suicide. We ask—why? Why should one family be singled out to suffer such hardships? Is it really God's will, or has the wheel of fate stuck on one number? Perhaps neither. We are probably seeing the deadly effects of stress and its different manifestations in different people.

You can't escape stress; you can only cope with it. What makes some people cope better than others? Perhaps genetic strength has something to do with it. Biologically, some families may have a greater capacity for adjustment, more efficient chemical coping mechanisms. Others may have (and generate) more environmental support—a stable family life, a network of friends, or many outlets. Maybe stress weeds out the "frail" people as part of nature's plan for the "survival of the fittest."

The human body is normally in equilibrium, or balance.

Anything that attempts to throw it into disequilibrium is a stress. Stress can be a physical disease, an allergic reaction, or a change in social and psychological spheres of life. It can be a single, terrible happening or an accumulation of minor insults. The strength of a person's coping mechanisms can determine the "stressor's" impact. Things that bounce off some people can incapacitate others. There is a wide variation in what individuals consider a strain. Humans have a great deal of physical and emotion resiliency, which is necessary for day-to-day living as well as major crises.

People respond to stress with conscious or unconscious "compensatory systems" that attempt to restore equilibrium. Some of these are psychological, some biochemical, and some a mixture of the two.

The Cerebral Pentagon

The most disturbed people are not necessarily the ones with the most problems; they're the ones who react the worst. They are unable—or, in some cases, simply don't know how—to cope. Coping begins in the brain, and if it's successful, stress doesn't do much damage to the body. The brain's attempts to solve these conflicts are called defense mechanisms, and each person employs a different set. The brain's choice of defense mechanisms depends on the severity of the conflict; and the conflict is between the person's raw instincts, her or his conscience (the values instilled by parents or society), and the real world.

Defense mechanisms are rarely conscious. Your brain concocts them automatically to alleviate short-term stress. It often doesn't consider the long-term consequences, though; so a defense mechanism can be successful in the short run and yet inadaptive and unhealthy in the long run. The healthiest mechanisms are highly productive—*sublimation,* for example, when you channel your stress into a work of art, a career, or a hobby. *Altruism* is also a defense mechanism; think of all the people who direct their frustration into doing good deeds for others.

The unhealthiest and least adaptive defense mechanisms

are those that significantly distort your perception of reality and disrupt or eliminate your relations with other people. The former include *denial,* when you refuse to acknowledge an accepted fact (the death of a loved one, for example, or the homosexuality of a son or daughter); or *delusion,* when you subscribe to irrational fantasies ("People are following me" or "Soviet agents are brainwashing me through fillings in my teeth"). Antisocial defense mechanisms include *projection,* when you project your own (often unacknowledged) inadequacies or feelings onto someone else (for example, thinking people are suspicious of you when it's you who are suspicious of them, or castigating someone for faults that you perceive in yourself); or *displacement,* when you direct your anger at someone or something onto someone or something else (from your boss to your child, for example, or toward yourself, as in some suicides or cases of self-mutilation).

Other unadaptive mechanisms are not so extreme, but they tend to complicate your life even as they help it. In *repression,* you "forget" something that you simply can't deal with; it would probably be okay, except that it takes energy to keep something repressed, and this leaves you psychologically drained and vulnerable. In *passive aggression,* you refuse to confront your aggression toward someone openly, and so hurt them indirectly (by neglecting them, if they're your children, or by being chronically late or inattentive). *Acting out* means blowing something out of proportion, externalizing it—as in a temper tantrum, for example; and the intensity of expression somehow keeps you from feeling it as deeply. *Dissociation* is the common defense of drinkers, who choose to remove themselves from the problem or situation instead of facing it. And in *rationalization* or *intellectualization,* you concoct mostly irrelevant theories to explain away a failure that hurts deeply ("I don't have friends because my intellect scares people away" or "I failed that test because the material bores me," for example).

You *have* to employ defense mechanisms—they're not abnormal in themselves. But the goal is to become conscious of them, and to employ them knowingly whenever possible. You have to understand *why* you yell at your kids for no reason, *why* you think the world hates you, *why* you have temper tantrums or drink too much. You can, with effort, adopt more "mature" methods of coping, and you don't necessarily need outside help. If you can't do it alone, a friend can sometimes point out things you can't see yourself. As a last resort, a psychiatrist or cognitive therapist (see Chapter 12, "Depression") can often give you insight into your own defense mechanisms and even steer you toward more effective ways of coping.

Fight-or-Flight System

The vegetative nervous system, also called the autonomic nervous system, is the most primitive we have. It regulates basic functions in the body that are not under voluntary control, such as breathing, body temperature, sweating, and digestion. The system has two distinct parts: the sympathetic and the parasympathetic systems.

The sympathetic system is the "uptight, fight-or-flight" system. When there is danger, either real or imagined, the sympathetic system raises blood pressure, increases the oxygen supply to the muscles, makes the heart beat faster (not always an advantage, since death is often caused by the fright reaction itself and not by the source of danger), and raises blood-sugar levels for rapid energy. Hans Selye, a pioneer in the study of stress, terms this reaction the "general adaptation syndrome." We could possibly live without the sympathetic system, but we could not tolerate any stress—not even a change in temperature.

The parasympathetic system, on the other hand, is calmer. It slows the heart, lowers blood pressure, conserves and restores energy. Together, both systems work to achieve a balanced internal environment.

Natural Killer Cells

The autonomic nervous system is not the only one in the body that responds to stress. The immune system does, too. This is the system that protects us from infectious disease, viral, bacterial, or fungal. We are only as good as our ability to fight off invading organisms. (The reason cancer is so lethal is that it can somehow fool, or incapacitate, the immune system.) All kinds of cells carry immune response, but the white blood cells are the main soldiers in the fight against unfriendly germs.

Little was known about the complexity of this system until the 1970s. Many of you who spent years in an allergist's office receiving batteries of skin tests, followed by batteries of shots, will agree—much of what allergists used to do was jabbing in the dark. In fact, allergy used to be the biggest joke in medicine, next to dermatology or diet doctoring. "At least they never killed anybody. That's a big plus!" we used to joke. Now allergists know more. And their most fascinating discovery of the past few years indicates that individuals who are under stress and develop the severe symptoms of anxiety or depression are probably more likely to have lower levels of "natural killer cell" activity. This, predictably enough, would make the body less resistant to disease.

Psychosomatics

Stress weakens various organs—makes them vulnerable to the cumulative effects of the body's own chemicals—and this could be the basis of psychobiologic (psychosomatic) disease. Diseases like peptic ulcer, migraine headache, and even heart disease—with its "Type A driving-ambitious" personality—have a psychobiologic component. Recent studies have shown that after a Type A personality has a heart attack, getting him or her to *relax* (with biofeedback) will dramatically reduce the chances of a *second* heart attack. Once an organ has been physically damaged, stress becomes an even more important factor. Peptic ulcer disease could be a result of the stress-mediating hormones. Stress signals the adrenal gland to produce more epinephrine; epinephrine causes the stomach to secrete more hydrochloric acid; prostaglandins that protect the lining of the stomach decrease; and with this protection gone, the hydrochloric acid can eat away stomach lining. Presto: a crater in your stomach.

Psychobiologic illness is essentially the violent interaction between personal biochemistry and external environment, provoking a nasty response in some target organ, be it the lungs, stomach, or skin. Nobody knows what determines the organ, but every person has a specific target area. Mine is my heart; I have palpitations. You may know some "skin reactors." Everything that happens to them shows up on their skin. They blush, flush, and break out in rashes, hives, and eczema. Their skin becomes "sensitized." In the presence of *any* stressor, be it psychological (like anxiety) mechanical (like cold), or chemical (a drug), their skin is likely to react.

Death of a Spouse

Mid-life is a more stressful period than most. There are identity crises, the beginning of chronic physical problems, changes in energy levels, and much more. But the most severe stress is bereavement, a survivor's complex reaction to the death of a significant person. The most powerful kind of bereavement is usually the death of a spouse. One story sticks in my head:

It was the end of a beautiful vacation, and I'd gone down to breakfast by myself to savor the last moments of a much-needed rest. The waiter sat me at a single table, and as I was enjoying my tropical breakfast, he seated a woman at the adjoining table. She was sobbing loudly, and he was apologizing profusely.

"I'm sorry," he said. "I didn't know. I didn't understand." But she kept on sobbing. Since our tables touched, and she was so distressed, I felt compelled to ask her what was wrong.

"My husband died last night," she said. All of a sudden this beautiful resort didn't look so beautiful. It was as if somebody had suddenly dumped a gray wash over the scenery.

"How?" I asked.

"A heart attack."

"Was he sick?" was the logical next question.

"No, he had never been sick a day in his life."

"How old was he?"

"Forty-seven."

I shuddered. How horrible to go on an exotic vacation and to fly home with your husband's body. I was amazed she'd had the strength to come downstairs and eat breakfast and told her so.

"It was better than staying up in the room crying," she said. "And I was fine, absolutely fine, until I got down and started waiting in line for a table. Do you know what the waiter said? He said, 'How many?' and I said, 'One,' and he said, 'Oh, one is always a problem! You'll just have to wait.' One is always a problem" she repeated, beginning to sob again. "Is that the way it's going to be for the rest of my life?"

"Not necessarily," I said.

"But I am a 'one' now, and what if I *do* have to live the rest of my life like this, alone? How am I ever going to stand it?"

Before her, though, were more practical problems: informing her children, aged thirteen and sixteen, that their father was dead; seeing to his transport home; burying him; and then enduring the intense period of mourning to follow. Yet she was looking beyond all that, into the bleak future and her sudden, unexpected oneness.

The time is never right for someone to die, and we are never prepared, even though we know that the ratio of widows to widowers is four to one, and that one-fifth of all new widows in any year are under the age of forty-five.

Mourning is female business, because women live longer, are usually younger than their husbands, and don't often remarry. A widow is faced not only with loneliness, loss of companionship, and unfulfilled sexual needs, but also problems of role definition: how long to grieve, how to act, which friends to keep, and where to get advice.

Few things can make you feel as alone as the death of a spouse. Though deep down most of us know that we are each very much alone, locked in our own little worlds and the victims of our own limited perceptions, a good or even not-so-good marriage can convince us that we are part of a unit. We can become dependent on a spouse in so many ways that his abrupt withdrawal can make us topple. A widow may look for her deceased husband at his desk or in the bathroom, or talk to him in the course of the day, because she's so *used* to telling someone about the little joys and annoyances of daily life, she's so *used* to being reinforced by his presence. Often his death won't really sink in for a month or two.

The mourning process varies from woman to woman but follows a somewhat similar formula: denial, depression, despair, and then a certain psychological distance. These feelings are extremely intense and can't be suppressed, and they activate the autonomic nervous system. This causes the physical symptoms of grief: rapid pulse, tightness in the chest, difficulty swallowing, palpitations, headache, stomach pain, sweating, tremors, dry mouth, irritability, weakness, and air hunger (represented by frequent sighing). These physical symptoms affect brain chemistry and can prompt more severe mental symptoms: vivid dreams, nightmares, and even hallucinations of the deceased (hearing his voice and seeing men who seem to look like him).

Where does help come from during this time? In the beginning, when the anguish is so intense that it becomes physical pain, the best help is often chemical. The minor tranquilizers—the benzodiazepams—can help you to function, to face the outside world, and do the tasks that must be done. After the first few weeks, these pills are no longer necessary on a day-to-day basis. They are extremely useful for sleeping, however. Many of the widows I know have had the most trouble during the night—nights filled with memories, sounds, scary noises, and the pain and cold of sleeping alone. A sedative and an electric blanket can mitigate all that. Take these pills as long as you need them. Most basically healthy people don't become addicted to drugs, even when they use them for a protracted period. Stories abound, it's true, of overtranquilized women stumbling over things, unable to make rational decisions; but they are the exception. The minor tranquilizers have been extremely useful in helping people to cope with early bereavement and grief, and they can make the process less physically grueling. Besides alleviating sleeplessness, diazepam relieves irritability, agitation, and esophageal spasm (that "lump-in-the-throat" feeling).

Most of my overweight patients have absolutely no difficulty eating, no matter how grief-stricken they are. They have enough adipose tissue to sustain them during a long fast, if necessary. For people of normal weight, however, a loss of appetite and refusal to eat can further enhance irritability, weakness, and agitation; and often physicians recommend soft foods or liquid supplements for necessary nourishment.

In the first weeks of the mourning period, friends become very important, and being around other people is helpful. But as time passes, some widows come to resent the woebegone faces and the "poor you" attitude. Some of them even avoid old friends, make new acquaintances, and do anything not to be reminded of their former life. They don't want to be professional widows. This reaction varies with the individual, however. On the other hand, widow-to-widow networks have been most successful in offering comfort, understanding, and direction, and they probably function far better than any professional counselor.

One of my widow friends suggests that the most constructive thing a new widow can do is go back to work as soon as possible—almost "cruelly soon," as she puts it. She says her boss forced her to go in long before she felt ready. Even though she went home and cried at the end of the day, she was distracted during those first terrible days of mourning. The longer a widow puts off the decision to go back to work (or to seek some outside distraction), the longer she will actively grieve—and the more severe her physical and emotional problems will become.

For most women, though, the stunning "acute" phase of mourning usually subsides within six to eight weeks, and then the chronic process of "reintegration" commences. The female begins to untie, one by one, the cords that bind her to her dead spouse.

Grief Work

Freud called this second stage, after the initial shock, "Grief Work" and pointed out that no mourning process could be complete without it. It can be ushered in by feelings of anger or rejection ("How could he leave me?") or feelings of worthlessness. Anger is often the most overlooked or denied component of grief.

As the work of mourning progresses and the female's life force (often called the libido) is gradually detached from the dead spouse, there is a surge of new feelings. Increased sexual desire is one of them; it is especially frightening because it is accompanied by guilt. This is only a sign that energy is returning, but many women find it so unacceptable that they displace it onto a need for adventure and variety: the urge to go on a marvelous trip, join a kooky religious order, or get a kinky permanent. Every woman has her own idea of what living is.

Ultimately, changes must be made, in life-style and perhaps in residence. Women redecorate their homes, their tastes changing from ultramodern to, say, French Provincial. They strive to break with their old world. Some women act too quickly. I had a friend who put her house on the market three weeks after her husband died. She had seen a condominium she liked just prior to his sudden death, and she panicked and reasoned that if the condominium were sold, she would never find another place where she wanted to live. Everybody, of course, jumped to the conclusion that she was selling her house because she couldn't manage it financially, which made her extremely angry. Luckily, her house didn't sell, and she was able to make the decision about what she wanted to do at a more opportune time.

Often during the latter part of the mourning period, a woman catches herself enjoying her freedom, suddenly realizing how many things she'd given up in the course of the marriage and how many compromises she'd made. Maybe she even realizes that there are some aspects of being alone that aren't so bad.

I have two close friends who are relatively recent widows, and each has handled the situation differently. Jean's husband died after a long illness, which some people think makes a big difference in the mourning period. (Other studies have disagreed, however.) If someone dies slowly, it is said, you can work off some of the inevitable guilt feelings ("I never really told him how much he meant to me" of "I never took an interest in his work") in his presence while he's still alive. By nursing him in his last hours, you "pay your dues." Guilt, on the other hand, can sometimes make people grieve longer than they would out of sheer love.

Jean shunned contact and clung to her depression after her husband died. Only now—two years later—can we get even a glimmer of a smile from her. Only her staunchest friends have stood by her, I'm afraid, and this is understandable. Other people can handle only so much active grieving before it begins to stir up anxiety and depression in *them*. It's not necessarily that they're being selfish; they simply begin to feel awkward and resentful, and they hate to be constantly reminded of their own vulnerability, of the fact that they or *their* husbands could die at any moment, too.

Long, protracted periods of grieving are healthy for neither the mourner nor the "audience." They are, frankly, a luxury, which many women can't afford emotionally, mentally, or physically. As a matter of fact, recent studies on the effect of stress and grief on the health of the surviving spouse have found that widows who have sustained the "grief reaction" the longest are the most likely to suffer severe physical consequences. There is some evidence that intense and prolonged grief weakens the immune system, making the person vulnerable to conditions as minor as a virus or as serious as heart disease and cancer.

In the year following the death of a spouse, women on the average have a higher incidence of physical disease. This is particularly true of the older widow. The stress of the situation activates any underlying diseases—rheumatoid arthritis, asthma, cardiovascular disease, and others—and medical treatment should be sought. The physician in this case has to distinguish between real illness and the physical pain of mourning. This is not an easy task, and I've seen physicians ascribe symptoms to patients' mental states when in reality they were having heart attacks. The more intense the stress, the more severe the physical repercussions. That is why it is so important to get on with living.

My other widowed friend, Helen, rapidly rejoined the living—or the living rejoined her. The support she received from friends and family after her husband's sudden death was tremendous, and she took advantage of it. She still cries, six months later, but she does it alone. She can also laugh, and *that* she does with others.

The widow who has had a healthy social life before her husband's death is not apt to be dropped afterward. Special efforts are often made to include her, and usually nothing is changed. After all, a bridge club or exercise class doesn't depend on your having a husband. If a woman was outgoing before her marriage, she will be so again—in time. If she was more private, however, and her husband was her "best friend"—well, she's lost her best friend, and she'll have to find another.

Sometimes the hardest part of the six-month-to-a-year mourning period is when the friends who have rallied around the widow no longer take so active an interest. Sometimes friends even begin to see the now-single woman as competition. That's when the new "oneness" really sinks in. The only thing to do is to confront that "oneness" and start to build a new, single life. Many women whose children have grown go back to work or school and, after the shock of increased contact with the outside world has passed, begin to fulfill themselves as never before. Some remarry. But the remarriage situation is imbalanced, unfortunately. Men have statistically shorter life spans, and there is an abundance of widows in our society. I know many charming and wealthy widows in their fifties and sixties who go begging for escorts, while uninteresting shells of men get snatched up. Some women retreat into their families, which can be helpful in the short run but can leave them frustrated and more dependent in time.

A House Divided: Divorce

Widowhood might be less traumatic than divorce in the long-term sense. Widows are severed, not "shredded." The cut is clean and absolute, and absent are the recriminations about faithfulness, child support, custody, and unpaid alimony. Also, a widow knows her finances and can plan her life accordingly. She has a better chance of being married again because her self-image is intact. She is left a loved woman, not a lost woman, and this is reflected in the way she relates to other people. One local pastor suggests it takes a year to get over the death of a spouse, but three years to get over a traumatic divorce. Mental breakdowns and suicide are more common after a divorce than after a death.

Divorce ranks just behind death as one of life's major stresses, and it's getting to be almost as natural. It's not an unfair situation, really—just inequitable. It's easy to see how the person you married at twenty might not be the person you want at forty; and if it were *only* a matter if personal and intellectual growth and change, the whole issue wouldn't be so troubling. Often, though, there's nothing intellectual about a male's cheating or request for divorce. Women do grow intellectually, but they don't grow younger, and *that,* too often, is the problem.

Divorce has its own grieving process. The pattern is less predictable than traditional mourning, but it likewise begins as a shock and ends with an adjustment to the separation. The shock comes at the first realization that the marriage is moribund.

Divorce is the artificial interruption of the normal life cycle of marriage, childbearing, child-rearing, and death, so it creates a lot of stress. The psychological defenses, often the first weapons the body employs, do not cope as efficiently under stress. The system is probably disarmed by the fact that psychic energy is tied up in bitterness and ambivalence. Ambivalence is that feeling in indecision—love/hate, right/wrong, my fault/his fault—and it prolongs the mourning process. It's a world without absolutes, and that's disorienting too.

Newly divorced women smoke more, drink more, eat less, and are less efficient at their jobs. For a while they may appear self-destructive. The nagging, dragging type of stress in divorce is hard on the body. In fact, more divorcees than widows seek medical attention during the first year after the loss.

The divorced female also loses her sense of well-being. "We had such a good relationship," she often moans—months after he's left. "He was my best friend." Obviously, it wasn't such a good relationship, and usually he wasn't her best friend. Why do women dwell on the former good times when they are being divorced? When men gear up for divorce, they say they've had ten, fifteen, twenty years of hell. Don't believe it. That's divorce talk—revisionist history—and don't let it get to you or dissolve your self-esteem. There is often no rhyme or reason for divorce, no questionnaires on which to check *A*, *B*, *C*, or *D* for what went wrong. Marriage isn't a fifty-fifty relationship. Somebody gives more, and if that person stops or changes and the other can't adjust, the whole thing can go down the toilet. Domestic life, as Edward Albee has dramatized, is a delicate balance, and a little less weight here or more there can upset the equilibrium and wreak enormous changes in everybody's psyche.

The fact that divorce is a reversible act also causes stress. From *The Philadelphia Story* to *Shoot the Moon* to Liz and Dick, our popular culture refuses to close the door on a marriage, always managing to stick a big, romantic toe in. Even if you slam the door, your "ex" still has the key. Will he use it? Will he creep back into your warm bed some night (you hope)? It's more likely, alas, that he'll creep in and steal your furniture. (That actually happened to a friend of mine. *Then* she changed the locks.) Certainly there are divorces that end in remarriage, but that's rare. You have to rebuild the friendship first, and that can be quite difficult.

About two out of every five marriages end in divorce, and everyone has a horror story, either her own or someone else's. Let me tell you a few of the hundreds I've heard, not to depress you, but to suggest how universal the experience has become.

Maxine, forty-six, discovered that her husband was not at the business meeting where he was supposed to be. Although he had been absent repeatedly to "take care of important business," one associate denied seeing him for six months. Maxine was so devastated when she realized what was going on that she phoned his psychiatrist. "Don't confront him with your knowledge," he told her. "It would destroy him."

Nora's husband, a professor, said he was tired of marriage, that it was too constricting, that he needed his freedom. He swore that there was no other woman. "He's like a little boy asking for permission to leave home," Nora's psychiatrist told her. "Don't allow him to." So every time Kenny said, "I want to leave," Nora said, "No, Kenny." Finally, when he was five hours late coming home and arrived to announce, "I can't stand this, I need my freedom," Nora, pushed to the limit, said, "Okay—go!" He picked up his electric shaver and in three minutes he was gone. Despite his earlier fulminations against marriage, he married one of his students as soon as the divorce was final.

Lois had nine pregnancies and produced two children with a man who beat her regularly. Finally she left him. She looked like a model.

Joy, forty-eight, walked her husband to the operating room before his cardiac bypass surgery. She looked lovingly into his eyes. Just before they pushed him through the O.R. doors, he whispered, "If I live through this operation, I'm going to divorce you." Joy was aghast. She rushed to his doctor. "The drugs made him a little crazy," the doctor said. "Or maybe his brain is anoxic [without oxygen] from the disease." Joy's husband survived the operation and left her, taking the family home and the Mercedes with him.

These stories illustrate certain truths we all suspect:

1. Marriages aren't made in heaven. Marriage is a man-made institution, created to uphold the fabric of society—which has gone from cotton and wool to polyester. Like it or not, the last stage in the modern marriage is its termination.

2. Divorce is democratic—it affects rich and poor, strong and weak, beautiful and ugly, young and old. No woman has to feel useless or inadequate because she has been dumped or things haven't worked out.

You notice that in all my stories the women are the victims. That's no accident; most mid-life women prefer not to change mates unless conditions are intolerable. Though this, thank God, is changing. More and more mid-life women are leaving marriages out of boredom and feelings of incompatibility. Many think there must be something better and are willing to go forth alone to find it. Inheriting money from a relative often makes this decision easier.

Be Aware

Before a marriage ruptures there are usually danger signals. Many of my patients and friends have repressed or pretended not to notice them until—well, the cancer has metastasized, so to speak, and the situation has gone out of control.

Here are a few of the warning signs:

1. Unaccountability
2. Nonverbal disapproval—smirks, dirty looks, a refusal to verbalize
3. Loss of interest in things that used to mean a lot
4. Loss of interest in extended family (mother-in-law, sister-in-law, and others)
5. Sudden increase in drinking or smoking
6. A loss of sexual appetite—particularly if he's prone to gluttony (they say a man who's cheating just for a little change of pace has better sex with his wife; but if he's really in love, forget it)
7. Irascibility; arguments plucked out of nowhere
8. Restlessness
9. Changes in appearance—a noticeable hair restyling or cosmetic surgery, particularly if he tends toward conservatism
10. Weight loss and preoccupation with fitness

Don't turn your back on these clues. Confront your husband with the discrepancies. Tell him you are worried or puzzled. Perhaps he has something to discuss with you? Don't get too worried about his answer. Most men lie quite gracefully right up until the time they leave. But at least he'll know your antenna is up. That could do one of two things: it could terminate his little fling (if it *is* a little fling), or it could drive him undercover—in which case he will be even more uncomfortable and will manifest a few more of the signs. Then you have to make a very important decision. Do you want to keep this marriage alive? Is it worth fighting for? Can you live with the idea that your husband has been unfaithful?

You might suggest marriage counseling or a vacation. Should you find out who the girl friend (or boyfriend) is and confront him or her? That is definitely the stuff of soaps, and sometimes it can be very effective. You can drop them in their tracks. Most other women don't like to get personally involved with the wife. It's rather like the murderer who doesn't want to talk to his victim, who then becomes a real live person. Or an even more difficult decision: Should you wait, hoping it will burn itself out? That's a real gamble. I've seen it go both ways. One piece of practical advice: the balance of power, in the long run, shifts to the cash, particularly if this is a guy who earned his money the hard way. In other words, if the female controls the money, the male is more likely to stay.

I'd like to say work at enriching your relationship, but that's hard to do if your husband is distracted.

Be skeptical for a while. Don't believe anything he says. I've seen men drop their wives after the most romantic vacation. But be sweet. Try to understand what deficiency in your personality drove your poor, lonely, misunderstood husband into the arms of another woman. When you finish that little feminine guilt trip and have found no such deficiency, you have several options. Sweetly turn the other cheek so that he can belt you again, or very nicely throw the SOB out, realizing that you have about a fifty-fifty chance that he will come back.

I know some women—very successful women—who threw their husbands out and felt so insecure without them that they wanted them back, but the old boys had had a taste of freedom and wouldn't return. So be very sure you can swing either way.

Be Prepared

If you can't prevent divorce (or loss of a spouse), prepare yourself for it. It's something to think about even in the happy times. I'm not being heartless; it's just a fact of contemporary life. Too many women have said, "This will never happen to me," only to choke on their words.

1. Prepare yourself financially to survive alone. If you don't have an inheritance, have a career—or the deed to your house.
2. Keep your sense of humor always.
3. Learn to enjoy the company of women—they can be fun. I'll bet you have more in common with your best friend than you do with your husband.

I once read a newspaper story about an all-female dinner party. The writer, a divorcee, discussed the experience as if it were a wake. She felt sorry for the other women, implying that each of them wished, more than anything, to be with a man. The article was more pathetic than the group. Can't women enjoy camaraderie and good food without men? I love my husband, but he's no Dr. Johnson at a dinner party. Neither are most of the married men I know. So why the fuss? Because women write articles about how dismal it is to have dinner with other women, and women believe it.

Being prepared is the best medicine. It doesn't matter if your precautions prove useless. Most precautions, happily, *are* useless. Besides, there is nothing wrong with being financially prepared, having a sense of humor, and liking women. It seems pretty natural to me.

If divorce becomes a reality *dissolve that cursed union*. Don't fantasize about reconciliation; try to live for the present and future. Give yourself a few weeks to carry on and then forget it. I see too many women waste too much time and energy having breakdowns or hibernating. One woman I read about emerged from a sanitarium after two years and complained, "Two years out of my life are gone. In two years I could have gone around the world, and for the same amount of money."

Ask yourself the following question:
"What was I getting out of this marriage?"

Companionship?
Warmth?
A bed partner?
Sex—good or bad?
A social life?
Child-rearing support?
High booze bills?
A TV hog?
Abuse?
Humiliation?
Compromise?
Frustration?
Financial support?
Constant sperm supply?
A carpenter?
Pleasant vacations?
Status?

Maybe seeing the facts on paper will make you realize how ridiculous the whole sorry affair was.

Keep as busy as you can. When men divorce, they find enjoyable outlets that have no connection with women. You should be able to read the books you always wanted to read, help with a political campaign, climb mountains, work, garden, listen to music, talk to strangers in safe places, go to lectures, and on and on. Don't fall into the trap of doing "couples things" (male-female couples, that is) until you are emotionally ready to handle them.

Specific Problems of the Divorced Female

An important component of good adjustment is how you see yourself. If a woman feels good about herself, she can manage failure, bad luck, and other stresses. If her self-image is poor, all the other problems are intensified.

Divorce, unlike the death of a spouse, leaves the female with lowered self-esteem, whether she is the divorced or doing the divorcing. Females are masochistic enough to blame themselves for all marital failures no matter *who* instigates the legal proceedings. Why do so many divorced women have a poor self-image? Because they have "tunnel vision" and focus only on the failed aspect of their marriages.

Men have marvelous self-image antennas, and they can sense a woman who doesn't feel good about herself. Pretty soon the new men in such a divorced woman's life begin to suspect there must be something wrong with her. And they say good-bye—reinforcing the image problem.

Analyze your self-image *without* thinking about the marriage. Think about the things you did *right* last week. You might find you have been concentrating on the unsavory side of your personality and dwelling on the low spots in your life. This is common in depression. Try to stand back and get a broader picture.

Do things to enhance your self-image, particularly in the area of self-*discipline*. Set one small goal after another instead of one impossible big goal. And learn to relax. For just a few minutes a day, sit down, close your eyes, and think of yourself living alone on a desert island and enjoying it. Each week you should enjoy it a little more. Pretty soon you might not even want to be rescued.

Economics is likely to be a serious problem. Get a good financial counselor. No matter how little money you have, professional advice could prove to be a saving. Women are now going into the financial-counseling business, and they are more responsive to the needs of other women.

Education is a good investment, but if you want to take a course, check out state and community colleges first. No matter how attractive the private schools appear, at $175 per credit hour they are not worth it for anyone on a budget. Adult education in high schools is often a minor financial investment and will give you many hours of pleasure.

Dating is apt to be a culture shock. The over-forty woman was raised with a different ethic. Her son or daughter may be living with someone, and she may have stumbled across a twenty-one-pill pack in her teenage daughter's bedroom, but nothing prepares her for the shock of the "meat market." I just got a call from a friend of mine who went to a resort with her fourteen-year-old daughter. "You wouldn't believe it," she screamed. "I walked into the bar to get a drink and there were guys all over the place. Most of them didn't even say, 'Hello, how are you?' before they propositioned me." Though she explained that she was a guest in the hotel, not a hooker, it made no impression. One ugly little creep said to her, "I like older women." "Call your mother," she told him. Another guy followed her to the elevator. "I'm coming to your room with you," he leered. "Are you nuts? I've got a fourteen-year-old sleeping up there," she said. "Yeah, I really believe that one," he slobbered in her ear.

Some people might say my friend was asking for it by walking into the bar alone at night. But she had every right to go in for a drink and to talk to anybody there. She also had the right to be free from harassment. Some men seem to think that all divorcees are so sex-starved they are just waiting to hop into bed with any man who comes along. So they feel quite charitable when they offer their services.

But if you avoid the singles bars, what happens? In a society of couples, where an extra man is a bonanza, an extra woman can be a drag. The male can marry a woman of any age with the blessing and even the envy of his contemporaries. The female who manages to date a younger man, on the other hand, is accused of being a cradle-snatcher; and the man is said to have a "mother complex." And though it really doesn't help your ego to seduce a nineteen-year-old, it can be terrific fun.

Many women complain that endless psychotherapy early in a divorce just keeps them wallowing in their misery and gives them no practical help—unless they feel the need for antidepressant medication. The new concept of "therapeutic divorce"—a team consisting of a lawyer and a social worker—has made it easier for some women to get through divorce phase one. But after a period of temporary relief when the divorce is finalized, they are often hit with another depression. It is during this period that a practical and cognitive therapist (see Chapter 12 on depression) can try to help the divorcee pinpoint pain spots and analyze feelings. Therapists can also help boost a shattered ego—but not by hopping on the couch with their patients. Except for getting medication during the early depression and a short period of therapy during the second depression, a good friend and confidant, a club, a consciousness-raising group, a professional association, and organizations such as Parents Without Partners might offer more help, support, and practical advice than a psychotherapist.

The plight of the older divorced woman is clear, and you

don't need a therapist to recognize the problem—nor can a therapist solve it. Older divorced women, though talented, have fewer outlets for their talent; though more interesting have fewer men interested; though willing to remarry have fewer opportunities to do so; though capable of happiness spend an average of three years getting over a marriage that just wasn't worth that kind of mourning.

Happy Endings

The stories earlier in this chapter have rather nice endings:

Maxine is married to a successful plumber who adores her. At first she thought it was beneath her dignity even to date him—he was a social disaster. But she taught him how to dress, gave him a little culture, and whetted his appetite for the finer things in life. What has emerged from her tutelage is a totally charming, well-rounded man with whom she enjoys life, even if she's not really in love.

Nora tried *est* and loved it. That, plus a younger lover, has made her glow again. She was originally a speech therapist, but after attending one *est* session, she liked it so much that she became an *est* therapist.

Lois finally realized her potential at thirty-nine, pursuing the modeling career she'd always wanted. The last I heard she had a boyfriend who owns a Learjet.

Joy managed to acquire a sizable chunk of her husband's business by proving in court that it had grown substantially during their years of marriage. Now she has her own public-relations firm—not too successful, but it's hers.

Women who don't destroy themselves through protracted rage, anger, or depression live and enjoy life again, often more than they did during their first marriage.

Part IV

THE COSMETICS OF AGING

Chapter 15

The Outer Wrapping

Facial Hair

Women get more facial hair as they age. It's not that they get more masculine; they just get less feminine. As estrogen supplies from the ovaries dwindle, the supply of the male hormone, androgen, remains the same. This change in the estrogen-androgen ratio sensitizes certain hair follicles, notably those in the male distribution pattern over the lips and under the chin. Estrogen replacement won't reverse this process. Electrolysis, an attempt to destroy the hair follicles, is still the best way to combat it—though as more androgen is secreted, more hair follicles will become sensitized. Interestingly enough, cimetidine, the histamine blocker used to stop acid secretion in the stomach, is now used to treat "hirsutism." Some scientists think it blocks the responsiveness of the hair follicles to androgen.

Skin

Skin is composed of the dermis, which provides the mechanical support for the fat and connective tissue, and the epidermis (''on the dermis''), which is the layer of dead cells that we see. It's the dermis that accounts for the skin's elasticity.

Loss of the normal lattice-like microscopic skin pattern, plus the biologic effects of chronic exposure to the sun's ultraviolet light, brings about rather rapid changes in the dermis and epidermis after the age of forty. The composition of the dermis layer becomes abnormal and causes fine wrinkling, a leathery look, and dilated (enlarged) pores. In addition, the dermis loses some of its water content, so the skin becomes dry and brittle. This is probably enhanced by a decrease in the number of sebaceous and sweat glands. Dry, itchy skin on the legs and arms, aggravated by harsh climate, brings many a woman to the skin doctor.

One dermatologist, I'm told, recommends bathing as infrequently as possible (except for sponge bathing of ''critical'' areas). I find this exceedingly funny, because the basic problem is internal, not external, and water is *good* for the skin—it plumps it up and softens it, if only temporarily. The thing to do is *grease* the outer layer well, particularly after a shower or a bath. Then it will hold its water longer. With what should you grease it? ''Bear grease,'' my favorite dermatologist says, but if that's too hard to get, any cooking oil will do.

What can you do about aging skin? First and foremost, protect it. Use sun blocks when the sun is at its strongest, even if you are not lying in it. Avoid extreme fluctuations of weight that damage the remaining elastic fiber. Try taking extra zinc tablets, which have some effect on skin elasticity; and rub some vitamin A and D ointments on particularly dry areas every few days. Use creams that will hold moisture in the skin. And take at least one tablespoon of corn oil a day; this can slightly stimulate oil secretion in the skin.

Adult Freckles

Pigment deposits become uneven as you age, and the more you're exposed to sun the more likely it is you'll get adult freckles—and the more likely you'll get skin cancer, particularly if you have white, fair skin. The good news is that only chronic, sustained exposure to sun does any real damage, and that damage is cumulative. So you can discourage adult freckles by staying in the shade and wearing a sun screen.

These brown patches are often called liver spots (no relation to the liver) or senile keratosis. Some women mistakenly think they acquire more melanin (pigment that gives skin a tan) as they age. Actually, they have less, but what remains is much more sensitive to the sun, so you end up having more color concentrated in less space. These patches can be flat or raised. If you have a raised one, it could mean trouble. You should check with your doctor to see if it should be biopsied to make sure it's not a "melanotic freckle," which looks the same as a normal freckle but is a premalignant lesion. If it isn't malignant, it can simply be scraped off so that it doesn't look so warty. If you want to get rid of these spots entirely, some dermatologists will jiggle the pigment around with an electric needle to lighten them. The bleaching creams available on the market are only weakly effective.

Figure Problems

In mid-life, thin women get fat middles—not beer bellies like men, but a pronounced thickening around the waist. What has happened is that from your neck to your pelvis you've compressed. If the same mass is put in less space, the shape is altered—that's a physical principle. This much of you:

) (

becomes this much of you:

) (

This is why stretching is so important: to try to prevent "telescoping" as well as the sagging of fat. Small changes don't have to spoil a good figure. Just change your wardrobe. Wear skirts and sweaters instead of blouses, and high and low waists instead of mid-waists.

The Legs Have It

Varicose Veins

Varicose veins are sort of like hemorrhoids that drop to your legs; both are symptoms of the female's sluggish vascular return system. More than half of all adults in this country have at least minor "varicosities," and at least one-fifth of those have significant ones. It's a woman's disease, four to one, and often there's a family history of it. Varicosities may be caused by an abnormal response of the veins to certain hormones, because they often appear for the first time in early pregnancy, even before the weight of the fetus compresses the leg veins and makes them pop out.

Varicose veins can cause aching, leg cramps, and fatigue, all of which grow worse as the day wears on. Standing aggravates them, causing valves in them to become "incompetent" and blood to pool in the lower extremities (because of gravity). Symptoms may worsen premenstrually or when a female is taking estrogen because estrogen tends to dilate them. In addition, estrogen itself is a salt-retaining hormone.

The first course of treatment for varicosities is simple compression and exercise. Walking is great—but this helps only the symptoms, not the cosmetics. If appearance bugs you, surgery is the only corrective treatment. Sclerotherapy, popular in England, is not commonly used in the United

States, and then only for small, dilated, superficial vessels. It consists of injecting a sclerosing solution in the vein, which causes the vein to thrombose (clot) and close. Then pressure must be applied for long periods of time to assure that the veins stay closed.

Leg Cramps

Aching or crampy legs are a chronic female problem—once again a "pooling" of blood in the lower extremities because of incompetent veins. Plasma (the fluid part of blood) leaks out of the cell, and swelling, or edema, follows. All of this interferes with your leg muscles' ability to consume oxygen, which in turn inhibits a vital exchange of calcium and potassium ions (atoms with an electrical charge). The result is that muscles don't contract efficiently. To make matters worse, some women take diuretics to counteract leg swelling. This works, but it also tends to further potassium and calcium loss. The combination of poor muscle oxygenation and flabby veins causes aching and cramping of the leg muscles and can also make you easily fatigued.

Doctors have tried various methods to alleviate leg cramps. Some work reasonably well. Potassium and calcium, taken by mouth, have provided great relief, probably by flooding the muscle with nutrients. Eight to 16 milliequivalents of potassium during the day or two to four (250-milligram) calcium tablets at night help about 70 percent of the problems. Vitamin E (400 International Units [I.U.]) also helps the symptoms, probably by allowing more oxygen to reach the muscle. Injections of vitamin B_{12} have proved successful in relieving general leg pain in the overweight female. (Overweights probably have more complicated circulatory problems, with some involvement of peripheral nerves, and B_{12} helps the nervous system to function more efficiently.) And simply elevating the legs on a pillow while you are sleeping has proved to be extremely helpful in soothing aching legs.

One contingent of physicians advocates leg-stretching exercises as a means of preventing leg cramps. Pushing against a fixed object with your toes, or alternately standing on your toes and then heels ten to twenty times daily, can help prevent further swelling. These exercises should be done after a warm shower or bath, when the blood vessels are dilated. Begin with five repetitions the first night, and work up gradually to a maximum of twenty.

Cellulite

Dimples in your cheeks might be fine, and even a couple of dimples in your rump are cute, but when the dimpling is all over the tops of your thighs, the cosmetic effect is terrible. It is more severe with obesity in the younger age group, but most women, unless they have spectacular thigh development, will have it at some point.

The word *cellulite* was originally coined by an exercise and beauty expert. Scientists were furious because of the *ite* ending, which implies that this is an inflammation of the cells. The word became so popular, however, that it's been reluctantly accepted.

There were so many quack remedies for cellulite that several teams of scientists were compelled to investigate this ugly puckering on the tops of many women's legs. They discovered that cellulite is not an abnormal disease state, but a hormonal type of fat deposit on female thighs. Fat on the top of female legs is compartmentalized between tough strands of connective tissue that act like little pouches. When you get an excess amount of fat on the tops of your legs, it pops out over the top of the pouch like too much popcorn in a brown paper bag. But you don't need to have too much fat to get cellulite. As you get older, your skin becomes looser, and those tough strands of connective tissue become less elastic and pull tighter. When the loose skin gives way, the existing fat—however small in amount—pops out. Men, incidentally, have an entirely different fat-storage system on the tops of their thighs. To begin with, they have much less of it, and the little they have is efficiently packed like a lattice, while their skin retains its quality and their muscles remain well developed.

Control of cellulite includes a diet to lose fat and exercise to firm and enlarge thigh muscles and to flatten the fat between the muscle and the skin. The *type* of diet does not matter so long as you lose weight. Firm massage, along with weight loss, can help push down that soft fat. Hand massage is fine—you don't have to be wrapped up in plastic or pushed in by a machine. Just place the palms of your hands flat against the sides of your thighs above your knees. Firmly press while sliding your hands up toward the top of the thigh. Repeat about ten times, twice a day. Even the rolling pin can be effective for this. Wrapping—or similar costly methods—removes the puckering only by pressing down and dehydrating the fat layer, so it isn't a permanent solution.

By the time this book is published, plastic surgery may have a treatment for cellulite. There is a device that can scrape away some of the fat on top of the legs and at the same time break up some of those tight connective-tissue strands. Then the plastic surgeon can sculpt the leg contour. It's an elaborate and expensive procedure—and not particularly necessary—but again, if your cellulite really bothers you, it's worth investigating.

Chapter 16

The Rewrapping

Plastic Surgery

Ginny sat in front of me. She looked great—she'd just lost thirty pounds. She gave me a sheepish grin. "I have something to ask you about," she said nervously. "It's my stomach. It's so ugly."

I looked down at Ginny's stomach. It did look a bit like a cantaloupe, but she was bone-thin everywhere else. In fact, except for that little bump, she had an extremely nice shape for a sixty-two-year-old female.

"I went to see a plastic surgeon yesterday," she confessed. "She said I had a separation of the stomach muscle, and if she repairs it, I can have almost a flat stomach. Then I told my own doctor about it, and he said it would be bad for my health to have an operation." She looked at me plaintively. "Do you think it would be bad for my health?" she asked. "Do you think I'm a silly old woman?"

I don't. As long as a woman's desirability is judged by her

age, she has the right to push back the clock and "buy time" if she wants to and can. I could lecture you on the meaninglessness of appearance, the beauty of the soul, and the uselessness of fighting the physical aging process. I could tell you to "go with the flow," that you may win the battle but you'll lose the war. But that would be imposing my values, not necessarily yours. For many women who look in the mirror and don't like what they see, plastic surgery is a Canadian Mountie come to whisk them off the tracks before they are flattened by the oncoming biological locomotive.

Plastic surgery belongs to everybody . . . who has the money to pay for it. It's stupefyingly expensive. The plastic surgeons, though, know how to play games with insurance companies and can defer your costs by telling Medicaid that the skin hanging down over your eyes is obstructing your vision, the stomach apron is giving you a rash on your thighs, and the clogged sinuses in your big nose interfere with your breathing. It's really nice of them to try to ease the financial burden on you by making a third-party payment possible, but I can't help feeling that if they didn't charge so much and didn't demand the cash up front (like no other branch of medicine), they wouldn't have to manipulate insurance forms so elaborately. One leading plastic surgeon, showing slides of some of his operations to a New York medical class, inserted a shot of his huge estate at the close of his presentation. Very funny—but the message was no joke; this can be a very lucrative profession. But those guys often think of themselves as "artists," not just as surgeons.

The most common question asked about plastic surgery is whether it will hurt. Yes, it will, but the operation itself won't. Plastic surgeons have premedication and local anesthesia down to an art, and even though you have to remain awake during surgery, you barely feel the first Novocain needle, which is the most painful. Noses, eyes, and face lifts are done under local anesthesia. I'm not sure why, except that general anesthesia is a little riskier.

The newest trend is to do whole facial procedures in the office instead of the hospital. This horrifies me for one reason. I once had a patient with a gigantic nose, and I felt compelled to suggest she get it fixed. The plastic surgeon she chose admitted her to the hospital to do, in his words, "the most atrocious nose I've ever seen." He put some local anesthetic into it and a few seconds later noticed she wasn't breathing. She had no pulse or blood pressure. Luckily, they were next to a cardiac surgery room, and part of a team was able to rush over and resuscitate her. She had had a cardiac arrest from an allergic reaction to the anesthesia. This is rare, but a doctor needs only one experience like it in a lifetime to be convinced that when you're doing potentially traumatic surgery—be it abortion, a delivery, or plastic or oral surgery—it's good to have a hospital nearby.

So the pain of surgery, except in cases like that one, is the least of the procedure. The pain afterward is a real shocker, however. "My face didn't feel like me for months," one of my patients said. "When I washed it, I wondered whose face I was washing. It was the weirdest, most uncomfortable sensation I've ever had." But pain never stopped anyone from having babies, and it won't stop anybody determined to change her features from having plastic surgery.

What about disappointment in the outcome? One woman confided to me that her face looked lopsided. It wasn't just the swelling, either. Her eye looked crooked and she couldn't stand what she saw in the mirror. Then one morning about three months after surgery she woke up and fell in love with herself. She said, "My face just suddenly came together. But why didn't the surgeon warn me that I would have the ugly interval?"

Cosmetic surgery for aging—face lifts, chemical peels, and so on—tends to create few psychological problems, but surgery that drastically alters appearance—a nose job or correcting a deformity, for example—might create a few. After all, people's personalities are partially shaped by their appearance, and you can't make a major change in one of your features without a corresponding change in self-image. Psychiatric counseling is now routinely provided to people who undergo drastic plastic surgery.

The state of the art? Faces are old hat. Mini-lifts, maxi-lifts, dermabrasion (for acne-scarred skin), and silicone injections for fine wrinkles are not commonplace. The new craze is breasts. In one day in my office I saw three remodeled breasts in a row, two reductions and an augmentation. It takes a special feel, so to speak, to do good breasts, and if that's what you want, investigate surgeons carefully. I've seen two atrocities in the name of breast surgery. One fifty-year-old female with pendulous breasts was left with pendulous flaps of skin with all the fat cleared out of them, and the other was a young girl minus nipples. She said they were thrown away by mistake. Lately, I've seen more tummy tucks, also a relatively simple, but uncomfortable procedure in which excess skin is removed and the stretched stomach muscle is "tucked under." If you're nice to the plastic surgeon, I'm told he or she might even cut out a few pounds of fat to save you the trouble of dieting.

The most exciting new operation, as I mentioned in regard to cellulite, is done with a knife and a suction curette. A small incision is made in the side of the groin, and the curette-knife is inserted in the pad of hip fat. The fat is then cut, scraped, and sucked out. This can remove the handlebars on the tops of your legs, the pouches on your hips, some fat on your derriere, and even a little fat on your ankles. The plastic surgeon can then sculpt the tops of your legs and give them a nice, smooth line. You walk away minus fat and a couple of grand, and you've had a blast watching yourself defatted.

For some this is the stuff of science fiction, even though it's real. For others, it can be a terrific cure for depression, at least temporarily. But it can be nightmarish if your surgeon isn't up to snuff. Check out the surgeon's credentials before surrendering to the knife.

Exercise

One of my fifty-year-old friends went to an exercise center. In the process of her evaluation, the instructor, a firm little nineteen-year-old female, pinched her middle and chided, "Look at all that fat." My friend was furious, and well she should have been; the remark wasn't just rude, it was totally inappropriate. My friend was five feet five inches tall and weighed only 118 pounds. There wasn't an extra ounce of adipose (fat) tissue on her, and her muscles were firm.

What happened to her body is what happens to many females past a certain age. The appropriate fat had dropped. Yes, fat does drop, It starts under the eyes, where it emerges as bags; the chin drops and becomes jowls; the hips droop into handlebars; and the tops of the legs become saddlebags. I could go on, but it seems a little sadistic. Why doesn't all that miserable fat slide all the way down to your ankles where it could easily be cut off? Because it is limited by fascial planes—wide sheaths of thin connective tissue that compartmentalize many parts of the body. The fat stops when it hits one of these natural planes. What the fresh, firm exercise instructor was pinching on my friend was loose skin and a small amount of appropriate fat that had fallen to her waistline.

Could my friend lose this by exercise and diet? Well, she tried like hell! She did every calisthenic known to humanity and went on a starvation diet to boot. But there's not much muscle to build up around the female waist, and the skin doesn't tighten up so fast at age fifty. So her face became thinner, but her middle remained virtually unchanged.

My feelings about exercise have changed a lot over the years. From being only moderately impressed, I have become a fanatic believer—but only in certain exercises, done certain ways, to achieve certain specific goals.

There are four basic types of exercises that perform different functions for the body. They include exercises that increase cardiorespiratory fitness, muscle strength, endurance, and flexibility.

Jogging is the most strenuous exercise and really does seem to make people thin. Except for what it does to your joints, *there is nothing else like it*—not swimming, biking, trampolining, or jumping rope (whick is equally bad for your joints). Jogging raises the basal metabolic rate, thins the blood, raises the level of good cholesterol (HDL), depresses appetite, lowers heart rate and blood pressure, kills pain, alleviates depression, helps protect muscle mass, increases fat burning, and does it quickly—in about thirty minutes. The other aerobic sports, though good for cardiovascular efficiency, take longer to produce the same results, because you are not responsible for moving yourself through space. Water, the wheel, and the trampoline do a lot of the work for you.

Jogging is tough on the female anatomy, however, and the mid-life woman, who has thinner bones, less muscle, loose pelvic supports, and bouncy breasts, is not really a good candidate for it. Sustained, brisk walking is the best aerobic cardiovascular sport for her.

But there's more to exercise for women than aerobics. Females have more problems with body shape, muscle flexibility, and strength than they do with cardiovascular fitness. (It's not too often, in contrast, that you see a male with a so-called buffalo hump or with the same degree of fat deposition on the shoulders and arms.) Therefore, in addition to aerobic exercises, a good exercise program for women should include stretching to improve flexibility and to prevent spinal-column compression (which, in effect, makes you shorter). Many women try yoga. Have you seen the figures on those yoga instructors in their sixties? They've got long, lean middles, and muscles as tight as possible for that age.

Yoga

Yoga is a particularly good, drug-free way for the mid-life woman to relax and yet limber up. You may laugh when someone tells you the sort of thing a yoga teacher intones: "To sail to the port of heaven, you must sail with the wind or against the wind, but you must sail, not drift or lie at anchor." But lying beside thirty other people, of all ages, on the floor of a loft or church basement, breathing evenly, feeling all the tension flow out of your body, you may wonder where our society has gone wrong, why it has never fully embraced more aspects of Far Eastern culture. Frenetic activity is the style today, particularly if you live in a big city where you can't cross the street without fearing for your life, or drive a car without getting into a drag race or having someone bear down on you.

You can't change anyone else, but you can control your own emotions. Control in an uncontrolled environment—that's yoga's banner, and for a lot of women it seems to work. Be only where you want to be, yoga seems to say. What a fine philosophy for middle and later life! No recriminations about a dead and buried past, no terror of what may come—only the belief in doing things to the best of your abilities in *this* place at *this* time. Philosophically, yoga embraces the union of body, mind and spirit.

This philosophy translates physically into a series of exercise systems, many of which revolve around breathing. Your breath, yoga says, is the very center of you, and concentrating hard on it helps you to go deep inside yourself. Then you are "centered," a concept of terrific importance in mid-life. At this age so many forces can knock you out of equilibrium. Balance is vital for your emotional and physical health. Emotionally, yoga teaches you how to center yourself anywhere to ease mental tension and stress. Physically, you learn to relax specific groups of muscles and to limber up stiff joints. Overall, yoga, if you take to it, can give you a real sense of autonomy.

The most serious deficiency in older females is in muscle mass. Older women are generally not muscular people to begin with, and with age, disuse, and lowered protein intake their muscles often diminish in size. At the risk of being gruesome, let me describe my cadaver in anatomy class. It was an eighty-year-old female, and her muscles were like paper. It's a wonder the poor lady could walk around when she was alive. So females should lift weights—small ones (five pounds). You should try to develop arm muscles particularly, because legs do get a certain amount of exercise anyway, even if on an involuntary basis. Remember, this is not a cardiovascular fitness exercise; it's just for strength.

If yoga is not your "thing," you can do stretching exercises instead. Ballet stretching exercises are good, but no twirls, please; your equilibrium is not as good as it used to be. The nice aspects of these exercises are that they can be done at home, they take only a few minutes, and anybody can do them—even if you have a bad back, knees, or heart. Stretching and muscle-strength exercises can be done in short periods of time, which makes them convenient for most women.

One word of caution: if you are out of condition, beware of overzealous physical-education instructors. Speed is not a prerequisite of exercise for strength and muscle tone. Bending and twisting too rapidly, especially if you are not limber, can cause severe back problems that tend never to go away. So easy does it when you start an exercise program. Learn to understand the limits of your own body.

For flexibility and strength there is no minimum amount of time you need to exercise, but it's a different story in weight loss. For that you want your body to use fat for energy, but for the first twenty to thirty minutes of exercise it uses primarily carbohydrates (glycogen) from the liver and muscles. After that, it begins to rely increasingly on its fat stores. This means that to lose fat as well as to strengthen muscles you should exercise for at least thirty consecutive minutes. It needn't be high-intensity exercise, although running is terrific for this. But whether it's running, walking briskly, or swimming, aerobic and cardiovascular fitness exercises should last a long time, because the basal metabolic rate (the body's consumption of oxygen at rest) stays elevated in proportion to the amount of time you exercise. Therefore, you will continue to burn more calories even after you stop moving—a true bonus.

In addition, in sustained exercise, actual metabolic and hormonal changes take place that depress hunger. The first metabolic change is a transient ketosis, or a rise in the level of free fatty acids in the bloodstream. This always occurs when fat reserves are being used without sufficient carbohydrate intake and gives rise to anorexia (loss of appetite). Also, exercise increases the breakdown product of muscles, creating more acidosis and aiding appetite suppression.

Finally, some interesting, though highly speculative, new studies have been made on long-distance runners. These suggest that runners secrete brain chemicals called enkephalins and beta endorphins, which might play a role in decreasing appetite. Both chemicals were discovered in 1975 and are being researched as possible natural painkillers manufactured by the body. Enkephalins exist in the brain and spinal cord. Within the cord they travel to certain receptor sites and act as chemical messengers. They then intercept pain messages being relayed to the brain. They may also block hunger messages.

Tai Chi and Me

I have never been adept at exercise. Being a typical endomorph (short, stocky, and slow), I'd rather exercise my brain than any of my other component parts. That's why I became very interested in Tai Chi Chuan. Tai Chi is a martial art, a slow version of karate. The manual I read calls it a sport, a skill, entertainment, a social activity, an art, and a method for curing sickness. "It will help you," the manual promises, "to improve your hands, brain, skill, character, energy and wisdom"—the perfect exercise for the middle-aged endomorph, I thought. But the manual further intoned, "Find a good teacher with a pure pedigree or you will waste your time and energy."

I was fortunate to locate a very pure pedigree who had come to this country only three years before to work as a dance instructor. He had a story: "I was a sick man many years ago," he told me. "I had a spot on my lung, and the doctors said I would never dance again. I went to the hospital, and there was a very old Tai Chi teacher, and I took lessons."

"What was the Tai Chi teacher doing in the hospital?" I asked. "Was he sick?"

"No," he assured me. "Most major hospitals in China employ a Tai Chi teacher, much as you in America have physical therapists. It helps people get better sooner. Six months after I started Tai Chi, the spot on my lung was gone, and I have not been sick since." Quite a testimonial, I thought. I was so impressed that I forgot to ask him if he combined Western medicine with Eastern exercise. I decided to find out about this exercise for myself. I entered a class filled with mid-life, slightly overweight females and young, romantic-looking males (a dynamic combination). Along with everyone else, I stretch, lean, pivot, point, and push the air for one hour with my out-of-condition body. It's fun, but hardly celestial; however, I am now unbelievably free of muscle aches and pains (before this I usually ached after just walking up the stairs) and have no back or leg pain from twisting myself into a pretzel. Is it my imagination, or am I more serene?

No, I'm not opening a Tai Chi center. But this exercise may be the American discovery of the century. It could replace sex, frustration, marriage, movies, and the Rubik's Cube. My teacher said don't be fooled, it may look slow and soft—but it's very strong. Just like us endomorphs, I thought.

Part V

LOSING WEIGHT, LOOKING BETTER, FEELING BETTER, LASTING LONGER

Chapter 17

The Body Balanced: What's Good for You

I know a woman who thinks she has the answer to eternal health. Her kitchen counter is crowded with hundreds of bottles of pills.

"Are you sick?" I asked when I visited her, wondering what rare malady could make all this medicine necessary.

"On the contrary," she replied triumphantly, "I am *well*. I take eighty vitamin pills a day, and I've never felt better in my life."

That's a lot of pills, and it's doubtful any well-nourished American could be that vitamin-deficient. But maybe we've focused too much on deficiencies. Scientists traditionally have defined vitamin needs by the amount necessary to prevent a deficiency. They have ignored, until recently, the notion that a lot of vitamins—a *lot*—might make people feel better, function more effectively, and stay healthy longer.

We all agree that vitamins and minerals are an essential

part of life, but how much do we actually need? And if a little is good, is a lot better?

Females tend to frequent doctors' offices with nonspecific complaints about fatigue, low energy, and mild depression. In their usual insensitive manner, the qualified male physician "works them up" for disease, and when that proves negative, advises them to (1) see a psychiatrist, (2) get a job, (3) get a good lay (sometimes with him), and (4) not to worry, "You'll live to be a hundred." Still feeling crappy (and that's the word), the hapless female tries other modes of health care: the chiropractor, nutritionist, naturopath, or holistic healer. She is invariably diagnosed as hypoglycemic, having a crooked spine, or in an "acute deficiency state." She is then given a therapeutic diet and a fistful of the clinic's own highly expensive vitamins and minerals. But the strange part (or is it strange?) is that many of these women feel far better leaving those offices than they felt leaving the doctor's office. Are vitamins just a placebo? Do women "think" themselves well? Placebo or not, I think that kind of response deserves some investigation.

That's precisely what happened to my friend. She frequented one doctor after another until her travels led her to a vitamin guru in another state, and to massive vitamin therapy. But the bottom line is that she feels better.

At this time of life, many women begin to feel themselves running down—slight lapses in energy, an ache here, a pain there. "I'm falling apart" is the expression I commonly hear. "Loosening up" would be more like it. The mid-life woman begins to look frantically for anything that will give her back the energy and vitality she had at twenty or thirty (if she ever had it).

As estrogen levels decline in the female, isn't it possible that more than just calcium is lost? Food intake is often restricted for cosmetic reasons, and the nutritional needs of mid-life women are really unknown. Absorption is often impaired as well. This means that you might take 1,000 milligrams a day of, say, calcium, but, if your body absorbs only 30 percent of it (that is considered average absorption), you're going to end up with only 300 milligrams, and you could be calcium-deficient. Sometimes the body won't absorb a particular nutrient from food, but will if you take it as a pill. So I think there is value in increasing some of the vitamins and minerals above the recommended daily allowances (RDA).

Deficiency means a *lack.* A vitamin and mineral deficiency is defined by a disease, or by symptoms caused by an insufficient amount. Toxicity, on the other hand, is an amount of a substance so large that it becomes poisonous. It is difficult to think of vitamins or minerals as being toxic, but if too much of them are ingested and cannot be excreted (as in the fat-soluble vitamins and some of the minerals), that is what happens. Almost any substance has the potential to be toxic in large enough quantities, including water, which theoretically can kill you if you drink too much.

In this country there are very few cases of outright vitamin deficiency. There are also very few diagnosed cases of people who overdose on vitamins. That leaves a simple question: What is the right amount? But it turns out not to be so simple. The Food and Nutrition Board of the National Academy of Sciences has set a standard recommended daily allowance that defines the minimum amount of a vitamin or mineral needed to protect against deficiency. But some scientists and researchers believe that vitamins and minerals, because of their unique effect on cellular metabolism, hold the key to preventing such diverse diseases as cancer, arthritis, and schizophrenia—and in doses much greater than the RDA. Perhaps minimum dose is the wrong concept. Maybe we should be looking at *saturation points* and ranges of effectiveness, instead of absolute numbers.

For most vitamins and other nutrients, undesirable or toxic effects are produced only with an increase of ten times or more above RDA standards. Within this tremendous range, the organism is able to maintain acceptable tissue concentration by control of absorption or excretion, or a combination of both. The margin of safety that separates the lower limit from deficiency and the upper limit from toxicity is different for each nutrient—and in some cases is very large—so why limit dosage requirements to an exact number?

Vitamins

Vitamins are organic compounds that perform *vital* actions in cells. They are found in small concentrations in foods and are divided into the fat-soluble and the water-soluble.

The Fat-Soluble Vitamins

These are the vitamins that dissolve only in fat and need the presence of fat and bile salts in the small intestine to ensure absorption. The fat-soluble vitamins are A, D, E, and K.

Vitamin A (retinol) This is found in pure form in animal sources, but its precursor (the pre-vitamin), carotene, is found in plants. Carotene is the substance that colors you yellow if you eat too many carrots, or too much melon or squash.

Vitamin A is absorbed in the intestines. Its absorption is hindered by aging (loss of absorptive ability of the intestinal tract), colitis (inflammation of the intestinal tract), infectious diseases, high fevers, and liver disease. A deficiency does not develop for three to twelve months because large amounts are stored in the liver. It is a heat-stable vitamin (it is not lost in cooking as are some) but is destroyed by oxidation. So if you take E (an anti-oxidant) with A, you enhance its absorption. Dose requirements of A are 4,000 I.U. daily, or 80 retinol equivalents. The accompanying E dose should be 12 I.U.

Vitamin A is especially valuable in stimulating epithelial growth (surface lining of skin, organ coverings, and other vital body parts), peripheral vision, and night vision. A deficiency will cause an increase in keratinization (hardening and scaliness) of the epidermis. Since this is found in normal aging, perhaps increasing A (along with E) could help to retard this process (see "Skin" in Chapter 15). Vitamin A might also play an extremely important role in the prevention of certain kinds of malignant tumors of the breast and other organs. Beta carotene (a precursor of vitamin A that is found in yellow vegetables) was recently reported to give some immunity against lung cancer.

Vitamin D (calciferol) Vitamin D is presently included in the fat-soluble vitamins, but it won't be categorized this way for long. It is now considered a hormone because it plays a critical role in maintaining blood calcium at normal levels. It regulates the intestinal absorption of calcium and the transfer of calcium into bone, and it maintains calcium homeostasis (balance) between intake, excretion, and bone. That's a hormone's job.

Food sources of this vitamin-hormone are notoriously poor. It's found in significant quantities only in fish-liver oils. The main source of vitamin D is from the interaction of the skin with ultraviolet light, either sun or artificial light.

Dark skin screens out ultraviolet light, so blacks and other dark-complected people tend to have deficiencies. It's also a problem for older people confined to nursing homes who don't get outside as often as they should, and for people who live in northern regions where the winter light is pale and short-lived. In all these cases, extra vitamin D fortification is important. An adequate dosage is considered to be 200 I.U. Excess vitamin D can cause too much calcium to be absorbed, causing "calcification" in various soft tissue such as muscle, or kidney stones. It can also cause hypercalcemia, dehydration, and coma. It can be a toxic drug.

Vitamin E (tocopherol) Vitamin E has often been called the vitamin in search of a disease. Though it has a long list of supposed virtues, few of them have been scientifically reproduced and documented. Some say it accelerates healing; others say it reduces the number of cysts in the breasts. Occasionally it is endorsed as a treatment for heart disease. It *is* important in the structure and function of all muscle and has been helpful in relieving pain caused by certain circulatory diseases of the legs. Perhaps it will prove useful in treating arthritis. The suggested daily dosage is 12 I.U.; but most regular users take 400 I.U. without any problems, although some women have complained of muscle aches with a dose that high. And women on anticoagulant therapy (to thin the blood after a heart attack or stroke) should be careful of vitamin E intake, because it interferes with clotting time.

The Water-Soluble Vitamins

The water-soluble vitamins (soluble in water), B and C, are my favorites. They make people feel better faster, and because excess is not stored in organs or adipose tissue, but excreted, they are relatively nontoxic even in large doses. If your B-complex pill has niacin, however, be careful. Niacin can cause flushing, elevated blood sugar, and in large doses over a long period of time, liver damage.

Vitamin B The B vitamins are the enzymes, or catalysts, of almost every chemical reaction that goes on in the body. They include thiamine (B_1), riboflavin (B_2), niacin, pyridoxine (B_6), biotin, folic acid, pantothenic acid, and cobalamin (B_{12}). Because these vitamins are widely available in nature, deficiencies are unusual, even though the body's ability to store them is limited.

I find two Bs particularly helpful in my practice. Vitamin B_6, 150 to 300 milligrams daily, acts as a diuretic and does much to relieve breast tenderness during post-reproductive life. And B_{12} by injection (2,000 micrograms) helps everything from simple aches and pains to numbness and tingling of hands and feet. It can also alleviate nonspecific fatigue. I realize using B_{12} for these reasons (without an absolute deficiency state) is a controversial issue. People who regulate health care programs have come down rather hard on physicians who give lots of B_{12} shots for lots of money. For some doctors it can be a profitable practice. But that aside, plus the obvious placebo effect of getting a needle in the butt, there are those of us who find B_{12} useful. In some nonspecific way, it gives many people a sense of well-being.

Vitamin C Experts are still arguing about how much vitamin C is good for you. The RDA is 60 milligrams daily, yet people *routinely* take 500 milligrams or more with no apparent ill effects. This type of discrepancy makes one wonder about the reliability of the standards.

Vitamin C seems to play a very special role in mediating cellular immunity. In my practice I see a lot of viral illnesses that occur when fat is lost. Even if a diet is well balanced and safe, losing body mass is a physical stress. The body is weakened by any stress, and it is more vulnerable to infection. In addition, some immune systems seem to reside in fat. So the combination of physical stress and loss of immunity makes you slightly more prone to illness.

So I prescribe a lot of vitamin C, which in females restores immunity and seems to protect cells against viral invasion. The supersaturating dose I use is 1,000 milligrams daily in the summer and slightly more in the winter. I have noticed that my current C-fortified patients do not get sick as often as my non-C-saturated patients.

Minerals

Your mineral requirements depend on how efficiently your kidney absorbs and conserves what you get—the kidney being the prime regulator of mineral levels in the bloodstream. A mineral is an inorganic substance that is essential to life. The most important minerals in the mid-life female are calcium, iron, potassium, and sodium.

Calcium Calcium is regulated differently from some of the other minerals in the body. When it's ingested, only about 30 percent of it is absorbed from the intestine. And a certain amount of calcium *must* be regularly excreted by the intestine and kidney, regardless of your intake. This is called an "obligatory fecal and urine loss," and it's completely independent of what the body has and needs. This strange process protects the neuromuscular system, because too little calcium would make the muscles go into spasm (called tetany).

We know that a fixed amount of calcium is going to be lost, so it's logical to assume that if intake is low, there will be a calcium deficiency in the bloodstream. But that doesn't happen. Blood calcium levels are tightly controlled and are normally between 9 and 11 milligrams percent. Why don't the levels drop? Where does that extra calcium come from? The answer is that the body "leaches" calcium from the *bone* in order to keep blood levels normal. Even though there's technically never a deficiency state, low calcium absorption probably contributes to the disease osteoporosis (see Chapter 8).

Since traditionally women have not lived much beyond their reproductive years, this system has seemed pretty efficient until now. At least it supplied the body with plenty of calcium in case of low intake. But now that women live longer, its effects are catastrophic; as a woman ages, bone simply can't regenerate fast enough to keep up with the losses. As I mentioned earlier (see Chapter 2), 1,500 milligrams of calcium daily with at least 400 or more I.U. of vitamin D (for better absorption) may help to protect bones, or at least to replace some of what's lost. If, however, there is an increased sensitivity of the bone to parathyroid hormone (see Chapter 2) as well as an actual deficiency state, the extra calcium will not be totally effective.

Potassium Potassium, an extremely important mineral, plays a vital role in supplying and maintaining muscle strength. The body absorbs *all* the potassium you give it, instead of just a small percentage, and the kidney regulates its blood level according to body needs. There are, however, certain chemical states in which the body loses so much potassium that the kidney can't keep ahead of the loss.

The most common of these is diuretic therapy, which is intended to block the kidney's absorption of sodium (because sodium holds water). But diuretics aren't selective. They block potassium absorption, too, and potassium isn't as easily replenished as sodium. It's not as abundant in food, and the body is more sensitive to its loss. A small loss can be significant—it can leave you weak and dizzy. I once prescribed a diuretic for a dentist because his blood pressure was elevated. He called me the next day, after *one* dose, to say he couldn't lift his arm to hold a drill. Other people can take diuretics for months and never go into negative potassium balance (losing more than you take in). Obviously, your reaction depends on how efficiently your kidneys protect their potassium, as well as on how sensitive you are to its loss.

Potassium levels also drop during dieting (see Chapter 19), particularly during the first few days when you lose the biggest water load. That's *extra*cellular potassium (outside the cell), which comes from blood plasma (the liquid part of the blood) and is the same potassium you lose with diuretics. The next time you lose potassium in dieting is more devastating and unexpected. It comes after the first month, when you've lost a significant amount of weight. You've just started to see a difference in the way you look, and you probably feel marvelous. Then you wake up one day and feel as if you've been run over by a truck. You feel headachy, irritable, slightly confused, and have insomnia. You may also have muscle cramps, pain, or little twitches. You've lost *intra*cellular potassium, and a lot of it. In fact, there is four times as much potassium inside fat cells as there is outside them. That's why it's helpful on a diet to eat a lot of *low-calorie* potassium foods (bananas, oranges, spinach, melons, tomatoes, lean meat) and, if you are under a doctor's care, to get a potassium supplement. An adequate potassium supplement for dieting is 8 to 25 milliequivalents per day (1 to 2 grams), depending on the severity of the diet. Liquid potassium has tasted vile in the past, so most people have preferred to take the tasteless potassium pills. The trouble with these is that they have a very thick coating and are often not absorbed well. They are thickly coated because concentrated potassium can cause stomach irritation, but coated for safety, they have lost much of their effectiveness. So the powder and effervescent pills, dissolved in juice or water, are the best supplements to use. They'll never replace ice-cream sodas, but they are much more palatable than the old liquid.

Iron Iron is the source of hemoglobin in the red blood cells, which supply oxygen to every single cell in the body. When you're iron-deficient (or anemic) your cells don't get enough oxygen, and this makes you fatigued and lowers your resistance to disease.

Iron deficiency is the greatest nutritional problem for females between the ages of fifteen and forty, the menstrual years. When you lose red blood cells, you lose a lot of reusable iron. After forty, when monthly blood loss diminishes and then stops, iron deficiency takes a back seat to

VITAMINS AND MINERALS	RDA	TOXICITY LEVEL
Vitamin A	Females: 4,000 I.U.	>25,000–50,000 I.U. over a period of 30 days
Vitamin D	Females: 200 I.U.	100,000 I.U. over a period of several weeks
Vitamin E	Females: 12 I.U.	Not available
Vitamin B_1 (thiamine)	Females: 1.0 mg or 0.5 mg/1,000 cal.	Excess eliminated in urine
Vitamin B_2 (riboflavin)	Females: 1.2 mg or 0.6 mg/1,000 cal.	Excess eliminated in urine

SYMPTOMS OF TOXICITY	DEFICIENCY LEVEL	SYMPTOMS OF DEFICIENCY
Joint pain, brittle nails, loss of hair, jaundice	<1,000–2,500 I.U. daily over a period of time	Night blindness; rough, dry skin; dry lining of mouth and gums; dryness of cornea
Hypercalcemia, vomiting, diarrhea, weakness, weight loss, kidney stones	<100 I.U. over a period of time	Rickets, soft bones, bowed legs, poor teeth, skeletal deformities
Not available	None known	Increased breakdown of red blood cells
Not available	<1.0 mg	Poor appetite, constipation, fatigue, beriberi (numbness in toes, stiffness in ankles, cramping pains, difficulty walking)
Not available	40% less than RDA over a period of time	Eye sensitivity; crackings in the corner of the mouth (cheilosis); shiny, red-purple tongue

VITAMINS AND MINERALS	RDA	TOXICITY LEVEL
Niacin	13 mg or 6.6 mg/1,000 cal.	Not available
Vitamin B_{12}	Females: 3 μg	Excess eliminated in urine
Vitamin C	Females: 60 mg	Excess eliminated in urine
Sodium	Approximately 2–7 g	Not available

SYMPTOMS OF TOXICITY	DEFICIENCY LEVEL	SYMPTOMS OF DEFICIENCY
Certain people are more sensitive to niacin. Smaller doses could cause flushing, itching, stomach distress. Larger doses could cause activation of peptic ulcer disease and liver damage	50% less than the RDA over a period of time	Weakness, loss of appetite, scaly skin, indigestion. In severe deficiency, the nervous system becomes involved leading to confusion, apathy, disorientation
Not available	Minimum requirement is 0.6–1.2 μg daily	Sore tongue, weakness, weight loss, back pains, tingling in extremities, apathy, mental and other nervous abnormalities, inability of red blood cells to develop normally
Not available; altered glucose tolerance with huge doses	<10 mg per day	Sore mouth and bleeding gums, weak-walled capillaries, poor wound healing, easy bone fracture
Edema (swelling)	Not available	Muscle cramping, loss of appetite, mental apathy, convulsions, ultimately coma and death

VITAMINS AND MINERALS	RDA	TOXICITY LEVEL
Potassium	No RDA; approximately 0.8–1.3 g recommended	Not available
Iron	Females: 18 mg	250 mg daily over an extended period of time
Calcium	Females: 800–1,500 mg	Not available

SYMPTOMS OF TOXICITY	DEFICIENCY LEVEL	SYMPTOMS OF DEFICIENCY
Weakening of heart action, mental confusion, poor respiration, numbness of extremities	Usually with diuretic use	Muscular weakness or cramping, paralysis, cardiac arrhythmia
Hemochromatosis (a disorder of iron metabolism); iron accumulates in tissues, characterized by bronze pigmentation of skin, cirrhosis, diabetes, bone and joint changes	Not available	Anemia (paleness, weakness, shortness of breath, lack of appetite, general slowing up of vital functions of the body)
Nausea, loss of appetite, fatigue, constipation, mental dullness, cardiac arrhythmia, dehydration	Not available	Anxiety, depression, irritability, psychoses, muscle cramps, convulsions, numbness and tingling, cardiac irregularities

calcium deficiency. Iron must still be regularly replaced, however, because the life of a red blood cell is only 120 days; and although some iron is reusable when a cell dies—it picks itself up and enters another cell—there is a constant turnover, and a significant amount of iron is lost in the process.

The best sources of iron in food are meat, fish, and poultry. (If you're a vegetarian, try spinach, chard, collard or beet greens, peanut butter, and legumes.) You normally absorb only 10 percent of the iron you consume, but if your body really needs it, it will sometimes absorb as much as 30 percent. Ascorbic acid (vitamin C) can triple your iron absorption. Seventy-five milligrams of C is all you need, but you must consume it *simultaneously* with the iron. This is called an "enhancing factor." Another absorption enhancer for iron is calcium, but it's much weaker than C.

Iron requirements are 18 milligrams a day (pre-absorption). Sudden and unexplained anemia in women over forty who aren't menstruating deserves attention. Don't write it off as simple iron deficiency; it sometimes signals a tumor of the large intestine. Immediately obtain a stool-specimen kit from your physician. This will monitor your stools for occult (hidden) blood, which could mean you're bleeding from the large intestine.

Sodium Sodium holds water, and it plays an important part in controlling fluid in the body. Actual requirements are very low, and deficiencies are rare. Most people try to cut down on their sodium intake, in fact, which translates into cutting down on salt (sodium chloride). The biggest controversy over sodium involves its relationship to high blood pressure. It has been noted that excessive sodium intake (more than 15 grams) causes blood pressure to rise; and a drastic deficiency (200 milligrams per day) causes it to fall. But no one seems to understand the precise mechanism of this action.

It has also been noted that weight loss without salt restriction causes blood pressure to drop; and weight gain *with* salt restriction can elevate blood pressure. Since water is lost in a weight-loss state, it would appear that the mechanism of action has something to do with fluid retention, with or without the influence of sodium.

In my diet practice I see women who are constantly preoccupied with the question of salt. Most of them have given it up even before coming to see me, not because they are hypertensive, but because they are bloated and retaining fluid. There's no doubt that restricting salt can take off a pound or so of water weight and can make you feel less bloated. And excessive fluid retention can be particularly troubling before menstruation, when it's often accompanied by headaches and depression.

However, I see no problem with a moderate amount of salt in nonhypertensive females. It doesn't crystallize in your blood vessels, as certain know-nothing nutrition gurus would have us believe; it won't give you high blood pressure; and it certainly makes food more palatable.

Chapter 18

Fat

She came into my office—color her gray. Her face was the original jowl. She carried a sheaf of papers with her. She weighed 231 pounds and was breathing heavily. I tried to talk to her, but she just kept shuffling the papers. "Tell me about yourself," I suggested, hoping she would relax.

"Oh, I have high blood pressure," she said, "and I'm on these pills." She showed me two bottles.

"Lose weight, and your blood pressure will come down," I said.

She appeared not to listen. "And I might have diabetes," she added.

"Lose weight and you won't be diabetic," I said.

"But when I diet my blood sugar gets too low."

"Sounds like you're telling me you can't diet," I said.

She ignored me. Another shuffle through the papers. "Oh, I should tell you I have a terrible problem with fluid retention. I swell up something awful."

"Diet will help," I interpolated.

"Oh, yes," she said, not really hearing me, "I have a hiatal hernia, too."

I got up from my desk. "Come with me," I said. We went into the examinating room. "Look in the mirror," I directed.

"Oh, I know I'm fat," she said.

"That not the message I want you to get. The message is: your problem is not your high blood pressure, your fluid retention, your low blood sugar, your hiatal hernia. Your problem is that body." I took the papers away from her and slowly tore them up. "Don't worry about these papers," I said. "Worry about your weight."

She didn't believe me. She bent over and began picking up the scraps of paper as if her life were nothing more than a bunch of diagnoses, a bunch of labels somebody had pinned on her. The bottom line was that she was comfortable with her ailments. When you've lived a long time with obesity, you do get used to it. But the older you get, the more problems excess weight can cause.

Weight gain is the most common nutritional problem in mid-life because at forty-five a woman's rate of metabolism slows down. She requires only two-thirds as many calories to maintain her weight. This is because the energy needed to keep her reproductive system functioning is no longer required. Most women are therefore forced to diet to lose weight—many for the first time.

Even though many women look better a little heavier at this age, they still worry about that extra weight. Figure changes can make even slight weight increases appear more marked. However, age is kinder to the female with a *little* more fat. Her face is less lined, her skin has more glow, and she might even have a higher resistance to certain diseases. There is nothing wrong from a health or cosmetic standpoint with the ten to fifteen pounds of extra weight women accumulate at this time. Studies have shown that this amount of excess weight does not impair physical health at all, even if you have always been thin.

Unfortunately, as the thin get a little heavier, the already overweight get heavier more quickly and lose weight more slowly. I constantly hear, "But I used to lose weight so easily. I could take off twelve pounds in two weeks.'' Now it sometimes takes two weeks just to initiate the process of weight loss. It's as if your body doesn't take you seriously. But regaining is disconcertingly rapid.

Obesity after forty is a different disease from obesity before forty. It is easier to catch, more difficult to control, and has many more dangerous complications. It's fun to be thin early in life, but it is *necessary* to be thin or thinner later, because obesity puts extra stress on an already beleaguered system.

What is Fat, and Why is it so Difficult for Females to Lose it?

Fat is nature's normal way of storing energy. Each sex has an appropriate amount of fat storage. Women, however, have twice as much body fat as men. The reason for this is that biologically they are supposed to have babies, and from the time a woman starts to menstruate, nature gives her enough reserve fuel to maintain a pregnancy when food supplies are not constant. This is a protective device to ensure survival of the species; in times of famine, a female can live longer than a male. The ''weaker'' sex is really much stronger.

The female hormone, estrogen, also supports this layer of adipose tissue by making it easier for food to be converted into fat. Estrogen is ''lipogenic''—it makes it easier for food to be converted to fat by encouraging a rise in blood lipids and stimulating the secretion of insulin. When a female loses weight, whether naturally (as in a famine) or induced (a diet), certain mechanisms are triggered to ''save'' her fat. Both her basal metabolic rate (energy-burning level at rest) and her level of T3 (a thyroid hormone that helps fat energizing) decrease. Because of this, she eventually gets into equilibrium with her food intake—even if it is as low as 300 or 400 calories a day. ''Isn't it a nice feature of human beings,'' a bright British physician said to me at an International Congress of Obesity meeting, ''that the body protects itself by hoarding fat?''

"Nice in famine," I replied, "but what if you're trying to diet?"

"You just have to be happy losing small amounts of weight," twinkled my pleasant friend.

"But my two-hundred-pound patients don't like losing a quarter-pound a week," I replied—to the empty air, because he had turned his back on me to give a dissertation to another doctor on how everybody uses up 1,100 calories a day, even if they are lying in bed. "Humbug!" I felt like saying. I know people who use only 500 calories when lying in bed. But he was a man, and men frequently don't understand female weight-loss patterns.

The normal male burns twice as many calories as his female counterpart. This is because of his greater size, muscle mass, bone weight, and his operative hormone, testosterone. Men have a higher basal metabolic rate, produce more heat, and greatly increase their oxygen consumption with all exercises. When a man starts on an exercise program, he often loses weight without curtailing his food intake..Meanwhile, the female is working out, doing calisthenics, playing tennis, and eating 850 calories, only to keep her weight the same. Her weight loss is always slower and more difficult. Biologically, socially, and behaviorally, being overweight presents many more problems to the female. And the problems become more pronounced with age.

Certain biologic cycles in females seem to deter the burning of fat. One of these is the monthly menstrual period—not the menstruation itself, but the fluid retention just prior to it. A fluid-retaining female does not burn fat so efficiently. Drugs can also cause fluid buildup in females. Steroids, nonsterodial anti-inflammatory drugs, antibiotics, and especially artificial estrogen in birth-control pills or menopausal supplements make it 10 percent easier for women to gain weight.

Fat cells want to survive. They might not have any brains, but they are tough, primitive organisms. They are a wily, unpredictable enemy. The longer you have them, the tougher they are. The older you are when you try to lose them, the tougher they are. The more you yo-yo up and down in weight, the tougher they are. Fat cells never die, either. They just go into temporary hibernation and lie around in their greasy cell membranes waiting for free fatty acids so that they can blow up again.

What is Obesity?

Obesity is the ability to produce and maintain too much fat. It is a physical, not a psychological, disease, characterized by weight gain that does not always seem to be directly related to calories ingested or energy expended. The female who has this disease is at a distinct disadvantage; her excess fat is zealously protected by the same mechanisms that protect normal fat. This makes her weight loss slower and tougher.

Obesity at times seems to be a problem of underburning as much as of overeating. Given the same diet, some women maintain their weight, some gain a small amount, and some gain a great deal. The reason for this discrepancy is obviously genetic. Some women are *genetically predisposed* to be fat.

People without weight problems, on the other hand, don't seem to get fat even if they eat too much. They seem to be able to convert excess food into energy while ''fat-prone people'' store the excess, either by enlarging their existing fat cells (called hypertrophic obesity) or actually increasing the *number* of their fat cells (hyperplastic obesity). The latter is the more serious obesity, because these new fat cells never go away.

What is it, then, that causes the fat to get fatter? Probably it is a sliding lipostat—a set point in the brain that drifts up when it should be fixed. This is like a thermostat set at sixty-eight degrees that doesn't shut itself off at the desired temperature, but continues to slide upward, allowing the temperature to climb. Other metabolic defects might be present in obesity. One fat-cell theory suggests there is a certain number of preadipocytes (fat cells) that each person is predetermined to have. Another postulates that when a certain level of fat-cell filling occurs, new fat cells bud out.

Psychiatrists and psychologists vehemently deny this. Most would have us believe that obesity is caused by overeating triggered by emotional problems, sexual frustration, or a desire to be strong and powerful. Or perhaps the overweight female is defying society, or overeating to mask feelings of dependency. Although some women probably do overeat to be powerful and impressive, most do not. Some women may overeat because they are unhappy, bored, frustrated, angry, and spiteful. Most do not. Some who do, do not become seriously obese.

What is Overeating?

What is overeating, anyway? Who makes this determination? Overeating is defined as eating too much, more than you need. What is too much? If a man sits down and eats a bowl of soup, a hot roast-beef sandwich with gravy, french fires, and a piece of pie, is that overeating? If a thin woman eats the same way, is that overeating? If a fat woman eats like that, is that overeating? Obviously, we've made the moral judgment that the fat woman is overeating, whereas everyone else is eating normally. The end results define the act, as they do too often in our society. Surprisingly, many overweight women eat a lot of salads and not a lot of hot-fudge sundaes. Surprisingly, many overweights do not overeat in an absolute sense. How did they get fat? you ask. They underburned. They didn't convert the food into energy efficiently, or they stored fat too efficiently.

Chapter 19

Taking it Off: The Dieter

Michelo was our young and thin Italian guide. When he discovered I had written two diet books, he sniffed his disapproval. "We don't need that over here," he said. "All *our* women are thin."

"But, Michelo," I said, as we passed a village with many amply endowed females, "what about them? They're overweight."

"Them?" He laughed. "They're not our women. They're our old ladies."

Discrimination against all women is a problem; discrimination against overweight women is a greater problem; but discrimination against the mid- and late-life overweight is an atrocity. There is no softening the blow, as in "She has such a pretty face," "She is pleasingly plump," or "She would be magnificent, if she just . . ." No longer held tightly in place by firm skin, her fat bulges, sags, puckers, dimples, and shakes. There is no place to escape; short sleeves, golf skirts, and tennis dresses are a disaster. Bathing suits are a joke.

This stupid, mindless fat manages to obscure the beauty, intelligence, and credibility of even the most gifted people—but only if they are female.

Therefore, dieting is especially helpful now. You can't get younger, but you most certainly can get thinner. There are some problems, though.

Weight Loss in Mid-Life

As I pointed out in my first book, this is a time of life when your body doesn't want to obey you anymore. Your skin doesn't fall into place the way it used to after you lost weight. Veins suddenly appear in your legs; your thighs are dimpled instead of smooth. Your tightly knit world begins to shift or even disintegrate. Your family structure may alter through death or divorce. More and more situations in life seem to be beyond your control. The key to weight loss in the forties is *concentration*. You must have the ability to focus on losing weight and block out anything extraneous to your purpose. You must realize that it is more important than ever for you to take care of your body and that you still can be an attractive human being. The forties can be anxious years; staying slim can make them easier.

Exercise is the key to increasing the speed of weight loss during these years—not sporadic sports, but sustained, brisk walking every day. Many women at this age prefer swimming, but swimming pools are not always accessible.

Weight loss in the fifties and sixties is often extremely slow, and this discourages women from staying on diets. It so markedly improves the way you look and feel, however, that it's worth every bit of extra effort.

Dieting—And the Diet

Here is a collection of diets and diet plans to satisfy all body types and all degrees of overweight. Most are diets that you can supervise yourself, although it's a good idea to have a checkup before you try to lose a lot of weight (more than twenty pounds). There are short diets, long diets, strict diets, and liberal diets (though not too liberal). There are no cute diets, no "You'll never have to diet again" diets, no "I love Poughkeepsie" or "Mamaroneck" diets. These are serious diets, but not *deadly* serious. You should be able to find a plan that fits your needs as a female in this very special time of your life.

Do-It-Yourself Dieting

I will give you three diets: one for fast losers, one for medium losers, and one for slow losers. How do you know which category you fall into? Read on.

Fast Losers—Normal Diet

Though it is rare after forty, you are a fast loser if you:

- could "eat like a horse" when you were younger
- have no menstrual problems, excessive bleeding, or hot flashes
- are not taking drugs, especially antidepressants, NSAIDs, or estrogen
- are "active" and do an hour of aerobic exercise a day
- have always been thin but suddenly put on ten or fifteen pounds

Medium Losers—Low-Calorie Diet

You are a medium loser if you:

- are not more than thirty pounds overweight
- have always had to be careful about food intake
- are not taking medication that could affect weight
- enjoy walking
- have not been on a major diet in the past year

Slow Losers—Very-Low-Calorie Diet

You are a slow loser if you:

- are more than thirty pounds overweight
- have just regained weight from your last diet
- stabilized for a while but suddenly can't stop putting on weight
- have a severe problem with fluid retention

- work the third shift (midnight to 8:00 A.M.), which alters your circadian rhythms so that you don't burn food so well
- can't exercise because of infirmity
- take medication that enhances weight gain
- have just had major surgery

There are many ways to lose weight, from the craziest and most dangerous to the most sensible and boring. Books have been written about all of them. I tend to stick to the sensible, with some spice and some surprises mixed in here and there for variety and excitement. In essence, I try to follow body quirks and anticipate problems.

You are as good as any diet center. In fact, all that separates you from them is a balance scale. That's right, a balance scale—not a step-on bathroom scale you have to squint to see and on which you can "wiggle off" a few pounds.

You are actually *better* than most diet centers. If you have a weight problem, you probably understand more about your body than anyone else does; many of the people who work at those places know little about the human body or obesity as a disease, except for the tidy and wholesome jargon they are taught and their own diet experience. They merely spoon-feed you a diet, and you pay lots of money to have somebody weigh you and pat you on the back. "Isn't dieting expensive!" you say. With a balance scale, a good diet, and a resolution to be completely honest with yourself, you can *do it yourself*.

Step 1

The first step is to buy your own scale. This is more important than an exercise bicycle, a trampoline, jogging shoes, or any other bit of exercise paraphernalia. It should be a balance scale, upright, with a bar. A digital scale, although much more expensive, isn't the same. Part of the *thrill* is moving the bar backward and jumping to a lower ten-pound level.

Step 2

Pick your own diet according to your needs (as determined by the previous guidelines).

Normal Diet

Breakfast. 4 ounces orange juice or 1 serving fresh fruit; 1 or 2 eggs and 1 piece dry toast with 1 teaspoon margarine, or 1 cup cooked cereal, or dry cereal, with ½ cup skim milk.

Lunch. 4 ounces beef, chicken, turkey, or fish; 1 slice bread (any type); lettuce and tomato (if desired); 1 piece fresh fruit.

Supper. 6 ounces lean beef, chicken, turkey, or fish (baked or broiled); unlimited salad with 3 tablespoons of diet dressing; 2 cups cooked vegetables (no corn, peas, lima beans, or potatoes—unless you substitute ½ cup of these for the fruit); 1 piece fresh fruit.

Snacks. Raw vegetables, dill pickles, diet gelatin, mushrooms (raw or boiled, but not in butter), stewed tomatoes (1 medium can), boiled cabbage (½ head), 8 ounces tomato juice or skim milk.

Beverages. Water (4 glasses)—obligatory; coffee (you may use whole or skim milk and a sugar substitute); tea; diet soda.

Supplements (daily). vitamin A (8,000 I.U.), vitamin C (1,000 milligrams), 4 spirulina or other protein tablets, vitamin B_6 (150 milligrams), vitamin E (400 I.U.), calcium (1,500 milligrams), vitamin D (400 I.U. or 5 milligrams), B complex (1 tablet), 1 tablespoon unprocessed bran.

You must follow certain rules on this diet:

1. Bread may not be eaten at supper. It must be eaten at lunch, or you forfeit it.
2. Meat must be eaten at one sitting. You cannot save some for later.
3. You can't save both fruits for evening.
4. Baked potato (plain) can be substituted for fruit at supper.

Low-Calorie Diet

Breakfast. Alternate 1 serving fresh fruit and 1 egg with 1 cup cold cereal and ½ cup skim milk.

Lunch. 3 ounces lean beef, fish or poultry; 1 piece melba toast (the 16-calorie type); 1 cup salad with 2 tablespoons diet dressing, or 1 cup cooked vegetables (no corn, peas, lima beans, or potatoes—save water to make low-calorie soup); 1 piece fresh fruit.

Supper. 4 ounces lean beef, fish, or poultry; 1 piece melba toast; unlimited salad (using all raw vegetables), with vinegar or lemon juice; 1 piece fresh fruit.

Snacks. Raw vegetables, dill pickles, diet gelatin, 8 ounces tomato or V-8 juice, 8 ounces skim milk.

Beverages. Unlimited: water (4 glasses)—obligatory; coffee (you may use whole or skim milk and sugar substitute); tea; diet soda.

Condiments. Mustard, ketchup, horseradish, herbs, spices, soy sauce, teriyaki sauce, onions as a garnish. Use diet salad dressing as marinade.

Meat and Fish (baked, broiled, or boiled). Cube or minute steak, round steak (partially freeze and slice in 3-ounce strips), tenderloin, chicken and turkey (no skin), seafood, all canned fish (drained of oil or water-packed), fresh fish (you may use 1 teaspoon of margarine in the preparation), pork (lean), lamb chops (lean), liver.

Supplements (daily). Vitamin A (8,000 I.U.), vitamin C (1,000 milligrams), 4 spirulina or other protein tablets, vitamin B_6 (150 milligrams), vitamin E (400 I.U.), calcium (1,500 milligrams), vitamin D (200 I.U.), B complex (1 tablet), 2 tablespoons unprocessed bran.

Very-Low-Calorie Diet

Breakfast. Alternate 1 orange and 1 egg (poached, scrambled, or deviled).

Lunch. 2 ounces lean beef, fish, or poultry (cooked weight); 1 cup salad or ¼ head lettuce with 2 tablespoons diet dressing; 1 cup cooked vegetables (no corn, peas, potatoes, or lima beans); 1 piece fresh fruit (no grapes or cherries).

Supper. 4 ounces lean beef, fish, or poultry (cooked weight); all the salad you want (using only green and yellow raw vegetables), with vinegar; 1 cup cooked vegetables (no corn, peas, potatoes, or lima beans).

Snacks. Raw vegetables, diet gelatin, 4 ounces tomato or V-8 juice; 1 bouillon cube in vegetable water (water that remains after vegetables have been cooked in it).

Beverages. Unlimited: decaffeinated coffee (you may use skim milk and sugar substitute); decaffeinated tea; diet soda (caffeine-free).

Condiments. Mustard, pepper, horseradish, herbs, spices, salt, soy sauce.

Meat and Fish (baked, broiled, or boiled). Cube or minute steak, veal patty (all-meat only), tenderloin of beef, chicken and turkey (no skin), seafood, all canned fish (water-packed), fresh fish.

Supplements (daily). Vitamin A (8,000 I.U.), vitamin C (1,000 milligrams), 4 spirulina or other protein tablets, vitamin B_6 (150 milligrams), vitamin E (400 I.U.), calcium (1,500 milligrams), vitamin D (200 I.U. or 5 milligrams), B complex (1 tablet), 2 tablespoons unprocessed bran.

Step 3: START!

Now that you have chosen a diet and you have the scale, weigh yourself. (Weigh a known weight to make sure your scale is accurate.)

Record your weight. It's amazing how many people forget their initial weight. Maybe they want to. When I was dieting, I would have my nurse weigh me while I had my eyes closed, and she would record it in some corner of a chart and hide it from me, just in case I went searching for it in a frenzy of curiosity. I did this to keep myself from getting discouraged about what I was losing, but it backfired—a few times we misplaced the weight, leaving me frustrated because I never knew how much I had lost. As your weight begins to redistribute, you feel much *thinner* than you are, giving you the illusion that you are wasting away. Never trust how thin you "feel." Knowing your weight, you don't get too cocky.

You should have an impartial monitor, not every day, but at least once a week. Ask your husband (if you are brave). Many women tell me their husbands have no idea how much they weigh. I find that hard to believe; my skinny husband knows each pound of my frame. In fact, there is a big celebration in our house when we reach the equinox, which in my house means the crossover—when my weight becomes less than his. If you don't want your husband to weigh you, ask a friend, a neighbor, or the mail carrier, and always on *your* scale. Don't weigh yourself on different scales; often there are discrepancies. Believe only your own.

Your Progress Report for Dieting

First Day of Diet You are going to be in the bathroom constantly. Where does all that water come from? When you eat fewer carbohydrates, a feature of all the diets, you immediately excrete a large amount of body water. Also, your body is using up its stored sugar (glycogen) from the liver and muscle, and glycogen is stored with water. Before you get too excited about all this rapid weight loss, remember you have to pay back that water debt at the end of your diet—when your liver again picks up its glycogen, it also picks up water.

You will be hungry, but it will pass; a few days on the diet and your head will realize you mean business. What about those stomach contractions? They take a few weeks to subside. They might resemble ulcer pain. If you have heartburn and feel as if stomach acid is sloshing around in your esophagus, don't panic. Your stomach is probably a little irritable because it's not getting fed. Take an antacid and you'll feel better.

Do not get on the scale yet. You've probably lost three pounds, but it doesn't mean anything. It's only water.

Day Two Today you will probably tire more easily. You probably think you're not getting enough food. That's true—the purpose of a diet is to make you use your fat for energy. But it takes a little while for your body to stop storing food and to start burning fat. By the fourth or fifth day of your diet you will have plenty of energy.

Rest today. If you're tired, don't push. Let your body get used to its new metabolic state. Don't get on the scale. You've probably lost two more pounds, but it's still misleading water weight and it won't go on too much longer. Some women think they'll lose at this rate for the whole diet and become so frustrated when they don't that they start eating again. So forget those unrealistic expectations. A good rule of thumb: figure out what you deserve to lose, divide that in half, and you'll never be disappointed.

Day Three Your arms and legs may feel like lead. You don't need food; you need *potassium*. Have you been drinking orange juice? If that upsets your stomach, half a banana will be fine—not as fast-acting, but okay. Other potassium-loaded foods that are lower in calories are spinach, white meat of chicken, tomatoes, and tomato juice.

Want to see some diet magic? Drink 4 ounces of orange juice with a pinch of salt and wait twenty minutes. Those tired legs and arms will feel much better. Or boil some fresh spinach and squeeze the liquid into a glass. (Use the spinach, chopped and mixed with minced onion, mustard, and a little yogurt, to stuff some tomatoes for your evening meal.) Add a little salt and pepper to the spinach water, or dissolve a bouillon cube in it, and drink. In twenty minutes you'll get the same results as with the orange juice, but with far fewer calories.

Don't worry about salt if you don't have high blood pressure. Cut down, not out. Salt makes food taste better. Besides, it has been shown that weight reduction without salt restriction lowers blood pressure by itself. Also, a diet high in potassium and high in animal protein lowers blood pressure. If you still don't like salt, that's okay—but don't complain that your food is tasteless.

You probably have bad breath. Your empty stomach is demanding nourishment. Unneutralized hydrochloric acid that you used to buffer with food in your stomach is the cause. If you don't want to alienate your friends, an antacid, pleasant-tasting and mint-flavored, will not only neutralize your gastric acids, but will take away any hyperacidity that's caused by dieting and is also low in calories. Eating is not the answer. Don't suck on sugarless candy for your breath. In the first place it's not sugarless (it does have a form of sugar), and in the second place you could be eating it all day.

Day Four Let's talk about vitamins. A well-balanced diet is supposed to give you lots of vitamins, but you're not eating very much food. Here are the dietary supplements I like:

A	**8,000 I.U. (twice the RDA requirement)**
B_6	**150 mg daily, for prevention of fluid retention (75 times the RDA). Feel more bloated? Take 300 mg.**
B_{12}	**200 μg (100 times the RDA)**
B_1	**250 mg (250 times the RDA)**
C	**1,000 mg in summer (take 250 mg four times a day; 15 times the RDA); 1,500 mg in winter (take 500 mg three times a day)**
D	**400 I.U. (RDA on target!)**
Calcium	**800–1,500 mg**
Protein	**2–4 tablets daily for filling purposes, and just in case your protein needs are not being met**

Why don't I want you to use single, multivitamin pills? Multivitamins may have analogues or blockers that you don't need, and taking individual pills gives you much more flexibility. Besides, you can take them at different times when you feel like putting something in your mouth. Take them when you're hungry or sleepy, in midafternoon or before supper. Take them with tomato juice or skim milk, if these beverages are on your diet. Do not take them with diet soda. Do not take them on an empty stomach. If you are fatigued and have a history of anemia, add some iron even if you are not having periods. If you're still having periods, you should also take iron, 18 milligrams a day. Iron may upset your stomach, so wait one week before you start taking it. Then you won't blame another pill or the diet for the cramps it might cause.

Day Five By now you've probably lost six or seven pounds. At this rate you'll lose twenty pounds in two weeks, right? Forget it—that's a fantasy. That much is not a woman's weight loss, I'm afraid, unless you're on a starvation diet, or you weigh 250 pounds. Your rate of loss will be slowing gradually.

If you find yourself drinking a lot of water, it's because you've lost a lot of fluid, and thirst is the body's attempt to replace volume. You don't need eight or ten glasses of water a day; four is sufficient. Drink the amount you are comfortable with, but enough to keep your urine light yellow (except in the morning). Light-colored urine means you are keeping plasma filtrate dilute, and that is important. Otherwise little stones might crystallize in your kidneys.

Day Six Perhaps you lost only a half a pound today. You're slowing down. Don't be disappointed. The worst is yet to come.

Don't worry about eating eggs every day unless you have a blood-cholesterol count of 400 or above or a history of severe heart disease in your family.

If you want to give up smoking now, you might fail at both your diet and your attempt to kick the habit. Nicotine is an appetite suppressant, and smoking more than a pack a day can also speed up your metabolism. Smoking can help you lose weight now. *After* your diet, give it up. Don't take up smoking if you don't already smoke, though. You'll only end up with two bad habits: smoking and overeating. Cigarettes, unless they are chocolate, will never replace food in a woman's life anyway.

Day Seven One-half pound today again.

Suppose your husband takes you out to eat. Do you feel you have to eat, to break your diet? There are always reasons to break your diet. There are always reasons to eat. There is never a convenient time to diet. You have to make the time. Fight those impulses to eat.

You can control what you eat at restaurants, but you must follow certain guidelines.

1. Pick the easiest type of restaurant in which to stay on your diet—not a pizza parlor.
2. Pick one that is expensive, where everything is priced à la carte.
3. Beware of sauces, even the "low-calorie" or "nouvelle cuisine" kind.

4. Eat slowly and talk fast to give the illusion you're having a good time, even if you are starving.
5. If you feel sorry for yourself, go home and eat a salad.

Day Eight Perhaps you lost no weight today. If you ate at a restaurant last night, you probably had larger portions than I specified. I know my diets give portions and not calories, but I've figured out the calories for you. If you exceed this, particularly in the beginning of a diet, with your sensitive, fat-storing system, you are going to interfere with your weight loss. But even if you didn't exceed your calories, your weight loss will still be slowing down.

Day Nine No weight loss again today? And you were perfect yesterday? This is the normal progression of things. Don't worry. Perhaps you feel like eating because you're so angry. That's not going to accomplish anything. Then you've wasted a lot of time. You can't defeat your body or your metabolism; you can only grit your teeth and work with it. If you take in few enough calories and exercise enough, you *will* lose weight.

Day Ten Suppose you gained half a pound today, even though you were perfectly faithful to your diet. This is only a "rebound phenomenon" that often happens during the first ten days of dieting. Your body is attempting to hold water to restore blood volume. Don't throw in the sponge. You *are* the sponge—some days a dry sponge and some days a wet sponge. That's not as bizarre as it sounds. It's why your weight loss is so unpredictable.

Day Eleven You might start having a craving now and want to binge. Well, part of that is psychological, because you were disappointed when you gained weight. If you are not getting positive reinforcement from your weight loss, you're probably recalling how nice and convenient it was to eat what you wanted. Is there any reason for your fluid balance to be screwed up? Your estrogen-progesterone balance may be off; perhaps it's right before your period. Taking 150 to 300 milligrams of vitamin B_6 is often helpful because it acts as a natural diuretic.

Day Twelve Perhaps you attended a behavior-modification meeting and the leaders didn't like the word *diet,* because "you can go on or off a diet." That's one of their silly word games. It doesn't matter what you call it—an eating program, a way of life, a food regimen. Whatever the name, I want you to stay on *"it"* as closely as possible. Dieting is often a word game, anyway. But it's the one game in which you want to lose.

Day Thirteen No loss. By now you may think you're constipated, that your unreleased bowels are keeping the scale up. Some of my patients have actually considered this and have tried prune juice in desperation! It doesn't help. Do you know what prune juice does to your intestinal tract? It works by irritating it. It gives you unnatural diarrhea. And it's loaded with calories. You are constipated because I took the bulk out of your diet. You will probably have fewer bowel movements because you aren't eating as much. Nobody has to have daily movements. It doesn't make you lose weight faster—well, the weight of the fecal mass, maybe. But that's all waste products, not fat.

Day Fourteen You have lost nine and a half pounds in two weeks, and that's quite respectable. People on other diets will lose four to five pounds, and some people will lose much more! Your husband probably went on a diet the same day and lost fifteen pounds. But *please* don't compare yourself to any other dieter except an over-forty, overweight female—not your daughter or a thin friend, and especially not your husband.

Week Three Perhaps this week you lost only two pounds and are irritated that you didn't lose more. But two pounds a week is an average, respectable weight loss. Women who gain weight easily do not lose weight easily. If you were an easy weight loser, you wouldn't be dieting for this length of time. So forget about the pounds magically dropping off.

Can you have more food, or different food, perhaps? Well, when I give a treat, it's generally one Chinese meal a week. With your Chinese meal, you may have the soup (chicken, hot-and-sour, or egg-drop soup preferred—no wontons) and anything that is not sweet-and-sour. No fried rice. And no dessert. That meal can be eaten in the house if you cook authentic Chinese (not "Chinese-American"), or it can be eaten in a Chinese restaurant.

If you don't like Chinese food, you're missing out on a good, low-calorie, filling, interesting way to prepare food. If you're overweight, you must learn to take an interest in low-calorie foods, because so many high-calorie foods will be denied you, unless science can figure out a way to make them low-calorie. But if you really don't like Chinese food, you can have one cup of rice fixed any way you want, twice a week.

You want to substitute a slice of bread at 75 calories for an ounce of meat that's about 100 calories? Sounds like a good substitution in calories. But it's not such a good substitution when you consider food type, and that makes a lot of difference in weight loss. As I have said, the purpose of this diet is to burn as much body fat as possible by reducing your caloric intake. When carbohydrates are available, less fat is mobilized, primarily because the increased insulin secretion induced by the carbohydrates inhibits the release of fatty acids from the fat deposits. That's why we want you to try to keep your carbohydrate level as low as possible. Meat has no carbohydrates, and bread is almost all carbohydrates. So, even though the calorie switch is equivalent, it's not equivalent in what it does in your body. And remember, you need protein. You can substitute one piece of bread for rice, though. When you are in the maintenance phase of dieting, you can eat complex carbohydrates and substitute as often as you wish (as long as you meet your minimum daily requirements for protein) because then you do not want to burn fat.

You might be more sensitive to the cold these days. Fat is fairly good insulation—though muscle is better—and you're going to be cold from now on, and getting colder. You might even have to go to bed wearing socks until your body adjusts to the loss of padding. It will adjust, though, if you stay thin long enough.

Week Four Your skin is dry? That's one of the mysteries of dieting. With all the free fatty acids that are broken down as you use your own fat, how can you possibly have dry skin? Female skin seems to rely on a certain amount of oil that goes through the normal process of digestion, and not on the oil being utilized from body fat. Add a teaspoonful of oil to your daily intake. It's only 30 calories, and it could make your skin moist. But use it where you'll enjoy it—add it to salad dressing, put it over some vegetables with chopped garlic and parsley, or brush it over a piece of fish before you broil it. You can use any oil you like, from walnut to safflower to olive. They all have the same number of calories. The degree of saturation differs, but you don't have to worry about that right now.

If you're wondering why I don't have soup on the diet, it's because canned soup has too much salt, too much fat, and too little protein. If you'd like it at this point as a change of pace, or if you feel the need for something hot, here is a simple soup recipe. A cup of it can be substituted for a fruit serving and a bowl (three cups) for a main course:

Boil together one large can of stewed tomatoes, one packet of dried vegetable-soup mix, the amount of water called for in the vegetable-soup mix, two chopped carrots, half a small head of shredded cabbage, two chopped celery stalks, one chopped onion, and any other green or yellow vegetable that you have lying around or left over. Simmer together for one hour, season with pepper or, if you like a sweet-and-sour taste, a tablespoon of vinegar and half a packet of artificial sweetener. You now have a low-calorie, low-fat soup. It can be refrigerated until you feel like eating it, and it freezes well, too. Freeze it in round plastic containers. It's handy to have on hand for a quick meal.

Week Five If you're having headaches, get your eyes checked first. If they are okay, look for other reasons. Skipping meals leads to ketosis—a metabolic deviation that could cause headaches. Tension about your "food program" puts a certain amount of strain on the muscles at the back of your neck. These muscles can cause pain to travel over your head, down your forehead, and around your eyes, causing headaches that feel like eye strain.

Dieting will make any medication you are taking more potent. This is called *potentiation*. Your blood vessels become sensitive to stimulation, and they react by going into spasm and causing pain, especially in the head. (By the way, the caffeine in drinks such as coffee is a common stimulant that also becomes more potent when you diet.)

Make sure to eat meals regularly, and try to relax. If the headaches persist for any length of time (two weeks), or become more severe, or are associated with nausea and vomiting, call your doctor. Also, headaches are common before a viral disease. Wait a few days; you might be coming down with something. No, it's not because you're not getting enough food; if you eat when and what you are supposed to, you will be satisfying all your nutritional requirements. Remember: you've got to make your fat burn.

Perhaps your headache is caused by tension. Does that mean you have hypertension? No, hypertension is high blood pressure and doesn't mean you are overly tense (see "Sodium" in Chapter 17). Women ask me all the time if their blood pressure is high because they've had a "bad day." The relationship between stress and blood pressure isn't so clear-cut, I'm afraid. You're probably tense because you have lost the tranquilizing effect of a high-carbohydrate diet. You've probably seen movies of animals that are vicious before they eat and tranquil afterward. That's what food does. Maybe some more protein will calm you down. Carbohydrates will do it better—they raise tryptophan (an amino acid—see page 248) levels in the brain—but you have to be careful with them.

If you're craving sweets, it's not because you need them. You're craving sweets because you like them and you miss them. Your body might, however, be signaling that it would like to replace some of your lost fat, and a carbohydrate signal is a good way to get that fat replaced. It's a general carbohydrate hunger signal, however, and you're interpreting it as a signal for sweets. It can be satisfied with a plain baked potato.

Week Six If you suddenly begin losing less weight, it could be because you're eating later. The time *does* make a difference. If you must eat your major meal of the day in the evening, keep it as small as possible. If your diet supper is normally 500 calories, subtract 100 for each hour after 7:00 P.M. that you eat. If you eat at 8:00, have 400 calories. If you eat at 9:00, 300. You must count the calories in booze, also.

What about alcohol? You can have two drinks a week free, provided they are made with water, diet soda, club soda, or tomato juice, and no more than a jigger of booze! If you're going out, you can also save your orange juice from breakfast and have it in a screwdriver. You can also have white wine or light beer. Alcohol has 7 calories per gram of energy, which is more than carbohydrate, less than fat. It might relax you so that you'll eat more, but an occasional drink is supposed to keep your coronary arteries open. Want more than two drinks a week? Then use them as your fruit exchange. I know it's not the same nutritionally, but that's why you're taking the vitamins—so that you don't have to worry about getting all your nutrition from food.

Week Seven Suppose you've lost no weight this week. This is just a plateau. You have reached a plateau either because you are eating too much for your present weight, or because you are exercising too little. Or you're retaining fluid for some reason. Or there's something else going on in your life. Perhaps you had a bladder infection and the doctor told you to drink cranberry juice (see "Cystitis" in Chapter 5).

Do you realize how many calories cranberry juice has? I know you are just following instructions, but those instructions are meant for normal people. No, you're not physiologically normal. You're overweight, and I think there's an important lesson for you to learn here. *Don't use food to treat illness if you are overweight. Use a specific noncaloric treat-*

ment for illness, no matter what your doctor says. He might instruct you to eat crackers frequently for hypoglycemia, and you might feebly protest, "But I'm dieting," to which the answer will invariably be "Don't worry about that now. We've got to take care of this other thing." Don't do it, I implore you. It will set your diet back two to four weeks. In the old days, when there was no sophisticated medicine, food was used to treat illness. But food is only for people who have no excess body fat from which to draw nutrient resources, whereas you want to use your fat, remember? You just need lots of low-calorie fluids, vitamins, and protein to sustain your muscle mass. You do not need ice cream for sore throats, chicken soup for colds, pudding and yogurts for upset stomach, mashed potatoes and rice for diarrhea, orange juice for a viral infection, or honey, tea, and whiskey for an upper-respiratory-tract infection.

That was my downfall. My dad had his own delightful regimen for treating me every time I was sick: tea, honey, and whiskey (all three of which I hate to this day), milk toast (which was buttered toast in hot milk with sugar, so the globs of fat floated to the top of the milk), little sugar pills that had tincture of belladonna in them, and an enema. This was his tried-and-true formula for all illnesses. The fact that I survived suggests that I was pretty hardy stuff. At that time there wasn't much else you could do when you were sick. There were few antibiotics except for sulfa and penicillin, no cimetidine (for ulcers), no decongestants for a stuffy nose, no diphenoxylate hydrochloride for diarrhea.

For *your* bladder infection, you should be taking sulfa, drinking eight glasses of water a day, and forgetting about the cranberry juice unless you can find the low-calorie kind. No matter what your doctor says. . . .

Your hair is falling out? It had to happen sooner or later. Female hair falls out periodically anyway, and this might be one of those natural periods. But it might also be your diet. Dieting by necessity lowers your intake of protein along with that of the other nutrients. This also lowers your metabolism, and that makes your hair thin. It also helps to make you cold.

If you think what you've got is bad, you should see the hair loss in semistarvation or protein-sparing diets.

Check for dandruff or scalp infection. If you see anything in your head that's not supposed to be there, get yourself to a dermatologist. If you see nothing, try zinc tablets, 30 milligrams a day, and some iron if you're not taking any. Sometimes thyroid helps. And wait it out. This is the regimen my dermatologist gave me. By the way, you don't have to choose between being fat and being bald.

Week Eight By now you'll be settling into a fairly steady two-pound loss per week. This is nothing to get frustrated about.

If you're having difficulty sleeping, if you lie down and feel your heart speed up and sometimes even flutter in your chest, it may be because you've had too much caffeine (see "Insomnia" in Chapter 5). There are those who say that coffee stimulates an instant respone in insulin secretion, which in turn stimulates appetite. I don't believe it often does—and I never insist that anyone give up coffee—but if you do have this symptom, caffeine could be causing it. Also, a high level of free fatty acids circulating in your body when it's in a weight-loss state makes you hyper-alert. Without a similarly high carbohydrate intake you are unbuffered, and you pick up the effects of stimulants more easily—such as the caffeine in coffee and diet colas. If you're snitching any chocolate, that would act as a stimulant, too.

Give up the caffeine. Switch to herbal tea, decaffeinated coffee, skim milk, tomato juice, grapefruit-ade (one part grapefruit juice to two parts water), diet lemonade, club soda, water, clam juice, or bouillon for your liquids. If you have cysts in your breasts, they'll become smaller and less tender when you give up caffeine, so you'll sleep better for more than one reason.

You're exhausted? And you're not losing that much water? Perhaps your gynecologist saw you last week and said your potassium is just fine, but that you need *more food*. Gee, I really wish those guys would stick to their hysterectomies and leave bariatric medicine to the people who know it. It's difficult to assess potassium need from blood plasma alone. There is four times as much potassium *inside* a cell as outside, and that's potassium you lose when you lose all those fat cells. I don't want you to eat more bananas and drink more orange juice to get more potassium; you need fewer calories at this point in your diet, not more. You get 1 milliequivalent of potassium for one inch of banana. In order to get the amount of potassium you need you would have to eat twenty-eight inches of banana—or three to four bananas—at the high cost of 300 to 400 calories. At this point you should use commercial potassium supplements, which have 20 or fewer calories and supply 25 milliequivalents of potassium.

Why aren't you losing as fast on this diet as you did on the one you were on three years ago? You are not the same person you were three years ago. As you have changed, so has the way you lose weight.

Why do you need less food at this point in your diet? Because there is less of you to feed. Also, your low carbohydrate intake has alerted certain systems in your body to lower your energy output to conserve fat. Finally, you're hungrier, too. The estrogenic properties of the fat you lost could have decreased your appetite, and since you no longer have that fat, your appetite may be a little stronger. That's not important, however. Estrogen might make you less hungry, but it also makes storing food as fat easier, so you are better off with a little less. Sometimes at the end of the diet you can be eating as little as 400 calories a day to continue to lose weight.

Now is the time to decide what you want to weigh. If you are more than twenty pounds overweight, it's going to be difficult to get down to your thinnest, or so-called normal weight, and almost impossible to stay there. Nature is kind to women who are chubby. They look extremely thin within ten to fifteen pounds of the "normal thin." What do I mean by "normal thin"? Well, the charts say that someone five feet three inches tall should weigh between 110 and 115 pounds. If you have usually hovered around 160 pounds, you will look extremely thin at 130 pounds, and there is really no need to knock yourself out to lose more now. Nature hides that extra padding. On the other hand, if you have always been a thin person weighing 110 pounds and have gone up to 130, you will look enormous and will want to lose that weight. When you decide on the weight you want, try to get down to exactly that level, and then go on to early maintenance for four months.

Harnessing the Amino Acids

You might need some chemical help during maintenance (or dieting), and you can get it from an unexpected source: amino acids. Amino acids are the building blocks of protein. There are twenty-two of them, of which eight are essential, meaning they cannot be manufactured in the body and must be ingested. Lately, the amino acids have been observed to have profound effects on mood, appetite, and sleep.

Like all of my patients, I still entertain the hope that one day a magic pill will appear that will cure obesity. In the past few years these natural amino acids and amino-acid-containing foods have been gaining some attention in the field of overweight—spurred on, I'm sure, by large numbers of non-medical people now involved in the treatment of obesity (who can't prescribe medications). The rationale behind using these amino acids involves the manipulation of certain brain chemicals, particularly *serotonin,* which are thought to suppress appetite. That's how I became interested in tryptophan.

Tryptophan—for Food and Mood

Because mid- and late-life women tend to be the most depressed, they take the most antidepressants. Antidepressants have a particularly disturbing side effect: they tend to cause weight gain, either by stimulating the appetite or by increasing fat production in some other way. Women gain weight easily enough without pills to help them. So when a speaker at a psychiatric conference announced that an antidepressant marketed in England did *not* cause weight gain and might even help people *lose* weight, I was very excited.

The active ingredient of the pill was tryptophan, an essential amino acid. Tryptophan has been used in sleep research and is supposed to reduce the time it takes to fall asleep by increasing brain serotonin. Serotonin-induced sleep is more natural and restful than sleeping-pill sleep. Both meat and milk contain high levels of this amino acid, and tryptophan might be the reason people feel drowsy after a big meal that contains a lot of meat, and why a glass of milk at bedtime makes it easier to fall asleep. But how does it work in weight loss?

New research from Boston reported that low levels of serotonin in the brain might have something to do with hunger and binge eating. Binge eating is at times related to premenstrual tension, which is at times related to depression, which may at times be alleviated by tryptophan. Now the puzzle starts to fit together. Decreased serotonin levels might have something to do with everything—hunger, binge eating, depression, and lack of sleep. Find something to raise those levels, and you might find a cure for everything. The answer could be tryptophan.

I tried it immediately on binge eaters and nighttime eaters (often the same people) and threw in a few depressed people also. I gave doses of 1 or 2 grams before meals or in the early evening. (Beware: drowsiness might be a problem.) I wish I could tell you it was the answer. Some women felt less hungry, some binged less, some slept better, but none felt less depressed. The overall results, however, are still faintly promising. It is certainly worth a try for uncontrollable eating or insomnia. And, as of this writing, it appears to be safe and nontoxic.

Phenylalanine—for Diet and Quiet

Equally promising is a moss-green pill called spirulina, which is derived from South African plankton. Spirulina is rich in many vitamins and amino acids, particularly phenylalanine. It has been the rage in California, touted as a miracle drug that protects against aging, hunger, and cancer. I do 't take all those claims too seriously, but when I hear that something curbs hunger, I investigate. I have found it useful in appetite control, probably because of its relationship to serotonin. I have given my patients two tablets two or three times a day for appetite control, and the results have been promising. There appear to be no unpleasant side effects, and the patients get mild but smooth appetite control. I can cautiously recommend spirulina. Many patients object to the smell and the dark-green algae color and won't even give the pills a fair try. I have heard that the pills are also quite effective in coloring goldfish.

Chapter 20

Keeping It Off: Weight Maintenance

Touchdowns count in football but not in dieting. Once you lose the weight, you have to keep it off, and often this can be the toughest part. If you were more than thirty pounds overweight before your diet, you may find yourself sliding slowly and relentlessly upward when you end it.

Scientists now think two factors are involved in the ease of regain. One is the way an empty fat cell refills—quickly, as I'll explain later. The other is the signal from the brain to eat more carbohydrates. This probably relates to maintenance of your original body mass: that giant computer in your head knows you are normally programmed to store so much in your fat cells and will bring all the body's defenses into play to regain that lost mass. So you have to fight not only your psyche, but also your biology.

Maintenance should not be haphazard. You still need a formal program—though not *too* formal—and will need one for as long as two years.

I divide maintenance into three stages: early, middle, and late.

Early Maintenance *(Up Through the Fourth Month After Your Diet Ends)*

Month One

Follow the weight-loss diet you used, keeping the protein and fat the same, but add one starch at one meal per day. One starch is defined as *one* of the following: 1 piece of bread, ½ cup rice, 1 potato, ½ sweet potato, ½ cup pasta, 1 tortilla, ¼ sheet matzo, ½ bagel, ½ roll, 1 small pita bread, ½ cup bulgur.

Weigh yourself *daily,* in the morning after you've emptied your bladder. If you gain more than two pounds in one day, or over several days, return to the weight-loss version of your diet. Think about the combination of foods that made you gain weight. After you've lost the weight again, return to maintenance, but avoid the foods that caused that quick gain.

Remember, the worst thing you can do is avoid the scale. No matter how much you wince, *weigh yourself daily.*

Month Two

After the first month is over, you may add one sugar two times per week in the form of a dessert or a main course. Sweet-and-sour chicken would be a sugar main course. Ice cream would be a sugar dessert. *Weigh daily again.* Follow the same rules as for month one.

Month Three

You may be more liberal with meat in both preparation and amount. Two times a week you can have a fancy or sauced meat dish (*not* to be combined with the sweet dessert). Try veal saltimbocca or beef burgundy. *Weigh daily.* Follow the same rules as before.

Month Four

Cautiously add regular salad dressing three times per week—but only if you really want it—limiting the amount to two tablespoons. This I add only as an afterthought because diet dressing is always a reasonable substitute, and you should try to develop a taste for it. I like to limit additions to foods for which there are no substitutes.

At this point in your diet, with this kind of eating, you don't have to feel left out. By weighing daily, you will know which foods are giving you the most weight trouble and which foods your body can't tolerate. Remember to exercise, exercise, exercise, to bring that citrate oxidase down. Citrate oxidase is an enzyme that, among other functions, promotes refilling of the fat cell after it has emptied. Levels of it will drop as normal people lose weight; but in overweight people it stays elevated for a longer period of time. Exercise helps lower it more quickly.

Middle Maintenance
(Month Five to Year Two)

Rules

1. You must always choose between consuming your calories in food or in alcoholic beverages when you are at a party or eating out.
2. Continue to exercise at least twenty minutes daily.
3. Avoid night eating, even of low-calorie foods.
4. Watch that 4:00 to 6:00 P.M. time when you tend to get hungry. If you're at home, prepare the meal earlier so that you are out of the kitchen by 4:00. Prepare most of supper after lunch if you have to.
5. Avoid snacks in cellophane bags.
6. Avoid fast-food restaurants (even their burgers are loaded with calories) unless they have salad bars.
7. Avoid vending machines.
8. You can find some type of diet food in most eating places, even cafeterias, some fast-food restaurants, and diners.
9. There is no reason to eat if someone dies. At a wake or shiva, for example, eating won't bring the deceased back, and you will be faced with both your sorrow and added pounds.

10. You will binge—it's human nature. But limit the binge to one food—the first one you pick—and don't jump around. Total the calories of the binge, then start subtracting for the next three days. Binge sensibly; see my binge list in Appendix 1.

Late Maintenance
(Two Years and Over)

If you have kept your weight down for two years, you have altered your metabolism and should now gain weight like a thin woman. This means about a pound a month if left unchecked. That's twelve pounds a year—a manageable gain. Fat women, on the other hand, can gain five pounds or more a month. That is *not* a manageable gain.

Remember, exercise, preventive dieting, and regular weighing will help to keep your weight down. If you have an illness or any kind of surgery that lays you up temporarily, eat as little as possible. This is a time when many women cripple themselves further by putting on twenty or thirty pounds and up.

Never allow your weight to get out of hand again; twenty pounds should be your *limit*. And keep up with advances in the diet field. The next big discovery could be the last.

Chapter 21

An Alternate Diet for Weight Loss

If you are tired of routine diets, or if none of them seems to be successful, try my Mix-and-Match Diet—for a week, a month, or longer. I call it Mix-and-Match because it mixes a liquid-protein supplement with one or two diet meals from the diets outlined in Chapter 19. It thus represents a rather severe curtailment of calories (between 600 and 700 a day), but without a drastic reduction in protein. Mix-and-Match is safe because I've used a zero-fat, calorically cheap protein in place of meat—60 calories and 9 grams of protein instead of the 200 to 300 calories you'd get from meat, cheese, or other protein sources.

This diet is good for people who normally skip meals anyway, never know what to eat, or are too busy to fix diet meals. It is also appropriate for people who, through either lack of exercise or advanced age, need to limit themselves to *very, very* few calories to lose weight.

Why bother with such a restrictive diet plan? The mid-life woman is a slow weight loser. The older and fatter she gets, the more slowly she loses. So we are faced with a dilemma: the woman who often requires the most nutrition also needs the fewest calories to maintain her weight.

My Mix-and-Match Diet provides adequate levels of protein and low levels of fat and carbohydrate. I have decreased fat because fat intake, plus obesity, has been implicated in cancer of the breast and colon. Besides, fat has 9 calories per gram, so the total calories add up quickly. I specify a low carbohydrate intake because I think the chemical defect in obese people is in burning carbohydrates, particularly simple and refined carbohydrates. All women seem to burn carbohydrates less efficiently, but it gets worse with age. Too much starch in middle or late life can stop weight loss altogether.

In nature, protein is attached either to fat as in meat, cheese, and eggs; or to carbohydrate as in beans and peas. If you must cut your intake drastically to lose weight, adequate protein is calorically expensive—80 to 100 calories per ounce of meat, and 400 to 500 calories per cup of beans. Does a protein exist in nature that has no fat or carbohydrate attached? Yes—egg whites are nature's only pure protein; and liquid supplements, whose main ingredient is powdered egg whites, are a fat-free, highly digestible form of protein.

It was with this in mind that I began using liquid-formula protein supplements that had been designed for the Protein Sparing Modified Fast Diet, a serious, semistarvation diet program developed at Cleveland Clinic. The liquid proteins are artificially flavored (I wish they were naturally flavored) powders that are composed of pasteurized egg whites, sugar, nonfat dry milk, vitamins, and minerals, and they can be reconstituted with water, skim milk, or diet soda. Each serving contains 9 grams of protein, 6 grams of carbohydrate, and no fat, for a total of 60 calories. This is mighty cheap protein calorically.

In the old days, certain drug companies of lesser repute manufactured liquid protein using a collagen form of protein derived from animal hooves and indigestible muscle fiber. They didn't put any carbohydrate in the formula either, so you got a poor-quality protein with no other nutrients. This led to serious problems. Without sugar and with only the poorest protein, the body, in its zest to find the most accessible fuel, used muscle sugar (glycogen) as well as fat. Unfortunately, the heart muscle was also attacked, and cardiac arrhythmias (irregular rhythm) abounded. Collagen protein mixtures have been virtually discontinued, but be sure to check labels and avoid those with "hydrolyzed gelatin" or "hydrolyzed animal collagen." These won't hurt you if you substitute them for one meal a day, but *never* rely on them exclusively for your protein.

Carbohydrate is also now added to all reputable mixtures as a "protein sparer." In other words, if carbohydrate is present in the mixture, there is less of a chance that the body will go after muscle when its own carbohydrate stores are depleted. I think the manufacturers may have gone a little overboard in the amount of carbohydrate they use today—patients become a little hungrier on the new liquid proteins. (Pure protein inhibits appetite.) But because there have been few, if any, adverse effects, the use of 6 grams of carbohydrate is probably justified.

The Mix-And-Match Menu

Breakfast. 4 ounces orange juice, 1 liquid protein supplement (mixed with water, diet soda, club soda, or skim milk), decaffeinated coffee or tea.

Lunch. 1 liquid protein supplement (mixed as above), 1 small salad with lemon juice and vinegar, decaffeinated coffee or tea.

Dinner. 4 ounces meat or fish, 2 cups salad with 2 tablespoons diet dressing, 1 cup cooked vegetables (except corn or peas; if you want corn or peas, reduce your portion to ½ cup).

The normal diet meal (described in Chapter 19) can be eaten for lunch or supper, and it may work even better if you eat it for lunch.

You should take the following supplements daily: vitamin A (4,000 I.U.), B-C complex (1 tablet), calcium (1,000 milligrams) with vitamin D (250 milligrams)—take these at bedtime if they don't bother your stomach—vitamin E (400 I.U.), potassium (800 milligrams).

This diet assures you of a two- to three-pound weight loss weekly, which you might say isn't very good. But on a regular three-meal-a-day balanced diet you would be losing only one-half to one pound per week.

This type of diet is especially helpful for the older dieter who eats alone, is not particularly hungry or motivated to take much trouble with meals, and needs a few highly digestible calories and an adequate protein intake. The older dieter should include a tablespoon of unprocessed bran sprinkled on the salad at noon.

If you are over sixty, you *must* have a physical examination before starting a program like this.

This Mix-and-Match Diet can be continued until weight is lost. However, the first maintenance phase (one month) should include two regular diet meals a day and one of liquid protein.

Chapter 22

Preventive Dieting

Preventive dieting is good for everyone. For the formerly overweight woman it is imperative. She has a marked tendency to gain weight rapidly, even if she's only eating larger quantities of nonfattening food or relaxing her carbohydrate control slightly. Preventive dieting is also valuable for people of normal weight who know that they are going to overindulge over a certain period of time, such as a forthcoming holiday season or a vacation.

Overweights (both current and former) tend to diet at inappropriate times. You rarely see heavy females indulging at dinner parties when the food is magnificent, or eating on sumptuous vacations, or during the holidays. At those fun times they are busy dieting. Having deprived themselves, they become so frustrated that they then go home and eat something unimportant.

They also waste their calories on unimportant food. Let's face it—a baked potato is *always* a baked potato, and mediocre bread is mediocre bread. Most of the time it isn't worth the calories. The times to eat are when you can get a great taste sensation in a lovely setting—not by yourself at 11:00 P.M., bolting down some packaged cookies or cold spaghetti, or munching cold french fries at some crowded fast-food restaurant.

Vacations are no time for dieting. Dieting should be done before the vacation to allow you a little more freedom in eating. Two nice things about vacation dining are different kinds of food and few distractions from the meal. It's a time to relax a little, to maintain weight instead of trying to lose it. The week before a vacation, when you're busy, is not a very interesting time to overeat.

The big holidays (Thanksgiving and Christmas) are a time to be careful (you could gain ten to fifteen pounds if you don't watch yourself) but not to starve. These weeks are filled with fun and food (which for many people can be synonymous with fun), and you should be able to indulge a little. By *indulge* I don't mean stuff. But taste, enjoy, sample something without feeling guilty, or eat out a little more without worrying about what will happen to your weight. Normal thin people eat more at holidays, but I've seen too many overweights who won't eat anything during the holidays because they've been eating right up to the beginning of them. Remember, it's not what you eat between Thanksgiving and Christmas that counts, but what you eat between Christmas and Thanksgiving.

That's why I think preventive dieting is so important. This concept takes into consideration that almost everybody overeats on occasion, and if you can prepare for those feast times, you'll do less damage. Holidays, vacations, and special occasions can leave you with an extra five pounds if you are of normal weight and an extra ten to fifteen if you are overweight. (Overweights put on twice as much, twice as fast, eating the same things.)

Preventive dieting is not crash dieting. Crash dieting goes for the quick, dramatic ten-pound loss, then allows you to go back to the same eating pattern you had originally. Since 80 percent of your weight loss the first two weeks of dieting is water, it's logical that if you stop dieting and reintroduce carbohydrates (that's the food that is commonly reduced on a diet program), the body will immediately restore its fluid volume plus some fat, and eight of the ten pounds will return. The trick in preventive dieting is *gradual refeeding,* so that the body has a chance to readjust to both fat and fluid loss, and by the time the "special eating occasion" comes you will be solidly down by five to ten pounds. Also, if you diet gradually, there is less tendency to overeat when you stop dieting.

For preventive dieting, use the diets outlined in Chapter 19. The first week use the Very-Low-Calorie Diet, the second and third weeks use the Low-Calorie Diet, and week four, if you need it, use the Normal Diet.

There are certain rules that you must follow on these diets:

1. Bread cannot be eaten at supper. It must be eaten at noon or you forfeit it.
2. Meat must be eaten at one sitting. You can't save it for later.
3. You can't save both fruits for the evening.

Note: If you have only five pounds to lose, do weeks one and three.

If you have ten pounds to lose, do weeks one, three, and four.

If you have more than ten pounds to lose, try the whole four weeks.

If you have practiced preventive dieting and preventive maintenance, you can have your cake and eat it, too. If you haven't, and you've gained weight, you need to jolt your body to start losing again after all that pigging out. Try my Restart Diet.

The Restart Diet

Day 1. Nothing but diet gelatin and liquids—coffee, tea, diet soda, tomato juice, skim milk, bouillon. Drink throughout the day, or divide the liquids into meals if you prefer.

Day 2. Add 9 ounces meat or fish (no pork or lamb), broiled, baked, or boiled. Divide into at least two meals and keep drinking the liquids.

Day 3. Add 2 large salads with 2 tablespoons diet dressing to the food for days 1 and 2.

Day 4. Add a breakfast of 4 ounces orange juice, 2 eggs, and 1 piece melba toast.

Day 5. Add 1 piece fresh fruit.

Days 6–14. Add another piece of fresh fruit, so that for the next eight days you will be eating all the food allotted in days 1 through 6.

Changing Food Preferences

Luckily, as metabolism slows down, many females seem to lose their taste for some of the high-calorie foods and "develop" a taste for foods of lower caloric density.

It is interesting to note the change in food preferences that comes with age. In most women, the sweet craze gives way to the starch craze. The statement "Sweets don't arouse me anymore, but I'd give anything for a piece of bread" is common. The bad news is that you can still get fat, because no woman lives on bread alone—it's bread and butter, cheese, jelly, peanut butter, or cold cuts. The woman who continues to like sweets above all other foods, though, is usually the one who is the heaviest.

The desire for red meat diminishes considerably in mature women. This presents a problem for dieters who eat out. Most "greasy spoons" can at least supply a hamburger on a plate with a bit of tomato and lettuce, but if you won't eat eggs because you're afraid of cholesterol, and you've lost your taste for beef, a casual lunch can become a problem.

Along with beef goes the taste for chocolate—well, not the taste, perhaps, but the ability to eat a lot of it comfortably. It's too rich. In both beef and chocolate the fat content is high, and both can make you feel uncomfortably full. You know you're getting older when you still have hot-fudge-sundae fantasies but the fantasies are better than the real thing.

Grapefruit, never a favorite with adolescents, zooms to popularity with the adult female. That and lemon juice are highly digestible citruses, and some people subscribe to the delicious myth that they burn adipose tissue ("acid dissolves fat''). I regret that even if you injected grapefruit or lemon juice directly into a mound of fat, it wouldn't dissolve a single cell. Grapefruits do help in weight loss, though, because their carbohydrate levels are low for fruits, and they don't stimulate as much of an insulin response as an apple or an orange does. Remember, ingesting sugar (a simple carbohydrate) causes insulin levels to rise. High insulin levels block the burning of fat. The main advantages of grapefruit are that it is filling, low in calories, and low in carbohydrates.

The popularity of mushrooms continues to rise with age. Often a teenager who rejected mushrooms learns, as she grows older, to appreciate their versatility and mildly moldy flavor—and the fact that five cups have only 100 calories.

The older we get, the more we seem to like foods with an unusual taste and texture—spinach, liver, and tofu (soybean protein), for example. This is probably because you have to acquire a taste for these foods—and when you're young, why bother? But as you get older, you realize that certain foods are good for you; they're easy to digest, low in calories, and versatile. And you *do* bother.

There is an amazing correlation, I've found, between age and love of spinach, and that love transcends climate. On one five-degrees-below-zero day, I counted ten women eating spinach salads for lunch in a posh club while the men were eating predictably ''hearty'' fare like beef stew and bean soup. One week while I was preparing a fancy seafood dish to be rolled up in pastry, I ran out of seafood. In desperation I looked around for something to substitute. The only thing I could come up with was two packages of frozen spinach. I put the frozen spinach in the dough (after suitably increasing its palatability) and hoped nobody would notice. Not only did they notice, but the spinach modification was actually more popular than the original seafood dish.

Why is spinach so popular? I think the reason is that women begin to come to grips with the fact that there are very few things they can chew that won't increase weight, won't turn them orange, and won't upset their stomachs—and spinach happens to be one of them. It's a remarkably digestible food, with none of the intestinal irritation caused by lettuce and none of the gas-producing qualities of the cabbage family. And it's loaded with potassium to make you feel energetic.

What happens to a woman between adolescence and age forty, when her repugnance and disgust at the mention of the word *liver* becomes instant salivation—especially when it's quickly sautéed with onion, bacon, apples, and a score of other things? Again, liver is nutritious, high in potassium and protein, low in calories, and easier to digest than red meat, but you should also be aware that it contains a lot of cholesterol.

Bran and prunes are other adult preferences. Teenagers probably disdain them because they are always associated with constipation, and constipation is always associated with old age. Just looking at these foods on the shelf can make them snicker with embarrassment. Comedians with their love of toilet jokes have never been able to pass up the connection.

In any case, it's helpful that we come to have instinctive preference for those foods that do our bodies the least amount of harm.

Chapter 23

You Be the Doctor

A very prestigious medical journal became famous for presenting a different case study each week. You were supposed to consider the questions and make a diagnosis. Then you would read how the experts approached the problem and arrived at *their* diagnoses, and then compare your methods and conclusions with theirs. The exercise was often challenging, and the results humbling. So let's try it. Read the following three cases and think about how *you* would treat each of these women and why, based on the information you've read in this book.

Case No. 1: Helen was a fifty-three-year-old female and had three problems: she was overweight, depressed, and had had a total hysterectomy. Her psychiatrist thought she needed an antidepressant, her gynecologist thought she needed estrogen, and her internist thought she needed to lose weight. Knowing the effects of estrogen and antidepressants on weight, what would you do?

Case No. 2: Carolyn, age forty-eight, 178 pounds, five feet four inches tall, came into my office taking four medications: propranolol (a beta blocker) to control her rapid heart rate, a diuretic to lower her blood pressure and to eliminate fluid retention caused by the propranolol, and three grains of thyroid. She was a borderline diabetic on oral antidiabetic medication and was told she should take anti-inflammatory drugs for multiple episodes of tendinitis. Her physical exam and EKG were normal, and blood chemistries revealed a minor elevation in blood glucose. She was still holding down a full-time job despite pain, discomfort, and depression. Every time she told her doctor she wanted to lose weight he told her not to worry, she had more pressing problems.

Case No. 3: Ruth, age fifty-five, five feet two inches, came into my office weighing 201 pounds. I had seen her at age forty-five, and she had weighed the same. At age forty-five, however, her physical exam, blood work, and EKG had been normal. She was raising four active children and, despite her obesity, seemed strong and vital. But at fifty-five things had changed drastically. She was taking nitroglycerin for heart pain, oral antidiabetic medicine for her diabetes, propranolol for her blood pressure, and a very strong diuretic for fluid retention. She had been told that her posterior coronary artery was almost blocked, but not to worry—if she had a heart attack, they said, it would be a minor one. Her physical exam revealed a blood pressure of 160/100 (high), her EKG showed minor ST wave changes (abnormal), and her SMA-12 blood test indicated that her blood sugar was at least 100 milligrams higher than normal. But more impressive, the amount of fat in her plasma was so high that when you looked at the serum part of her blood in a test tube it resembled cream.

All three women represent the multisystem breakdown of the overweight older woman. Nature dramatically protects women of childbearing age from chronic debilitating disease; after the childbearing years are over, however, the mechanisms required to keep her in good health deteriorate rapidly, leaving her as debilitated as if she had had physical problems her whole life.

In the case of Helen, you would technically be right no matter what you said. Her psychiatrist wanted to treat her depression, her gynecologist wanted to treat her hormone-depletion state, and her internist wanted to treat her obesity. All of them *should* have been able to coexist peacefully in this case. There were several questions you should have asked, however, before you decided on the *order* of treatment. What happened first—her depression, her hysterectomy, or her obesity? If her depression came first, it was unrelated to her surgery but still could have been related to estrogen slowdown. Was it a realistic depression or a nonspecific depression? How intense was it? Was she a suicide risk, or just unhappy? Was she functioning? Was she having severe premenopausal symptoms after her surgical castration? (If you still have your ovaries, you don't have menses, but you can still have the cyclic hormonal disturbance.) Were the symptoms interfering with her sleep and general well-being? How fat was she? Was she merely a thin woman who wanted to be thinner or was she obese?

Helen was depressed before her surgery because she was overweight. She had no menopausal symptoms immediately after surgery, but she did have a marked weight gain that depressed her even more. She was not suicidal in the general sense, although it could be argued that she was trying to eat herself to death. The treatment of choice? Diet, of course. She went on my Very-Low-Calorie Diet, lost sixty pounds, and felt much better. She became less depressed but began to have severe menopausal symptoms, including hot flashes. At that point the smallest possible dose of estrogen was initiated. This resulted in a ten-pound weight regain, but this did not distress Helen that much—it relieved her hot flashes, and she was still much thinner than she had been before.

This case illustrates that the right treatment is often a matter of timing. Only the psychiatrist was off base. It also points out that a physician tends to zero in on the organ system he knows best and often fails to look at the patient as a whole. A woman is more than just the sum of her parts. Helen's fat gave her enough estrogen to keep her symptoms from being too severe; and if she had undergone estrogen replacement *before* she lost weight, she would have gained even more weight and would have become more depressed.

What did you think about Carolyn? If you said weight loss first, you would have been right. And then she should have been slowly taken off her pills. With every ten-pound loss you could try to de-drug her. First, the diuretic would go—because after a ten-pound loss her blood pressure would probably drop to normal. After the second ten pounds you could decrease her thyroid by one grain. (Balanced thyroid—or T3 *and* T4—is not that valuable in weight loss.) Another ten pounds and you could try to take her off the propranolol for her rapid heartbeat. Because she has lost weight, increased her exercise, and decreased her thyroid, her pulse rate should now be normal. Another ten-pound loss and you could take her off her thyroid totally—in spite of her protests. (You would then monitor her, of course, to see if she really needs it.) Her internist did all these things. After three weeks blood tests showed that her thyroid function was normal. But she complained so bitterly about not being on it that he eventually let her take one grain. The end of the story? She ultimately weighed in at 138, looked and felt fine, and from taking seven pills a day to live she was down to taking one to placate her. A repeat glucose tolerance test for diabetes was normal.

And what did you say about Ruth? If you said get her to a hospital, you were right. She was a sick cookie and was inches away from a heart attack. If she had been a male, she would have had one already. The cornerstone of her treatment, however, was also diet and exercise. After she lost thirty pounds, her angina decreased in frequency. She was able to discontinue her antidiabetic medication, although she still had to use her beta blocker and nitroglycerin.

What is important for you to learn in all three of these cases is that obesity influenced the course of all these disease processes.

Chapter 24

Finding the Right Health Mate

Life for the woman over forty occasionally degenerates into a wrestling match with nature, and women should learn to thrive on those challenges. A good tussle and a little pain can make you a much more interesting and aware human being. Besides, science is doing its best to provide you with awesomely sophisticated weapons in your struggle; and if the other sophisticated weapons it has devised don't leave this planet looking like the moon, you probably have many productive years ahead of you.

But it means staying in the best possible physical and mental health. This means respecting your body and keeping it primed with exercise, rest, and proper nutrition; not taking foolhardy risks by poisoning it with tobacco, alcohol, or too much food; and striving always to learn and grow, never to stagnate in ignorance and complacency. All this you can do for yourself, and I hope I've given you enough information in this book to understand and to anticipate the changes in your body in the coming years.

Another factor in staying healthy is good medical care. Perhaps I've advised you to see a physician too often in the course of these pages to make this a bona fide "self-help" book. But I have a very deep faith in modern medicine—that's why I practice it—and I only wish that high-quality health care were accessible to everybody who needs it. We may not have socialized medicine, but in some ways we're better off. We can choose our own physicians. My son once spent a summer in Spain with an upper-middle-class family. His Spanish "father" had a severe progressive lung disease and was quite ill. He had no private doctor, however. He had to go to a clinic and take a number . . . and wait, and wait. He didn't know whom he was going to see, and it didn't much matter, because whomever he saw didn't see him for very long.

In this country it's different. You pay more, but you get more, and you can *expect* more. Unfortunately, too many older women settle for shoddy, indifferent, and otherwise callous care. Many are tyrannized by their doctors, living in fear that they will inadvertently make them "mad." I know one physician who threatened a woman patient who wanted to see her old gynecologist for a yearly pelvic. He told her, "If you go someplace else for your checkup, I'll never take care of you in an emergency." She actually believed that creep, and he nearly scared her to death. She shouldn't have worried, though, because in a true emergency she'd have ended up in a hospital, where there's always somebody to take care of you.

The scare tactic, I am afraid, is all too common in medicine and is employed only on women. (I've never heard of a male physician telling another male that he'd better not go to another doctor.) The male ego is fragile in sex and in medicine, and a male doctor scorned is a menace. A friend of mine couldn't comply with an unreasonable demand from her psychiatrist, and when she called him in tears to tell him how upset she was, he hung up on her. She was amazed. "After spending all that money on him, he didn't even say goodbye," she said.

What kind of doctor do you want? I know you want someone who is kind, caring, intelligent, dedicated, reasonable, rational, and who doesn't overcharge.

Now let's get back to reality.

Location

First, you should decide geographically where you want your doctor to be. Remember, close is convenient, but not absolutely necessary if you don't expect to be sick that often. If you live miles from anywhere in a small town, you can't drive, and there is only one physician, you don't have much choice. But if that physician is intolerable, take a half-hour bus ride to a different one. It's worth the trouble. If you do have a medical condition that might call for frequent office visits, it's handy to have someone nearby. But that is not important enough to stay with an unsatisfactory physician.

I have patients who come to me from faraway places. This is ridiculous because you have to see a diet doctor at *frequent, regular* intervals for a *sustained period of time*. Although it is exceedingly flattering to have somebody fly to Connecticut from Texas or Georgia, it's not practical or logical—and worse, it doesn't work. These long-distance relationships work out only if it's a one-shot consultation; and then you can go back home and let your own doctor carry on the treatment. No matter how enthusiastic you are about a doctor, in any long-term therapy your enthusiasm will be dimmed by distance.

Male or Female

Gender could be an important consideration in choosing a physician. Women happen to make excellent doctors, especially if well trained. (Thank you, thank you.) One of the things that hurt female performance in medicine in the past was that many women were denied good residencies, did not complete their training, or were forced to interrupt practice for family commitments. In this decade, female physicians seem to be made of sterner stuff, and they remain on their goal-directed paths no matter what obstacles they encounter. I think this has been possible, in part, because of a new breed of young men who are delighted to see women pursue careers and will assist them in the tricky problem of combining them with family life. The trouble with choosing a female doctor is that there are still not many around, particularly in the primary-care specialties like internal medicine, and obstetrics and gynecology.

Age

I prefer middle-aged physicians because they don't have to learn on you, and they'll be around for your life expectancy. Don't get me wrong; young physicians are bright. You never know more than when you get out of medical school. That's the trouble. You know so much that you don't realize how much you don't know—humility has not set in. I heard a story about a woman who asked to be appointed to the admissions committee of a prestigious medical school. When somebody asked her why she wanted such a thankless job, she replied, "Fourth-year medical students at —— are so insufferable that I want to find out if we make them that way or we take them that way."

Don't be afraid that the older physician is out of touch with things. In today's medical world, "recertification" is a fact of life, at least for the specialties. The medical societies and the specialty boards insist that physicians obtain a certain amount of postgraduate training every year; and the caliber of this training at seminars, annual meetings, and intensive courses is very high. Periodically, the medical boards offer a test to make sure the doctor is up on general medicine. Occasionally, though, some previously well-respected but now senile physician slips through. So be alert to noticeable incoherence or lapses in memory in an elderly doctor.

Training

You might want to choose your doctor by the schools he or she went to or the residency training he or she received. This will assure you of some pretty bright people, because most of those high-powered residencies are almost impossible to get into—particularly in the big-city teaching hospitals. And they pyramid doctors out ruthlessly. That means that ten residents will start a program, but there will be only five slots at the top, so five people will have to go. The person who survives is often tough and calculating. And if that person spent his or her premed career sabotaging other people's experiments (to squash the competition) and has ended up a chief resident, how much humanity can there be left?

The internship, by the way, used to be a year of general training that followed medical-school graduation. It wasn't specialized. Interns rotated through the different departments of the hospital so that they could see which branch of medicine appealed to them most. Or, if they knew what they wanted to do, they could at least get a surface acquaintance with some of the other specialties. This was the year to tie it all together—academics mixed with practical work. This system, however, was gradually replaced by an internship in one specific branch, because many students resented having to do a stint on pediatrics or urology if they wanted to be an allergist. Then the internship was phased out entirely and the medical school took over that part of the training, allowing its senior students to do more and more practical work.

People seem to be deciding on specialties much earlier these days. I asked an obnoxious ten-year-old what he was going to be when he grew up. "An ophthalmologist," he answered, "because that has a nice blend of medicine and surgery, there's not much night call, and the pay is good." I feel sorry for his patients already.

Head of the Department (the Professor)

There are always people who want to see the "head of the department." No one else will do. Heads of departments love this ego support, but often they don't love patient care. They're good for one consultation, if you can catch them between lectures and seminars; if your particular problem interests them; and if the department makes it attractive enough financially for them to put in the extra time and effort. But remember, heads of departments and professors are there because they like to do research, teach, have long summer vacations, take sabbaticals, and attend meetings all over the world. That doesn't leave much time for patient care, and certainly not consistent patient care.

Many times the only reason they take private patients at all is that the department lets them keep the money; or else they need to do it to justify their salary. They aren't always the best practical physicians. Many live in a cloistered world. I had two patients who insisted on going to the heads of departments and left very competent physicians in the process. One ended up with a complete hysterectomy for what should have been a one-day, in-and-out, minor surgical procedure; and the other had to have disc surgery not once, but twice. "That was because your doctor was twice as good as anyone else," I always kid her.

Specialty

It's nice to have a primary-care physician, a "personal doctor" who knows you and can give you reasonably comprehensive care. In choosing this physician, you may ask which specialties—meaning the field or fields of specific expertise—will come in handiest in treating you. I feel that a good gynecologist with a knowledge of psychiatry and medicine, or a good internist with a knowledge of psychiatry and gynecology, would be the specialists of choice. It depends on your age—gynecologists are handiest before menopause, and internists in post-reproductive life.

Unfortunately, gynecology has really missed the boat by acting like a *surgical* specialty. It is, in theory, the specialty with the greatest continuity-of-care possibilities for a woman from puberty to menopause. Gynecologists could be involved in general female health care, sex counseling, psychotherapy, weight control, and treatment of uncomplicated female illness. They aren't, though. Once you pull them away from their bleeding uteri and warm vaginas, they become totally disoriented. Which reminds me of the time I took a course in "Office Gynecology for the Family Physician" in Boston. I accompanied the chief resident for an entire day, and all we did was fit diaphragms, put in IUDs, check vaginal bleeding, and look at cervical infections. I never saw a patient's face. Finally, as we were seeing our last patient, the male resident turned to me and said, in all seriousness, "How can you stand looking at fat people all day?'' Different strokes, I guess.

Since the gynecologists have generally fallen down on the job, the logical choice for the mid-life woman would be the internist who can practice general medicine. An internist might also have a subspecialty, an area in which he or she is superspecially trained—such as the digestive tract (gastrology), glands (endocrinology), joints (rheumatology), kidneys (nephrology), and so on. It is expedient to pick a physician with a subspecialty in an area in which you've previously had problems. If you have always had a sensitive stomach, for example, it would make sense to choose an internist with special training in gastrointestinal disease. This rather narrows your choices, but it often saves you from having to find a superspecialist if your stomach acts up again.

How to Find Him or Her

How do you go about finding a physician? The best impersonal and objective ways are looking through a reference book or calling your local medical society.

Two books are available in libraries. One is the *American Medical Directory,* which gives you the following information: geographic location by state and town, address, Board Certification, subspecialty, year in which license was issued, and type of practice (group, hospital, part-time). The second book is much more complete and is called the *Directory of Medical Specialists*. This is arranged by specialty, then broken down into regions. It includes the year in which the physician was certified (and recertified), age, degrees, places of training, and positions and appointments currently held.

The local medical society will give you a pristine list of three ''approved'' specialists from a list that they continuously rotate for the sake of fairness. At least this weeds out the egregious quacks, but it still won't tell you much about the physician beyond the *curriculum vitae*.

Consulting advertisements is the worst way to choose a doctor. Maybe some savvy gynecologist will start a trend someday with Broadway-style quote ads: ''Best damn hysterectomy I've ever had!''—Jane Jorgins, Springfield. ''Sheer good fun! I warmly recommend Dr. Jacob's stirrups! I can't wait to go back!"—Dottie McGee, Watertown.

I recommend you ask an intelligent female friend or a nurse. Never ask a man—there's usually a difference between a physician's treatment of a male and his treatment of a female. A hospital nurse (from the doctor's "floor") will have had a chance to observe a physician's "handiwork" over the months and years, as well as his or her treatment of patients. Nurses often rate the doctors among themselves; they're in as good a position to judge overall competence and personality as anyone.

Say you have chosen a doctor and go for a first visit. How can you judge a physician's competence? Staff privileges at a good hospital and/or recommendations from reliable people probably indicate competence. If you notice alcohol on his breath or needle marks on her forearm, though, he or she might be "decompensating." Watch for a stagger, slurred speech, and pin-point pupils.

Do you like this physician? Don't stay with a doctor out of respect, fear, or because you are too lazy to move. You should *like* your doctor. I saw a patient the other day who complained bitterly about her gynecologist because he always insults her weight. She had developed a vaginitis, and I asked her whom she was going to see now.

"Oh, I guess I'll go back to him," she said, referring, of course, to her old doctor.

"Why?" I asked. "You can't stand him."

"Well, he has my records," she said lamely.

Records can be transferred. You should be comfortable with your physician and relate to his or her personality. And what about a doctor's attitude? Is your doctor open? Talkative? Phony? Or do you have to pull every word out of his or her mouth? Are you charged by the minute, or is an office visit an office visit? Is your doctor possessive and insecure (a horrible combination for a physician)? Do you like to see an office crawling with people, like a mill, with brisk, svelte, impersonal nurses; or do you prefer a quieter office with a less homogeneous, more informal staff?

A good indicator of a physician's attitude is the office

staff. For the most part, they tend to reflect their bosses. Don't let anyone tell you that a doctor doesn't know what the nurse or medical assistant is doing. A doctor has to be told only once about poor behavior, rudeness, or indifference, and if he or she cares, that will change. The nicest doctors I know have the sweetest office help, and, unfortunately, the reverse is also true.

Unacceptable behavior in a male physician is making passes when you don't want him to, or insulting you about your weight since that's not why you came to see him. In *all* physicians, unacceptable behavior is not returning phone calls, not providing adequate coverage for patients when he or she goes away, and not being reachable much of the time.

Appendix 1:

Binge List

If you feel an uncontrollable urge to binge, binge my way. The rules of the binge list are:

1. You must binge consecutively.
2. You may skip no foods.
3. You may go backward on the list once you have eaten something on it.

For instance, to get to fruit on the list below, you must eat your way through eight categories. If you go as far as fruit on the binge list, you will hold your own or gain only slightly. Higher than fruit and up to ice milk, you will gain about one or two pounds per week. Higher than item 16, you can gain up to five pounds per week. But remember, a binge list is to be used only if you feel you must binge; its purpose is not to encourage bingeing but to give some kind of order to your binges. Follow it from the top every time you binge, starting with raw vegetables. Most of my patients get to about item 4 or 5, then quit in disgust; they find it is too much trouble to work down to the food they crave.

If you follow the list, there is a good chance you can successfully fight a sudden, irrational desire to go off your diet.

1. Raw vegetables
2. Cooked vegetables
3. Eggs
4. Hard cheese
5. Soft cheese
6. Fish—canned, frozen, fried
7. Meat, plain
8. Cold cuts
9. Fruit
10. Plain popcorn
11. High-fiber bread
12. Rice
13. Potatoes
14. Fruit juice
15. Crackers
16. Ice milk or sherbet
17. Ice cream
18. Peanuts
19. Potato chips, etc.
20. Food served creamed or with gravy
21. Noodles
22. Cookies
23. Cake
24. Pie

Appendix 2:

High-Fiber Diet

A high-fiber diet should provide a normal diet with emphasis on the addition of high-bulk foods such as cellulose. This diet emphasizes bran, all whole grains, raw fruits and vegetables, legumes, and beans, Fiber tends to decrease colon transit time, improve regularity and produce bulk in the stool.

Breads and Crackers. 3 or more servings daily, whole-grain or enriched

Cereals. 1 serving daily, with emphasis on bran and other whole grains

Desserts. Emphasis on raw fruits

Potato or Potato Substitute. 1 or more servings of white or sweet potato, macaroni, noodles, rice, spaghetti; emphasis is on unrefined grains

Soup. as desired, with emphasis on bean, pea, and legume soups

Vegetables and Vegetable Juices. 2 or more servings daily, one of which should be dark green or deep yellow; emphasis on raw vegetables, legumes, and beans

Bran. 2 teaspoons to 2 tablespoons unprocessed bran daily, mixed in food or juice

Appendix 3:

Routine Blood Work

This specific series of blood tests is performed on an interim basis to enable the physician to make an evaluation regarding a patient's health. In our office we order SMA-24 (Sequential Multiple Analysis) and CBC.

g = gram
mg = milligram
mEq = milliequivalent
u = unit
l = liter
dl = deciliter
µg = microgram
I.U. = International Unit

1. *CBC*—complete blood count
a. *RBC (Red Blood Count)*. A red blood cell is a hemoglobin-containing cell that carries oxygen to the tissues and is responsible for the red color of blood. Red blood

count is also an indicator of anemia. Norms: males, 5.4; females, 4.8.

b. *Hemoglobin*. The oxygen-carrying pigment of red blood cells. Norms: males, 16 g%; females, 14 g%.

c. *Hematocrit*. The volume percentage of red blood cells in whole blood. Norms: males, 47%; females, 42%.

d. *WBC (White Blood Count)*. A white blood cell does not contain hemoglobin and has the function of protecting the body against infection. Norms: male and female, 7.8.

Differential of White Blood Count

a. *Poly*. A polymorphonuclear leukocyte. Norm, 50–75%.

b. *Lymphocytes*. Mononuclear leukocytes produced from lymphoid tissue; they aid in cell-mediated immunity. Norm, 20–40%.

c. *Monocytes*. Mononuclear phagocytic leukocytes. Norm, 0–10%.

d. *Eosinophils*. Leukocytes with cytoplasmic inclusions readily stained by red and prominent in allergies. Norm, 0–5%.

e. *Basophils*. Granular leukocytes. Norm, 0–3%.

2. *Liver Profile*—a blood evaluation of liver function consisting of the following tests:

a. *Albumin*. A major protein of human blood plasma. Reliable index of severity and prognosis in patients with chronic liver disease. Norm, 3.0–5.5 g/dl.

b. *Alkaline Phosphatase*. An enzyme that synthesizes the phosphate esters of carbohydrates. Elevated when bile ducts in liver are obstructed. Norm, 30–115 u/l.

c. *Bilirubin*. A bile pigment that normally circulates in plasma in combination with albumin. Norm, 0.2–1.2 mg/dl.

d. *LDH—Lactic Dehydrogenase*. An enzyme widely distributed in the liver that catalyzes the oxidation of lactic to pyruvic acid. Norm, 60–200 u/l.

e. *SGOT—Serum Glutamic Oxaloacetic Transaminase*. An enzyme in the liver released into the serum as the result of tissue injury; hence the concentration may be increased in acute damage to liver cells. Norm, 0–41 u/l.

f. *Globulin*. A group of proteins. Norm, 1.5–3.5 g/dl.

g. *SGPT—Serum Glutamic Pyruvic Transaminase*. An enzyme in the liver released into the serum as the result of tissue injury; hence the concentration may be increased in acute damage to liver cells. Norm, 1–45 u/l.
h. *Total Protein*. Norm, 6.0–8.5 g/dl.

3. *Lipid Profile (Blood Fats)*—a blood evaluation of lipids in the body achieved by the following tests:
a. *Cholesterol*. A pearly, fatlike alcohol found in animal fats and oils, bile, blood, brain tissue, milk, egg yolk, the liver, kidneys, and adrenal glands. The body must manufacture a certain amount of it. Norm, 150–250 mg/dl. (Some physicians think any cholesterol above 200 mg/dl is too high.)
b. *Triglycerides*. Neutral fats synthesized from carbohydrates for storage in adipose cells. They release free fatty acids in the blood upon breakdown. Norm, 30–175 mg/dl.
c. *Lipoprotein Electrophoresis*. The technique used to measure and characterize lipoproteins into HDL and LDL.
   i. *HDL (High-Density Lipoproteins)* are scavengers of cholesterol in the body. They aid in flushing cholesterol from the cells and delivering it to the liver for excretion. Norm:

Serum HDL (mg/dl)	*Risk of CHD*
25 or less	highest risk
26–35	high risk
36–44	moderate risk
45–59	average risk
60–74	below-average risk

   ii. *LDL (Low-Density Lipoproteins)* aid in carrying cholesterol to arterial placques. LDL cholesterol binds to the same cell surfaces as HDL cholesterol. Therefore, if there is a greater concentration of HDL, less LDL will be available for absorption and accumulation.

4. *Kidney Profile*—a blood evaluation of kidney function
a. *BUN (Blood Urea Nitrogen)*. Urea is the end product of protein metabolism. Norm, 10–26 mg/dl.
b. *Creatinine*. A nitrogen-containing compound found in urine and muscle. Most of it is produced in the body. Norm, 0.7–1.5 mg/dl.

5. *Electrolytes*

a. *Sodium*. A mineral in the extracellular fluid of the body which along with other electrolytes controls proper water balance. Sodium is also necessary to carry nutrients across the cell membrane and for glucose absorption. Norm, 136–146 mEq/l.

b. *Potassium*. A major mineral found in intracellular fluid, important in energy metabolism. Low potassium levels cause weakness. Norm, 3.5–5.0 mEq/l.

c. *CO_2 (Carbon Dioxide)*. An odorless gas formed in the tissues and eliminated by the lungs. Norm, 24–32 mEq/l.

d. *Chloride*. Combines with sodium in extracellular fluid and aids in maintaining fluid balance and body base balance. Norm, 96–106 mEq/l.

6. *Uric Acid*. A product of protein metabolism, produced from protein in diet. An elevation found in gout. Norms: males, 3.9–9.0 mg/dl; females, 2.2–7.7 mg/dl.

7. *Parathyroid Profile*—a blood evaluation of parathyroid function

a. *Calcium*. Found in bones and teeth, giving them strength and rigidity. It is also responsible for the relaxation and contraction of muscles. Norm, 8.5–10.5 mg/dl.

b. *Phosphorus*. Needed by every cell in the body, part of DNA and RNA (genetic code determinants). Norm, 2.5–4.5 mg/dl.

8. *Iron*. A component of hemoglobin (gives color to red blood cells) that aids in transporting oxygen to the blood. Norm, 40–50 mg/dl.

9. *Thyroid Profile*—a blood evaluation of thyroid function

a. *T4 (Thyroxine)*. Iodine-containing hormone secreted by the thyroid gland. Its chief purpose is to increase the rate of cell metabolism. Norm, 4.5–12.5 μg%.

b. *T3 (Triiodothyronine)*. An iodine-containing hormone with several times the biological activity of thyroxine. Norm, 25–35%.

c. *TSH (Thyroid-Stimulating Hormone)*. A hormone released by the pituitary gland when the amount of thyroid hormone is decreased in the serum. This causes the thyroid gland to produce more cells and increase in size to create more hormone. Norm, 1.0–10.0 I.U./ml.

10. *Blood Glucose*. The principal source of energy for living organisms, made by the incomplete breakdown of starch. There is often impaired glucose metabolism in conditions that cause high blood-fat levels. Norm, 70–120 mg/dl.

Appendix 4:

Directory of Common Drugs

Anti-Anxiety

Also known as the minor tranquilizers, these drugs are used to control neurotic anxiety states.

Benzodiazepine: Benzodiazepine acts on multiple nerve pathways throughout the central nervous system. The action is mainly inhibition.

1. *Ativan* (lorazepam)
2. *Tranxene* (chlorazepate dipotassium)
3. *Valium* (diazepam)
4. *Xanax* (alprazolam): a new drug touted as being extremely effective in panic states

Meprobamate: This has been shown in some studies to act at multiple sites in the central nervous system.

1. *Equanil* (meprobamate)
2. *Miltown* (meprobamate)

Antidepressants

Three general types of drugs used as antidepressants are the tricyclics, named for their chemical configuration; lithium, a mineral; and MAO inhibitors, named for their mode of action.
Tricyclics: The exact mechanism of action of tricyclic antidepressants is not known. One theory suggests that they may restore normal levels of neurotransmitters by blocking the re-uptake of these substances.

1. *Elavil* (amitriptyline hydrochloride)
2. *Etrafon* (amitriptyline hydrochloride)
3. *Sinequan* (doxepin hydrochloride)
4. *Tofranil* (imipramine hydrochloride)
5. *Triavil* (perphenazine and amitriptyline hydrochloride)

Lithium: The exact biochemical mechanism of lithium is not known. Some studies have shown, however, that lithium can alter sodium transport in muscle and nerve cells.

1. *Lithium carbonate*

MAO (Monoamine Oxidase) Inhibitors: Monoamine oxidase inhibitors interfere with certain enzymes within the nerve endings. They interact adversely with tyramine and dopamine to release norepinephrine from nerve endings, which causes acute hypertension and at times results in death. To prevent possible drug interaction, foods containing tyramine and dopamine must be restricted. These include:

Beverages: alcoholic beverages, including ale, wine, and beer
Fats: soured cream
Breads and Bread Substitutes: homemade yeast breads with large amounts of yeast, breads or crackers containing cheese
Fruits: bananas, red plums, avocado, figs, raisins (permitted on diets not restricted in dopamine)
Vegetables: Italian broad beans (pods contain tyramine), eggplant, green bean pods

Meats and Meat Substitutes: liver, canned meats, aged game, yeast extracts, stored beef liver, chicken liver, salami, sausage, aged cheese—blue, Boursault, brick, Brie, Camembert, Cheddar, Colby, Roquefort, Stilton, Emmentaler, Gouda, mozzarella, Parmesan, provolone, Romano; salted dried fish such as herring, cod, or camlin, pickled herring

Miscellaneous: yeast concentrates, soup cubes, products made with concentrated yeast, commercial gravies or meat extracts, soups containing restricted items, soy sauce, any protein food that has not been properly stored or might be spoiled—that is, all except those foods that have been properly prepared

1. *Nardil* (phenelzine sulfate)
2. *Parnate* (tranylcypromine sulfate)

Anorectics—Nonamphetamine Diet Pills

These are currently used for appetite control over short periods of time (up to twelve weeks) when accompanied by a total diet program.

1. *Fastin* (phentermine hydrochloride)
2. *Ionamin* (phentermine resin)
3. *Plegine* (phendimetrazine tartrate)
4. *Pondimin* (fenfluramine hydrochloride)
5. *Prelu-2* (phendimetrazine tartrate)
6. *Sanorex* (mazindol)
7. *Tenuate Dospan* (diethylpropion hydrochloride)
8. *Tepanil* (diethylpropion hydrochloride, N.F.)

Over-the-counter diet pills: These types of pills employ an antihistamine that has a weak appetite-depressing effect.

1. *Anorexin* (phenylpropanolamine caffeine)
2. *Dietac*

Diuretics

These drugs remove water from the body.
Spironolactone:

1. *Aldactone* (spironolactone): causes increased amounts of sodium and water to be excreted, while potassium is retained; therefore care is advised when taking supplemental potassium; acts both as a diuretic and as an antihypertensive drug

Thiazides: (named for their chemical configuration)

1. *Diuril* (chlorothiazide)
2. *Enduron* (methyclothiazide)
3. *Esidrix* (hydrochlorothiazide)
4. *HydroDIURIL* (hydrochlorothiazide)
5. *Dyazide* (triamterene, plus hydrochlorothiazide): a diuretic/antihypertensive drug combination. This is a combination of a thiazide and a spironolactone, so care should be advised when taking supplemental potássium.

Other Types:

1. *Hygroton* (chlorthalidone): an oral diuretic with prolonged action (48–72 hours)
2. *Lasix* (furosemide): an oral diuretic that acts rapidly and inhibits primarily the reabsorption of sodium and chloride, not only in the proximal and distal tubules, but primarily in the loop of the Henle (other parts of the kidney)

NSAIDS—Nonsteroidal Anti-Inflammatory Drugs

These are used for a variety of inflammatory joint and muscle conditions, including bursitis, tendinitis, and arthritis. The mechanism of action of these drugs is not known exactly. We think they inhibit prostoglandins.
Phenylbutazones:

1. *Butazolidin* (phenylbutazone)
2. *Tandearil* (oxyphenbutazone)

Others:

1. *Clinoril* (sulindac)
2. *Motrin* (ibuprofen)
3. *Naprosyn* (naproxen)
4. *Tolectin* (tolmetin sodium)

Thyroid

Natural Thyroid:

1. *Armour Thyroid:* prepared by a special process from fresh, desiccated animal thyroid glands; thus, the active thyroid hormones L-thyroxine (T4) and L-triiodothyronine (T3) are available in their natural state
2. *Euthroid:* levothyroxine (T4) USP and liothyronine (T3) combined in a constant 4:1 ratio in order to simulate as closely as possible the physiologic and metabolic effects of normal thyroid
3. *Proloid* (thyroglobulin): obtained from a purified extract of hog thyroid

Synthetic Thyroid:

1. *Cytomel* (L-triiodothyronine): contains only liothyronine; 24 μg is equivalent to approximately 1 grain desiccated thyroid and 0.1 mg L-thyroxine. Cytomel has a rapid cutoff. Its metabolic effects persist for a few days following discontinuance.
2. *Letter* (sodium levothyroxine)
3. *Synthroid* (levothyroxine sodium): L-thyroxine is the principal hormone secreted by the normal thyroid gland
4. *Thyrolar* (liotrix): a combination of the active thyroid hormones levothyroxine and levothyronine in a ratio of 4:1 by weight

Others

1. *Catapres* (clonidine hydrochloride): an alpha blocker used to treat hypertension and also as an alcohol detoxifier.
2. *Tagamet* (cimetidine): a histamine blocker that inhibits gastric acid secretion.

Glossary

Adenoma: a benign tumor.
Adipose: of or relating to fat cells.
Anemia: a condition in which the blood is deficient in red blood cells.
Antigen: a substance that, when introduced into the body, stimulates the production of an antibody.
Aphrodisiac: any drug that arouses the sexual instinct.
B.M.R.: basal metabolic rate; the rate at which heat is given off by an organism at complete rest.
Cholecystectomy: surgical removal of the gallbladder.
Cholesterol: a steroid alcohol present in body fluids that is important in body processes and implicated experimentally as a causal factor in arteriosclerosis.
Collagen: connective tissue.
Collagen disease: a disease that affects connective tissue.
D and C: dilation and curettage; stretching the cervix and removing growths or other material from the uterus wall.
Disease: a definite morbid process having a characteristic train of symptoms; it may affect the whole body or any of its parts.
Diuresis: increased secretion of urine.
Diuretic: a substance that causes increased secretion of urine.
Dysuria: painful or difficult urination.

Ectomy: excision of an organ or part.

Electroshock (electroconvulsive therapy, E.C.T.): the induction of convulsions by the passage of an electric current through the brain.

Enzyme: any of numerous complex proteins that are produced by living cells and catalyze specific biochemical reactions.

Flatulent: having gases in the intestine or stomach.

Gland: a cell or group of cells that selectively removes materials from the blood and secretes them for further use in the body.

Hematocrit: the percentage of red blood cells in whole blood; norms = male, 47; female, 42 (normals may differ slightly).

Hemoglobin: the oxygen-carrying part of the red blood cells; norms = male, 5.4; female, 4.8 (normals may differ slightly).

High risk: increased exposure to hazard or danger.

Hormone: a product of living cells that circulates in body fluids and produces a specific effect on the activity of target and specific cells.

Hyper-: a prefix signifying "above," "beyond," or "excessive," as in *hyperthyroidism*.

Hypo-: a prefix signifying "beneath," "under," or "deficient," as in *hypothyroidism*.

Hypoglycemia: abnormal drop in blood sugar, which may lead to tremors, cold sweats, and headaches and may be accompanied by confusion, hallucinations, and bizarre behavior. The blood-sugar level for hypoglycemia is usually below 55 milligrams.

Hysterectomy: the operation of taking out the uterus, performed either through the abdominal wall or through the vagina. In a *complete hysterectomy* the uterus and cervix are completely removed. In a *partial hysterectomy* the corpus or body of the uterus is removed, leaving the cervix in place. This is not commonly done at present.

-itis: suffix signifying inflammation of (*gastritis* = inflammation of the stomach).

Mammography: X-ray of the breast.

PRL: post-reproductive life, my name for menopause or climacteric.

Pap (Papanicolaou) smear: a method of staining smears of various body secretions from the respiratory, digestive, and particularly the female genital tract. This is done for the detection and diagnosis of various conditions, mainly malignant and premalignant.

Primary: first in order or in time of development; principal.

Secondary: second or inferior in order of time, place, or importance; derived from a primary event or thing; for example, primary—menopause; secondary—depression.

S.M.A.: sequential multiple analysis; used to designate a series of blood tests.

Symptoms: subjective evidence of disease or physical disturbance; for example, a cold is a disease; a cough is a symptom.

Syndrome: a set of symptoms that occur together.

Index

ABOUT THE AUTHOR

BARBARA EDELSTEIN, M.D., was born in Massachusetts and attended Bucknell University and the Hahnemann Medical College in Philadelphia. She has been a psychiatric resident at Eastern Pennsylvania Psychiatric Institute in Philadelphia and at the Institute of Living in Hartford. In addition to articles in national publications, Dr. Edelstein has written *The Woman Doctor's Diet for Women* and *The Woman Doctor's Diet for Teen-age Girls*. She has an active practice in Bloomfield, Connecticut, and lives in West Hartford with her husband Stanley, a gynecologist, and their three children.

We Deliver!

And So Do These Bestsellers.

- ☐ 05042 **HEARTS WE BROKE LONG AGO** by M. Shain $10.95 (A Large Format Book)
- ☐ 22646 **SOME MEN ARE MORE THAN PERFECT** by Merle Shain $2.95
- ☐ 22649 **WHEN LOVERS ARE FRIENDS** by Merle Shain $2.95
- ☐ 05035 **OUT ON A LIMB** by Shirley MacLaine $14.95 (A Hardcover Book)
- ☐ 01457 **YOUR ACHING BACK** by A. A. White III, M.D. $7.95 (A Hardcover Book)
- ☐ 23029 **HAVING IT BOTH WAYS** by E. Denholtz $3.50
- ☐ 23568 **GET A JOB IN 60 SECONDS** by Steve Kravette $2.95
- ☐ 23355 **'LUDES** by Benjamin Stein $3.50
- ☐ 22616 **THE DEMON SYNDROME** by Nancy Osborn Ishmael $2.95
- ☐ 23563 **THE ONLY INVESTMENT GUIDE YOU'LL EVER NEED** by Andrew Tobias $3.95
- ☐ 23188 **BEVERLY HILLS DIET LIFETIME PLAN** by Judy Mazel $3.95
- ☐ 22661 **UP THE FAMILY TREE** by Teresa Bloomingdale $2.95
- ☐ 22701 **I SHOULD HAVE SEEN IT COMING WHEN THE RABBIT DIED** by Teresa Bloomingdale $2.75
- ☐ 22576 **PATHFINDERS** by Gail Sheehy $4.50
- ☐ 22585 **THE MINDS OF BILLY MILLIGAN** by Daniel Keyes $3.95
- ☐ 22736 **A MANY SPLENDORED THING** by Han Suyin $3.95
- ☐ 22771 **THE GREATEST SUCCESS IN THE WORLD** by Og Mandino $2.75
- ☐ 23271 **WHY DO I THINK I'M NOTHING WITHOUT A MAN?** by Dr. P. Russianoff $3.50
- ☐ 23296 **BH&G STEP-BY-STEP HOUSEHOLD REPAIRS** by BH&G Editors $3.50
- ☐ 20621 **THE PILL BOOK** by Dr. Gilbert Simon & Dr. Harold Silverman $3.95
- ☐ 23111 **GUINNESS BOOK OF WORLD RECORDS—21st ed.** by McWhirter $3.95

Prices and availability subject to change without notice.

Buy them at your local bookstore or use this handy coupon for ordering:

Bantam Books, Inc., Dept. NFB, 414 East Golf Road, Des Plaines, Ill. 60016

Please send me the books I have checked above. I am enclosing $______ (please add $1.25 to cover postage and handling). Send check or money order —no cash or C.O.D.'s please.

Mr/Mrs/Miss ________________

Address________________

City__________ State/Zip__________

NFB—9/83

Please allow four to six weeks for delivery. This offer expires 3/84.